A DICTIONARY OF CRIMINAL JUSTICE

A Dictionary of Criminal Justice is the only dictionary that deals with criminal justice from a UK perspective, and in doing so provides a comprehensive guide to all aspects of the British criminal justice system, including its historical context and contemporary operations.

The first three sections of the book explore in turn key definitions, key pieces of legislation and key documents that have helped to shape the operations of the criminal justice system, whilst the fourth details websites of particular relevance to this field. As such, this dictionary provides an extensive but accessible introduction to the important terms that relate to both the development and the contemporary processes of criminal justice. It also succeeds in placing the UK criminal justice system within an international setting through the inclusion of entries that acknowledge the global setting in which British justice operates.

Guides to key legislation and documents are included, and each definition is accompanied by references for further reading, making this book an invaluable learning tool for both students and practitioners of criminal justice.

Peter Joyce is Principal Lecturer in Criminology at Manchester Metropolitan University. Recently published works include *The Politics of Protest* (Palgrave, 2002), *Criminal Justice* (Willan, 2006) and *Criminology and Criminal Justice: A Study Guide* (Willan, 2009).

Neil Wain is Chief Superintendent in the Greater Manchester Police and divisional commander of Stockport. He was a BCU commander for three years, with considerable experience of working in partnership with local criminal justice agencies. Publications include *The ASBO – Wrong Turning, Dead End* (Howard League for Penal Reform, 2007) and numerous articles on youth crime.

A DICTIONARY OF CRIMINAL JUSTICE

Peter Joyce
and
Neil Wain

Routledge
Taylor & Francis Group

LONDON AND NEW YORK

First published 2010
by Routledge
2 Park Square, Milton Park, Abingdon, Oxon, OX14 4RN

Simultaneously published in the USA and Canada
by Routledge
270 Madison Avenue, New York, NY 10016

Routledge is an imprint of the Taylor & Francis Group, an informa business

Typeset in Times New Roman by
Florence Production Ltd, Stoodleigh, Devon
Printed and bound in Great Britain by
MPG Books Group, UK

British Library Cataloguing in Publication Data
A catalogue record for this book is available from the British Library

Library of Congress Cataloging in Publication Data
A dictionary of criminal justice/Peter Joyce and Neil Wain.
p. cm.
Includes index.
1. Criminal justice, Administration of – Great Britain – Dictionaries.
2. Criminal justice, Administration of – Dictionaries.
I. Joyce, Peter. II. Wain, Neil.
HV8195.A2D527 2010
364.03 – dc22   2009051849

ISBN13: 978–0–415–49245–4 (hbk)
ISBN13: 978–0–415–49246–1 (pbk)
ISBN13: 978–0–203–85030–5 (ebk)

To our respective families
Julie, Emmeline and Eleanor Joyce
and
Jane, Jessica, Hannah, Esther and Samuel Wain

Contents

Introduction   ix

Section One: Definitions   1

Section Two: Key Acts   261

Section Three: Key documents   275

Section Four: Internet sources   299

Index   315

Introduction

This dictionary is designed as a study aid to those embarking on the study of criminology and criminal justice or to those entering a career in the criminal justice system. It assumes no prior knowledge of the subject area.

The dictionary is organized into three sections

Section One provides definitions of a number of key terms that students and practitioners are likely to encounter in their early years of study or work. The section provides detailed definitions of a number of key aspects of criminal justice. On a number of occasions, related terms have been placed under one broad heading in order to provide awareness to the reader of the inter-relationships between various major criminal justice themes and concepts. Additionally, each of the major definitions includes key references which may be consulted in order to provide a more detailed examination of issues raised in connection with the definition.

Section Two gives a brief account of a number of key pieces of legislation which have exerted an important influence on the subsequent development of the criminal justice system. This section is highly selective and is designed to supplement material that is considered in the previous section.

Section Three examines a number of key documents that have helped to shape the operations of the criminal justice system by providing the basis on which subsequent legislation or executive decisions were based. Each entry is accompanied by a reference to the source of the documents and in some cases additional references are provided to enable the reader to secure additional knowledge regarding the content or context within which the document was produced. Again, this section is highly selective, offering no more than a brief snapshot of a number of key developments affecting criminal justice policy. Its main intention is to add to the reader's store of knowledge derived from material presented in section one.

Peter Joyce
Neil Wain
November 2009

Section One
Definitions

A

absolute discharge

See **sentences of the criminal courts**

accountability

Accountability (which is sometimes referred to as 'responsibility') is a political concept whereby individuals or agencies to whom responsibilities have been delegated are required to submit to the scrutiny of another body (or bodies) and justify their actions. Accountability thus constrains the autonomy enjoyed by criminal justice agencies and practitioners.

In addition to being required to answer for their actions ('answerability'), accountability requires that the body to whom the individual or organization is responsible possesses sanctions which may be deployed if actions that are proposed or which have been already undertaken are deemed to be unacceptable. These sanctions may be imposed within an organization (for example at a disciplinary hearing) or from outside of it, by a separate body or agency.

There are two forms of accountability. The individual or organization which discharges functions may have to seek permission before acting. Alternatively, accountability may entail an individual or organization being free to undertake actions but required to report what has been done to another body. The latter is termed *ex post facto* accountability.

Accountability underpins the operations of the criminal justice system at a number of levels. Those who are involved in enforcing the law are subject to the constraints which this imposes on them regarding the performance of their responsibilities. They are required to act within the law and failure to do so may result in penalties being imposed on them.

The professions which operate in the criminal justice system have codes of practice which may impose sanctions on members whose conduct falls below the standards that are expected of them. These standards of behaviour hold professionals accountable for their actions, one example of which is the code of professional standards for police officers.

Some agencies in the criminal justice system operate in a hierarchical fashion so that the actions of one body may be overruled by a higher one. Thus the decisions of a Crown Court may be overruled by the Court of Appeal to which the former is ultimately accountable for its decisions. Alternatively, the actions of one agency may be subject to review by another to which it becomes accountable.

Agencies and individuals within the criminal justice system may be accountable to ministers who can deploy disciplinary sanctions against persons or bodies whose conduct they deem unacceptable. For example, magistrates and judges may be disciplined by the Ministry of Justice which has an Office for Judicial Complaints to investigate complaints (Evans and Hirsch, 2009).

Criminal justice agencies may also be accountable for their actions to the general public. Consultation is one mechanism through which communities may be involved in criminal justice affairs. Consumer-

ism is another approach through which this objective might be achieved. This has been developed as an aspect of new public management since the 1980s which has sought to enhance the rights and responsibilities of members of the general public through market choice rather than formal political mechanisms of accountability (Brake and Hale, 1992: 37).

Practitioners and agencies of the criminal justice system are also informally accountable for their actions. The media is an important mechanism through which actions undertaken within the criminal justice system can be scrutinized and through which changes in practice may be influenced.

See also: constabulary independence, consultation, judges, criminal court system England and Wales, magistrates, new public management

References and further reading

Brake, M. and Hale, C. (1992) *Public Order and Private Lives: The Politics of Law and Order.* London: Routledge.

Evans, R. and Hirsch, A. (2009) 'Names of Misbehaving Judges "Should Be Made Public"' *Guardian* [Online] http://www.guardian.co.uk/politics/2009/mar/16/judges-discipline-freedom-of-information

accredited programmes

Accredited programmes are utilized by the prison and probation service to ensure that interventions directed at offenders are of a high quality in terms of both content and the way they are delivered. The aims of these programmes are to aid an offender's reintegration into the community, to enable an offender to desist from crime in the future and to reduce the risk of harm to those who might otherwise become victims of crime.

There are a wide range of accredited programmes which include cognitive behavioural programmes. These may be delivered within the community, or in prison, or in both settings. Offenders may be required to participate in designated programmes by a community order issued by a court under the provisions of the 2003 Criminal Justice Act, or involvement may be a condition of a prisoner's post-release licence.

The Prison Service has made use of cognitive skills programmes since the early 1990s which 'aim to teach offenders the process of consequential thinking in order to avoid patterns of thinking which lead them to offend' (Cann *et al.*, 2003: 1). The key programmes have consisted of the Reasoning and Rehabilitation Programme (introduced in 1992 following its success in Ottawa, Canada, in significantly lowering recidivism among adult offenders) and the Enhanced Thinking Skills Programme (commenced in 1993). Both target offenders with convictions relating to sex, drugs or violence (Parkin, 2002: 295).

Accredited programmes were initially certified by the Correctional Services Accreditation Panel (CSAP) (formerly known as the Joint Prison/Probation Accreditation Board) that was set up in 1999.

Following the creation of the National Offender Management Service (NOMS), the CSAP became a non-statutory body in May 2005 whose role was to assist the Ministry of Justice in developing and implementing high-quality offender programmes. One consequence of the establishment of NOMS as an executive agency within the Ministry of Justice is the likelihood of programmes of this nature being increasingly delivered by the private and voluntary sectors.

An important aspect of accredited programmes is that their success (or otherwise) should be capable of evaluation. They thus constitute an important aspect of the criminal justice policy 'What works?' agenda.

See also: cognitive behavioural programmes, desistance, National Offender Management Service, political oversight of the criminal justice system, prisons, recidivism, What works?

References and further reading

Cann, J., Falshaw, L., Nugent, F. and Friendship, C. (2003) *Understanding What Works: Accredited Cognitive Skills Programmes for Adult Men and Young Offenders.* London: Home Office Research, Development and Statistics Directorate, Findings 226.

Parkin, J. (2002) 'Offending Behaviour Programmes' in M. Leech and D. Cheney, *The Prisons Handbook.* Hook, Hampshire: Waterside Press.

actuarial assessment

See **assessment tool**

administrative law

Administrative law is a branch of public law that relates to the rules and regulations that control the operations of government agencies or of agencies that have been granted statutory powers of administration.

Administrative tribunals constitute an important mechanism to adjudicate disputes arising between the citizen and the state and to review decisions undertaken by government agencies (Cane, 2009).

They are viewed as a more effective manner for matters of this nature than civil courts because of the cost and delay which aggrieved members of the public would be likely to experience in the courts.

Tribunals grew up in an *ad hoc* manner which resulted in 'wide variations of practice and approach, and almost no coherence'. It was argued that the current arrangements seemed to have been developed 'to satisfy the needs and conveniences of the departments and other bodies which run tribunals, rather than the needs of the user' (Legatt, 2001: para 1.3). This resulted in a number of reforms seeking to establish a unified system which includes regulatory supervision and appeal mechanisms.

In 2006 the Tribunals Service was set up as an executive agency of the Ministry of Justice to manage administrative tribunals and in 2007 the Tribunals, Courts and Enforcement Act (TCEA) replaced the Council on Tribunals (which had been set up by the 1958 Tribunals and Inquiries Act to review the constitution and operations of a number of stipulated tribunals) with the Administrative Justice and Tribunals Council.

The TCEA provided tribunal judges (the new name given to legally qualified tribunal members) with the same guarantees of independence as is possessed by judges. Members of administrative tribunals are appointed by the Judicial Appointments Commission. The legislation created a two-level tribunal system consisting of a First-tier Tribunal and an Upper Tribunal, both divided into areas of specialization (although some tribunals including the Industrial Court and the Special Immigration Appeals Commission remain outside of this system). The Upper Tribunal possesses limited appellate functions arising from decisions made by First-tier Tribunals and possesses enforcement and supervisory/guidance functions.

The legislation also set up the office of the Senior President to exercise management and supervisory responsibilities, performing a role akin to that carried out by the Lord Chief Justice for the court system.

Although tribunals were established to perform functions of a judicial nature, they perform a range of other functions that include the administration of government policy. This is sometimes reflected by their designation as 'Board', 'Authority' or Commission.

Additionally, they are also used to settle certain types of disputes between two private parties. Examples of the latter include industrial tribunals which were created by the 1964 Industrial Training Act and deal with a very wide range of issues concerned with disputes between employers and employees in connection with employment rights (covering issues such as unfair dismissal, redundancy payments and sexual or racial discrimination). The remedies available to employment tribunals include awarding compensation or reinstatement.

See also: judges, judicial review

References and further reading

Cane, P. (2009) *Administrative Tribunals and Adjudication.* Oxford: Hart Publishing.

Legatt, Sir A. (2001) *Tribunals for Users: One System, One Service.* London: Department for Constitutional Affairs.

adversarial justice

Adversarial justice underpins the operations of a legal system in which 'evidence against the defence is presented by the prosecution and tested by the defence before an impartial adjudicator' (Walker and Starmer, 1999: 182). The proceedings take the form of a contest, at the end of which those arbitrating the dispute declare the defendant to be guilty or innocent of the charges that have been laid against him or her.

Adversarial justice is associated with countries possessing common law legal systems and has its origins in the medieval system of trial by battle. 'Under this model one is usually judged by one's peers (the jury) and the system emphasises oral presentation of evidence' (van Koppen and Penrod, 2003: 3). Rules of evidence are drawn up to ensure that jurors are presented with evidence that is reliable and the trial judge plays an important role in determining fair play between the contestants by strictly enforcing these rules. These determine, for example, what evidence is appropriate for the jury to consider.

Adversarial justice permits those accused of crimes to be represented by lawyers who put their client's case to the court. Although the role of advocates is to present evidence, they face considerable pressure to 'win' a case and the outcome of the trial may depend on their skilful questioning of witnesses, the evidence they choose to bring forward and how this is presented to the court.

Adversarial justice rests on the principle that an accused person is regarded as innocent until proven guilty by the prosecution and does not normally require defendants to testify in court or face cross-examination. In the United States this right is enshrined in the fifth amendment to the constitution. However, since the enactment of the 1994 Criminal Justice and Public Order Act, juries in England and Wales have been able to draw inferences if a defendant has refused to answer questions put to him or her by the police in the investigation conducted before the trial and subsequently declines to give evidence in open court.

See also: judges, jury system, right to silence, rules of evidence

References and further reading

van Koppen, P.J. and Penrod, S. (2003) (eds) *Adversarial versus Inquisitorial Justice: Psychological Perspectives on Criminal Justice Systems.* New York: Kluwer Academic/Plenum Publishers.

Walker, C. and Starmer, K. (1999) *Miscarriages of Justice: A Review of Justice in Error.* Oxford: Oxford University Press.

Anti-social Behaviour Orders (ASBOs)

Anti-social Behaviour Orders (ASBOs) were put forward in the 1998 Crime and Disorder Act as a response to activities that caused concern to local communities (and thus increased their fear of crime) but which did not constitute criminal actions to which enforcement measures available to the police could readily be applied.

ASBOs built on the approach adopted in the 1997 Protection from Harassment Act and were directed at nuisance in a way not previously catered for by legislation. The term 'anti-social behaviour' embraces an extremely wide range of activities.

ASBOs may be directed at individuals or groups (such as families) and can be applied to children as young as 10 as well as to teenagers and adults whose actions cause, or are likely to cause, 'harassment, alarm or distress to one or more persons not of the same household' but which fall short of actual criminal behaviour.

ASBOs are issued by Magistrates' Courts at the behest of (initially) the police or a local authority. The civil law standard of proof – the balance of probabilities – must be met to obtain an ASBO. There is no need for the victims of anti-social behaviour to make a formal statement as the basis for action by the police or a local authority. Hearsay evidence and (in certain circumstances) video evidence is acceptable and, additionally, evidence provided by professional witnesses (such as council officials or police officers) may be used as the basis for obtaining these orders.

ASBOs last for a minimum of two years (with no upper limit) and breach of them is a criminal offence that is prosecuted by the Crown Prosecution Service (CPS) and could result in up to five years' imprisonment for an adult or a detention and training order for a juvenile. Attaching the threat of a prison sentence to what is in effect a civil injunction blurs the distinction between civil and criminal law and provides a potentially easier route to prosecution.

Tackling anti-social behaviour has been an important priority of post-1997 Labour governments and was a key aspect of the 're-spect agenda' adopted during the government's third term. The cam-paign against anti-social behaviour formed a crucial aspect of the government's objective to create 'strong and cohesive' communities (Home Office, 2004). Additionally, they addressed behaviour that has been viewed as the starting point of future manifestations of criminal behaviour (Home Office, 1997), seeking to nip it in the bud.

There are several strengths of ASBOs. They offer protection to vulnerable groups suffering harassment such as the elderly, the disabled, racial minorities, gays, and children on their way to and from school. They are relatively cheap to administer, are extremely flexible and can be applied to a very wide range of activities.

However, there are several difficulties associated with ASBOs. They deal with the symptoms of a problem and not the cause of unruly behaviour itself (Squires and Stephen, 2005: 7) and may be used in a vindictive manner against marginalized persons. It has been argued that ASBOs perform a 'street cleaning function' (Burney, 2005: 101), since they are directed against certain types of 'problem people' (such as beggars, youths, prostitutes, drunkards and persons with mental disorders) who have been targeted 'simply by being in the street' (Burney, 2005: 36), thereby heightening their sense of social exclusion.

Critical criminologists see ASBOs as an unwarranted extension of the state's power to intervene against actions which were more akin to bad manners than incipient criminality (Blaikie, 2004). The use to which ASBOs have been put accords to the concepts of 'net widening' and 'mesh thinning' associated with the 'dispersal of discipline thesis' (Cohen, 1985) whereby an increasing number of minor social transgressions become subject to new mechanisms of social control whose effect is to draw people into the criminal justice system earlier than is necessary.

In addition to ASBOs, other measures to tackle anti-social behaviour have also been pursued. An extra-statutory development, the Acceptable Behaviour Contract (ABC), was introduced to combat anti-social behaviour and may be used by Crime and Disorder Reduction Partnerships to tackle anti-social behaviour, especially that committed by those aged between 10 and 18 years of age. ABCs are voluntary agreements entered into by a person committing anti-social behaviour and rely on multi-agency responses to combat it. They may be used as a warning to an offender to change their ways or face a court hearing at which an ASBO could be issued.

The 2002 Police Reform Act initiated important developments in connection with ASBOs. Henceforth they could be valid throughout the country, and the courts could impose an ASBO when convicting an offender for any criminal offence at a youth, Magistrates' or Crown Court. This procedure is variously referred to as 'ASBO bolt-ons' or 'CRASBOs'. This Act further enabled registered social landlords and the British Transport Police to apply for ASBOs.

Further measures to tackle anti-social behaviour were contained in the 2001 Criminal Justice and Police Act that introduced Penalty Notices for Disorder (PNDs) across England and Wales. The 2003 Anti-social Behaviour Act also introduced the new power of dispersal notices. These would be applied to areas that suffered from persistent and serious anti-social behaviour that justified the issuance of an authorization notice by a senior police officer (to which the local authority had to consent) that lasted for a period of up to six months.

The authorization notice provided the police (or Police Community Support Officers) with powers to remove groups consisting of two or more persons from the designated area and also to return unsupervised persons below the age of 16 in a public place between the hours of 9 p.m. and 6 a.m. to their place of residence. This power would be applied when it was reasonable for a police officer to believe that members of the public had been 'intimidated, alarmed or distressed' by the presence of the group.

One danger with this approach is that it may merely displace a problem to another area and in this sense has been described as 'an excellent tool to protect middle-class areas from trouble overflowing from nearby estates' (Pakes and Winstone, 2005: 9).

See also: out of court disposals, Police Community Support Officer, zero tolerance

References and further reading

Blaikie, T. (2004) 'It's About Manners, Stupid', *The Independent*, 28 November.

Burney, E. (2005) *Making People Behave: Anti-social Behaviour, Politics and Policy*. Cullompton, Devon: Willan Publishing.

Cohen, S. (1985) *Visions of Social Control*. Cambridge: Polity Press.

Home Office (1997) *No More Excuses – A New Approach to Tackling Youth Crime in England and Wales*. London: TSO, Cm 3809.

Home Office (2004) *Confident Communities in a Secure Britain: The Home Office Strategic Plan 2004–2008*. London: Home Office.

Pakes, F. and Winstone, J. (2005) 'Community Justice: The Smell of Fresh Bread' in J. Winstone and F. Pakes (eds) *Community Justice: Issues for Probation and Criminal Justice*. Cullompton, Devon: Willan Publishing.

Squires, P. and Stephen, D. (2005) *Rougher Justice: Anti-social Behaviour and Young People*. Cullompton, Devon: Willan Publishing.

Wain, N. (2007) *The ASBO. Wrong Turning – Dead End*. London: Howard League for Penal Reform.

appellate court

See **criminal court system England and Wales**

assessment tool

An assessment tool seeks to establish the future risk that an offender poses to society and is used to guide the courts and agencies such as the National Probation Service in devising an appropriate response to the offender's offending behaviour. The information derived from assessment tools is incorporated into practical use in formats that include pre-sentence reports and sentence plans. It also aids decisions taken by bodies such as the Parole Board in determining whether to recommend the release of prisoners.

There are various forms of assessment, one of which is *actuarial assessment*. This is primarily concerned with establishing the risk of the offender causing serious harm and his or her risk of re-offending rather than seeking to discover the causes of offending behaviour or using assessment as the basis to devise practical measures to reduce these risks. This approach seeks to predict future offending habits by comparing the offender's individual profile with information that has been gathered from a large sample of offenders.

A difficulty with this approach is that it may de-personalize the offender who is defined according to characteristics such as 'the type of offence, previous record, education and employment history, family size and income, residence, alcohol and addictions and relationship problems' (Hudson, 2003: 162). The aim of actuarial techniques of offender risk assessment 'is to place offenders into the categories of risk, and then isolate and exclude the high-risk, allowing only the low-risk to be punished by proportionate penalties' (Hudson, 2003: 163). This approach was embodied in the bifurcation principle governing sentencing in the late twentieth century.

The assessment tool used with adult offenders in England and Wales is the Offender Assessment System (OASys). This seeks to evaluate the risk posed by offenders and also to assess his or her individual needs in order to prevent future re-offending. It has become integral to the work of the National Offender Management Service and is viewed as an important aspect of the 'What works?' strategy that is based upon the development of standardized intervention programmes and assessment procedures (Merrington, 2004: 51). OASys is now used by the Probation and Prison Services in an electronic form, eOASys. One advantage of this latter procedure is that it aids the production of standardized pre-sentence reports.

Much of OASys involves the use of a structured interview. It consists of five components, the first of which seeks to assess the risk of reconviction and the factors that might cause re-offending behaviour. The issues that are examined include current and previous offending habits, social and economic factors such as accommodation, education, personal relationships, substance misuse, emotional and mental health issues, cognitive abilities and attitudes towards offending and supervision.

The second component seeks to assess the risk of causing serious harm to others including persons known to the offender and the public at large. This enables offenders to be graded as posing low, medium, high and very high risk. The third component consists of a summary sheet which annotates the risks and needs that have been identified and which become incorporated into the fourth component that relates to sentence planning (which is formalized in a sentence plan). The fifth component is a self-assessment questionnaire. This covers a range of social and individual problems and an offender's perceived likelihood of future re-offending (Moore, 2007: 1).

Youth Offending Teams use a different assessment tool, ASSET, in connection with evaluating juvenile offenders (aged 10–17) which also includes an element of self-assessment by the offender.

Assessment tools that seek to predict risk and identify factors that are relevant to offending behaviour are regarded as a more reliable predictor of future actions than judgements made by criminal justice practitioners relying solely on their professional knowledge and experience. Additionally, these tools help to promote consistency in the approach adopted towards the assessment of risk and the devising of appropriate interventions. However, the effectiveness of these methods is dependent on a number of extraneous factors that include the relationship between the offender and the assessor and the ability of the assessor to interpret – and if necessary probe – information that is provided through interviews and questionnaires.

Although assessment tools are routinely used in connection with offenders, they can also be used to evaluate the risk of victimization. One example of this is MARACS (Multi-Agency Risk Assessment Conferences) which are used in connection with those (and their children) who are deemed to be at very high risk of domestic violence.

See also: bifurcation, desistance, National Offender Management Service, Parole Board for England and Wales, Probation Service, What works?, youth justice system

References and further reading

Hudson, B. (2003) *Understanding Justice.* Buckingham: Open University Press, second edition.
Kemshall, H. (2003) *Understanding Risk in Criminal Justice.* Buckingham: Open University Press.
Merrington, S. (2004) 'Assessment Tools in Probation' in R. Burnett and C. Roberts (eds) *What Works in Probation and Youth Justice: Developing Evidence-based Practice.* Cullompton, Devon: Willan Pubishing.
Moore, R. (2007) *Adult Offenders' Perception of the Underlying Problems: Findings from the OASys Self-assessment Questionnaire.* London: Home Office, Research, Development and Statistics Directorate, Findings 284.

Association of Chief Police Officers (ACPO)

See **Police Staff Associations**

attorney general

See **political oversight of the criminal justice system**

attrition

Attrition in criminal justice refers to the gap that exists between the number of crimes that are committed and the figure for which a conviction is obtained.

There are a number of stages involved in the prosecution of crime. Crimes are weeded out at each stage resulting in the number of convictions constituting only a small percentage of crime that has been carried out.

In order for a crime to be investigated by the police, it has first to be reported to them, so attrition is initially caused by the non-reporting of crime. Historically, police practices played a considerable part in explaining the reluctance of victims of some crimes to report their experiences. Victims of racial, domestic and sexual violence were reluctant to inform the police in the belief that the police service (and other agencies within the criminal justice process) would be unsympathetic. The police service could also influence the attrition rate by not recording the crimes reported to them. The difference in the two figures is referred to as the 'grey area of crime' and one of the explanations for this is the procedure known as 'cuffing' (Coleman and Moynihan, 1996: 36).

Crimes reported to the police and recorded by them are then investigated. A file is prepared which forms the basis of the decision by the Crown Prosecution Service as to whether a prosecution should be mounted. Attrition occurs at this stage since the CPS may decide to discontinue a case.

Attrition finally occurs in court where a person who has been prosecuted for a crime is either found not guilty or the case is thrown out. Guilty persons may escape conviction for a variety of reasons that include the quality of the evidence presented against them and the high balance of proof required to obtain a successful prosecution. Attrition is a particular problem in connection with sexual offences. In 2002, 11,766 allegations of rape resulted in only 655 convictions (5.6 per cent) (Kelly *et al.*, 2005: 94). Court procedures (whereby features of the victim's lifestyle was frequently presented as mitigation by the defence) is one explanation for this high rate of attrition.

See also: Crown Prosecution Service, crime statistics, detection rates, criminal court system England and Wales, re-balancing the criminal justice system

References and further reading

Coleman, C. and Moynihan, J. (1996) *Understanding Crime Data: Haunted by the Dark Figure.* Buckingham: Open University Press.

Kelly, L., Lovett, J. and Regan, L. (2005) *A Gap or a Chasm? Attrition in Reported Rape Cases.* London: Home Office.

Audit Commission

The Audit Commission was created by the 1982 Local Government Finance Act and was set up in 1983 as an independent watchdog to regulate the external auditors of local authorities in England and Wales. Its remit was subsequently extended to a wide range of other bodies (such as the police service in the late 1980s and the Health Service in 1990) and other services that spent public money. Its functions relating to Wales were transferred by the 2004 Public Audit (Wales) Act to a single audit office for Wales under the control of the Welsh Auditor General.

The Audit Commission aims to ensure that public services are delivered to a high standard of quality through the attainment of the three 'E's' of economy, efficiency and effectiveness. It operates through inspections whose findings are contained in reports. Its contemporary role encompasses auditing local public services (that include the police service and community safety) to promote the principle of value for money, assessing the performance of these services, conducting research into contemporary issues affecting local public services with a view to recommending best practice and facilitating data-matching between public bodies with a particular aim of eliminating fraud. The National Fraud Initiative, introduced in 1996, spearheads this latter approach, involving agencies that include police authorities and local Probation Boards.

The Audit Commission played an important part in advancing new public management by devising performance indicators for public organizations that included the police service. Initially a range of central bodies were involved in this process, but following the 1992 Local Government Act, devising performance indicators became the sole function of the Audit Commission. In 1995 it published the National Performance Police Indicators which defined targets and priorities for this service.

Following the enactment of the 2007 Local Government and Public Involvement in Health Act, the Audit Commission has played a leading role in assessing the effectiveness of partnership working conducted by local government and other locally oriented agencies. It performs this role by conducting Comprehensive Area Assessments in conjunction with existing inspectorates that include Her Majesty's Inspectorate of Constabulary (HMIC), Her Majesty's Prison Inspectorate and Her Majesty's Probation Inspectorate. These seek to secure a more coordinated and targeted system of inspection and assessment.

Reports by the Audit Commission have played an influential role in developing criminal justice policy in a number of areas. The development of Basic Command Units (BCUs) as key structures within which contemporary police work is delivered was influenced by this body (Audit Commission, 1990) which, commencing in 2000, led to the introduction of targets, performance indicators and inspections for BCUs. The reform of the youth justice system in the late 1990s was heavily influenced by an investigation (Audit Commission, 1996) carried out by this organization. Its influence over police affairs will be further developed when, commencing in September 2009, police authorities become subject to a process of inspection conducted jointly by HMIC and the Audit Commission.

Although the Audit Commission is independent of government, its role with regard to criminal justice agencies has tended to reinforce policies favoured by central departments such as the Home Office.

See also: Basic Command Units, new public management, police authority, Probation Service, youth justice system

References and further reading

Audit Commission (1990) *Reviewing the Organisation of the Provincial Police.* London: Audit Commission, Police Paper 9.

Audit Commission (1996) *Misspent Youth.* London: Audit Commission.

B

bail

Bail is a procedure whereby a person suspected of having committed a crime can be released from custody either by the police (in order for further enquiries to be made as to whether the suspect should be charged with an offence) or by a court (in cases where a trial will be held at a later date).

The procedure governing the granting of bail by a court (which is usually a Magistrates' Court) is contained in the 1976 Bail Act and is applied to defendants who plead not guilty or to those who are remanded to appear in court at a future date. Bail (to which conditions may be attached) enables an accused person to remain out of custody until they return to court in connection with the charges laid against them.

The general assumption of the 1976 legislation was that bail would usually be granted on the grounds that a person is presumed innocent until proven guilty. The refusal of magistrates to do so can be challenged in a higher court. However, the granting of bail became a politically contentious issue during the 1990s when arguments were made that those freed on bail went on to commit further serious offences. Thus the 1994 Criminal Justice and Public Order removed the right to bail from a person charged with a further indictable offence whilst already on bail. The 1998 Human Rights Act required that decisions by the courts to grant or refuse bail should be compatible with the European Convention on Human Rights (Slapper and Kelly, 2001: 428). The 2003 Criminal Justice Act amended provisions related to bail, reversing the presumption that it would be granted in some cases, and extending the prosecution's right to appeal to a Crown Court against a decision to grant bail (that had initially been provided for in the 1993 Bail (Amendment) Act).

The police may also grant bail under two circumstances. The first is when a suspect is released from police custody without charge so that further enquiries can be made in order to decide whether to charge him or her with a criminal offence. If this course of action is preferred, the suspect will be required to return to the police station at a later specified date. The second circumstance is when the police decide to charge a person but release him or her from custody with a requirement to attend a court hearing at a later date.

The system of police bail was initially provided for in the 1976 Bail Act and is now governed by the 1984 Police and Criminal Evidence Act as amended by the 1994 Criminal Justice and Public Order Act which enabled the police to attach conditions to bail such as restrictions on a person's movements. The ability to impose conditions ('conditional bail') may result in fewer suspects being detained in police stations but also to a reduction in the numbers granted unconditional bail hence resulting in an element of net widening (Hucklesby, 2001: 441).

Decisions relating to police bail were traditionally made at a police station by the custody officer whose position was created by the 1984 Police and Criminal Evidence Act. However, the 2003 Criminal Justice Act introduced a system of 'street bail' whereby a police officer could grant bail to a person who had been arrested without having to convey him or her to a police station. The main rationale for this reform was to enable police officers to spend more time out on the streets.

Persons who fail to adhere to their bail conditions or fail to turn up in court when required may be arrested and remanded in custody. It is likely that bail will be refused in the future. Those refused bail and remanded in custody (that is, detained in a custodial regime) are subject to time limits beyond which the court is required to release them on bail unless the prosecution can obtain a prior extension from the court. For a trial in a Magistrates' Court, a person may be remanded in custody for no more than 56 days.

See also: criminal court system England and Wales, magistrates

References and further reading

Corre, N. and Wolchover, D. (2006) *Bail in Criminal Proceedings.* Oxford: Oxford University Press, third edition.

Hucklesby, A. (2001) 'Police Bail and the Use of Conditions'. *Criminology and Criminal Justice,* 1: 441–63.

Slapper, G. and Kelly, D. (2001) *Sourcebook on the English Legal System.* London: Cavendish, second edition.

barristers

See **legal profession England and Wales**

Basic Command Units (BCUs)

Basic Command Units (BCUs) (or divisions as they are referred to in some police forces) are responsible for providing a wide range of police services to part of the area covered by a police force. They are typically headed by a Chief Superintendant.

BCUs have not developed in a standardized fashion and their structure and organization is subject to considerable variation across England and Wales. They differ in size, some comprising over 1,000 officers whereas others have below 200 (HMIC, 2004: 76–77). They are not necessarily coterminous with local authorities or Crime and Disorder Reduction Partnerships (CDRPs).

Basic Command Units deliver most everyday policing services and they also gather criminal intelligence, conduct criminal investigations and provide rapid responses to emergencies (Loveday, McClory and Lockhart, 2007: 10). They perform an especially important role in delivering neighbourhood policing have been described as the key level 'at which there is engagement between the police and local communities' (HMIC, 2001: 15), in particular through BCU involvement with CDRPs.

The importance of BCUs in contemporary policing is reflected in the fact that performance measurement includes assessments of the operations of individual BCUs. Data relating to their performance was initially published in 1999, and in 2001 measurements allowing comparative analysis of BCU performance were introduced. BCUs were grouped into 13 'families' that were defined on the basis of socio-economic and demographic characteristics. This enables a comparison to be drawn of the performance of BCUs in comparable areas.

BCU commanders have become important figures in the community whose role is increasingly oriented to local concerns through mechanisms that include Local Area Agreements. The inevitable consequence of the community empowerment agenda will be that responding to local concerns and needs will dominate BCU activities in the future. This may influence the current police hierarchy since lines of accountability linking the BCU commander and the chief constable may require to be loosened (Loveday, McClory and Lockhart, 2007: 9) with BCU commanders effectively becoming 'mini chief constables' in their areas.

However, the enhanced autonomy of BCUs from control by force headquarters will need to be balanced by alternative mechanisms, including increased accountability of policing to local government.

This situation may also require BCUs to possess enhanced financial autonomy through developments such as delegated budgets to enable BCU resources to be deployed in response to local needs (Audit Commission, 2001).

See also: Crime and Disorder Reduction Partnerships, empowerment, joined-up government, Police Service England and Wales

References and further reading

Audit Commission (2001) *Best Foot Forward: Headquarter's Support for Police BCUs.* Abingdon: Audit Commission.

Her Majesty's Inspectorate of Constabulary (HMIC) (2001) *Report for the Year 2000–2001.* London: TSO.

Her Majesty's Inspectorate of Constabulary (HMIC) (2004) *Modernising the Police Service: A Thematic Inspection of Workforce Modernisation – the Role, Management and Deployment of Police Staff in England and Wales.* London: Home Office.

Loveday, B., McClory, J. and Lockhart, G. (2007) *Fitting the Bill: Local Policing for the Twenty-first Century.* London: Policy Exchange.

Best Value

Best Value was an initiative pursued by post-1997 Labour governments to secure efficiency in the delivery of public services. Its aim was to ensure that these were performed in innovative ways that provided the consumer with good value for money.

Best Value replaced the former policy of compulsory competitive tendering (CCT) as the main structure within which the public sector purchased services. Whereas CCT had placed priority on securing the cheapest form of service delivery, Best Value looked beyond cost to embrace other aspects of value for money such as quality of service.

Although many of the ideas embraced by Best Value had their origins in reforms associated with new public management, the approach was now underpinned by legislation. The principle of Best Value was introduced by the 1999 Local Government Act and imposed a requirement on local authorities, police authorities and fire and rescue service authorities (termed Best Value Authorities) to secure continuous improvement in the delivery of its services in order to achieve the objectives specified in the legislation of 'a combination of economy, efficiency and effectiveness'.

Best Value also imposed an obligation on Best Value Authorities to consult with stakeholders (including service users) thus enabling services to be tailored according to the needs of those living in the locality.

In order to assess the attainment of Best Value, the government laid down standards that were required to be met and the indicators that would be used to assess attainment. The latter were termed Best Value Performance Indicators (BVPIs). From 1 April 2000, police authorities were required to develop a five-year rolling programme of service reviews and to summarize their findings and planned actions for improvement (accompanied by measures and targets) in an annual Performance Plan (Spottiswoode, 2000: 9), the aim of which was to ensure continuous improvements in their standards of service delivery.

Their review took into account the 'four C's' – challenge (questioning how and why a service was provided), compare (judging their performance in comparison with other service providers, with a view to improving the services for which they were responsible), compete (ensuring that the service they provided was efficient) and consult (seeking the views of local taxpayers, service users and the business community (Martin, 2003: 168). A fifth 'C', collaboration, was subsequently incorporated into the review process.

The process was subject to a system of independent audit conducted by the Audit Commission and by Her Majesty's Inspectorate of Constabulary.

An important aim of Best Value was to enable service providers to compare their performance with that of the best deliverers. It thus embraced a measurement of comparative efficiency. However, when the Home Office published comparative performance data about police forces in England and Wales for the first time in 2003, an attempt was made to avoid comparing the performance of individual police forces against a national average for a given performance measure and instead to use specific comparison groups for each force, enabling the performance of 'most similar forces' to be compared.

Subsequently a new Policing Performance Assessment Framework (PPAF) was put forward by the Police Standards Unit to assess police performance (including cost) across the full range of policing responsibilities for all forces in England and Wales (Martin, 2003: 173).

To do this, PPAF divided policing responsibilities into six outcome areas (or domains) that consisted of citizen focus, promoting safety and security, resource usage, investigating crime, reducing crime and helping the public. A seventh area, measuring force performance against local priorities, was also included in the PPAF. The attainment of these was measured by a number of key performance indicators and, commencing in 2004–5, the BVPIs were incorporated into the PPAF.

See also: Audit Commission, police authority

References and further reading

Martin, D. (2003) 'The Politics of Policing: Managerialism, Modernisation and Performance' in R. Matthews and J. Young (eds) *The New Politics of Crime and Punishment.* Cullompton, Devon: Willan Publishing.

Spottiswoode, C. (2000) *Improving Police Performance: A New Approach to Measuring Police Efficiency.* London: Public Services Productivity Panel.

bifurcation

Bifurcation is an approach to sentencing policy whereby offenders are differentiated according to the seriousness of the crimes they have committed: the more serious the crime, the more severe is the sentence that those who commit it will receive. The term was coined in the 1970s (Bottoms, 1977) and is sometimes referred to as a 'twin-tracking' approach (Powell, 1999: 193).

Legislation that included the 1972, 1982 and especially the 1991 Criminal Justice Acts sought to introduce the principle of 'bifurcation' into sentencing policy. This approach sought to draw a distinction between serious offenders and the less serious and to give more severe sentences to those who were to deemed to pose a danger to the general public (or who were viewed likely to re-offend) while treating non-serious offenders more leniently. In practical terms this resulted in imprisonment being reserved for the former category of offender with a range of non-custodial sentences being directed at less serious offending behaviour.

Bifurcation principles also influenced other decisions taken within the criminal justice system such as the granting of parole, and in connection with juvenile crime it provided 'a convenient justification for the continued use of both justice and welfare measures within the same youth justice system' (Pickford, 2000: xxxi).

The rationale of this approach was in part economic – community penalties were cheaper to administer than custodial sentences. However, a problem associated with this approach was the perception that offenders who escaped imprisonment had 'got off lightly'. There are various reasons for this belief, which included non-custodial sentences not being seen by the public or sentencers (that is magistrates or judges) as adequate forms of punishment.

The principle of bifurcation was undermined by the penal populism of the 1990s whose retributive focus sought to give criminals their just deserts and to promote imprisonment as a sign of success that the government was succeeding in its mission to 'get tough' with criminals. However, attempts to preserve a twin-track principle of sentencing have been evidenced in the sentencing provisions of the 2003 Criminal Justice Act.

See also: cautioning (formal), judges, magistrates, non-custodial sentences, punishment (aims of), youth justice system

References and further reading

Bottoms, A. (1977) 'Reflections on the Renaissance of Dangerousness'. *Howard Journal*, 16: 70–96.

Pickford, J. (ed.) (2000) *Youth Justice: Theory and Practice.* London: Cavendish.

Powell, M. (ed.) (1999) *New Labour, New Welfare State? The 'Third Way' in British Social Policy.* Bristol: Policy Press.

binding over

See **sentences of the criminal courts**

boot camps

A boot camp is a custodial regime whose environment is based upon military-style discipline.

Boot camps originated in the United States and were initially associated with the tough training regime that was undergone by recruits to the US Marine Corps. During the 1980s this approach was applied to some penal institutions for young offenders which sought to shock them into changing their behaviour.

Aspects of this approach were adopted in the UK. The 1982 Criminal Justice Act introduced the 'short, sharp shock' regime into four selected detention centres where inmates were subject to military-style discipline. Subsequently, the approach was selectively applied to persistent young offenders in the 1990s following a visit by the then Home Secretary, Michael Howard, to America in 1994 when he visited a boot camp in Texas.

A High Intensity Training (HIT) regime (to which the term 'boot camp' was applied) was set up at the young offender institution (YOI) at Thorn Cross in 1996 and at the Military Corrective Training Centre at Colchester in 1997 (where a small number of offenders were accommodated in separate accommodation that constituted a YOI).

Persistent young offenders aged 18–21 undergoing custodial sentences, who were deemed suitable for open conditions and were physically fit and mentally able to cope with the HIT regime were given the opportunity to volunteer for what amounted to the 'last chance saloon'.

At Thorn Cross, the HIT regime was divided into five phases, each of five weeks. In the early phases the emphasis was placed on drill and physical education, but later phases introduced vocational training, therapy to aid the control of temper and anger, and sessions whereby offenders discussed the nature of their offending and the impact of their crimes on the victims, in order to prepare them for release. The fifth phase was a work placement away from the institution. The Colchester regime devoted greater emphasis to physical activities.

Experiments conducted during the 1980s were deemed to have been unsuccessful since the 'short, sharp shock' was stated to have had 'no discernible effect' on the re-offending rates of trainees (Home Office, 1984: 243). The HIT regimes of the 1990s achieved mixed results.

An evaluation of these regimes suggested that there was no significant difference in the proportion reconvicted two years after release between the Thorn Cross experimental group and a control group. However, the Thorn Cross experimental group took longer to re-offend and committed significantly fewer crimes.

However, findings suggested that the cost savings from the smaller number of crimes more than outweighed the extra cost of the Thorn Cross regime compared with a standard regime – at least £5 was saved for every £1 expended. The Colchester experimental group committed slightly fewer crimes than a control group, but their crimes were more costly – at least 89p was lost for every extra £1 expended on the Colchester regime (Farrington *et al.*, 2002: 1).

The Colchester 'boot camp' was closed in March 1998 but the Thorn Cross regime has continued.

See also: youth justice system

References and further reading

Farrington, D. Ditchfield, J., Howard, P. and Jolliffe, D. (2002) *Two Intensive Regimes for Young Offenders: A Follow-up Evaluation*. London: Home Office Research, Development and Statistics Directorate, Findings 163.

Farrington, D., Ditchfield, J., Hancock, G., Howard, P., Jolliffe, D., Livingston, S. and Painter, K. (2002) *Evaluation of Two Intensive Regimes for Young Offenders*. London: Home Office Research, Development and Statistics Directorate, Home Office Research Study 239.

Farrington, D., Painter, K. and Jolliffe, D. (2006) 'Military Corrective Training Centre: An Evaluation' in G. Towl (ed.) *Psychological Research in Prisons*. Oxford: Blackwell. Home Office (1984) *Tougher Regimes in Detention Centres: Report of an Evaluation by the Young Offender Psychology Unit*. London: HMSO.

Bourbon system of policing

The 'Bourbon system of policing' refers to the system of policing used in France in the period before and after the French Revolution (that commenced in 1789).

Policing was controlled by central government and was characterized by the use of arbitrary powers and spies to combat political dissent to the government. The perception that a reformed system of policing in England would emulate this model and thus undermine the prized rights and liberties of English people was a potent argument against police reform in the late eighteenth century. This was evidenced in the unsuccessful attempt by the government to promote a police Bill in 1785 in the wake of the 1780 Gordon Riots (Critchley, 1967: 36–7).

The desire to avoid implanting a Bourbon system of policing in England exerted a considerable impact on the nature of police reform when this was eventually introduced during the nineteenth century. Outside London (where the Home Secretary was the police authority under the 1829 Metropolitan Police Act), a considerable degree of local control over policing was allocated to local elites who composed Watch Committees in the towns (first created under the 1835 Municipal Corporations Act) or who served as magistrates in rural areas (whose role over policing was initially provided for in the 1839 Rural Constabulary Act). Local control over policing was provided by the 1856 County and Borough Police Act and has been exercised since the 1964 Police Act by police authorities.

The excesses associated with the French system of policing also helped to shape the functions of the reformed English policing system and the manner in which these were discharged. The role of the police as spies was considerably developed during the French Revolutionary period by Joseph Fouché who held the post of Minister of Police in 1799–1802, 1804–10 and 1814. He also briefly occupied this position during the early days of the restored Bourbon monarchy in 1815 when he was responsible for unleashing the 'White Terror' against the new regime's opponents.

The desire not to use the police in such a political manner ensured that the ethos of policing in England was preventive, performed by uniformed officers. The use of police officers in plain clothes was kept to a minimum. The outcry arising from the infiltration of a plain clothes police officer, William Popay, at meetings of the National Political Union of the Working Classes in the early 1830s evidenced popular opposition to a system of policing that infringed civil and political liberties (Bunyan, 1977: 63).

This situation also helped to explain the slow development of detective work in reformed English police forces. The Metropolitan Police did not develop a detective branch until 1842 (which became the Criminal Investigation Department in 1878).

See also: accountability, new policing system, old policing system

References and further reading

Bunyan, T. (1977) *The History and Practice of the Political Police in Britain.* London: Quarter Books.
Critchley, T. (1967) *A History of Police in England and Wales.* London: Constable.
Emsley, C. (1996) *The English Police: A Political and Social History.* Harlow: Longman.
Rawlings, P. (2001) *Policing: A Short History.* Cullompton, Devon: Willan Publishing.

Bow Street Runners

See **thief takers**

British Association for Women in Policing

See **Police Staff Associations**

British Crime Survey

See **victimization surveys**

'broken windows'

The 'broken windows' theory holds that 'disorder and crime are causally linked' (Vito *et al.*, 2007: 359). Failure to combat disorder effectively will ultimately result in a neighbourhood becoming a haven of crime.

The concept of 'broken windows' was put forward by Wilson and Kelling (1982) to describe a situation whereby the overt display of minor forms of disorderly behaviour (such as vandalism, graffiti and anti-social activities) within a community gives an impression that 'no one cares'. If this situation is unchecked, a downward spiral of community disintegration occurs in which informal mechanisms of community self-regulation break down and the community slides into a situation of being perceived both by residents and outsiders as being 'out of control'.

Citizens are more likely to encounter disorderly behaviour committed by 'disreputable or obstreperous or unpredictable people' than they are criminal activities. The absence of meaningful intervention against disorder and unruly behaviour creates a sense of insecurity among residents which is characterized by a perception on their part that crime is on the rise.

This causes them to shun 'getting involved' and they withdraw from communal interactions in favour of an insular, self-preservation approach that is lived behind locked doors and bolted windows. The 'control of the streets' is thus ceded to the unruly which provides a setting for the commission of more serious criminal acts because of the absence of challenges that the community is willing or able to mount to their behaviour.

'Broken windows' helps to explain the impact that disorder and low-level criminality can exert on social cohesion and also as a rationale for crime control agencies adopting a firm approach towards activities of this nature. Effective responses to disorder are put forward as a necessity to combat crime that will inevitably arise if unruly behaviour is unchecked. This affirmed the role of order maintenance as a key police priority alongside that of investigating serious crime. In the UK this approach has been delivered through methods such as neighbourhood policing that involve placing a more visible uniformed presence within communities.

See also: Anti-social Behaviour Orders, neighbourhood policing, reassurance policing, zero tolerance

References and further reading

Vito, G., Maahs, J. and Holmes, R. (2007) *Criminology: Theory, Research and Practice*. London: Jones and Bartlett, second edition.

Wilson, J. and Kelling, G. (1982) 'Broken Windows: The Police and Neighbourhood Safety', *Atlantic Monthly*, 249(3): 29–38.

C

cautioning (formal)

Formal cautioning is a procedure whereby minor offenders are officially warned that their behaviour is unacceptable. A formal caution constitutes a 'shot across the bows' which is designed to discourage further offending behaviour that might result in more severe penalties being applied.

A formal caution is delivered orally to a person who admits to having committed a minor offence and would otherwise be prosecuted. It is delivered by, or under the authority of, a senior police officer at a police station: this does not constitute a conviction (since the person has not been taken to court) and does not result in a criminal record. However, it is recorded on the Police National Computer and may be taken into account in any subsequent court proceedings if the person who has been cautioned commits a further offence. The administration of a formal caution for a minor offence constitutes a sanction detection.

The police exercise wide discretion in deciding whether to issue a caution. This resulted in wide variation in the use made of cautions that the Home Office sought to address through circulars specifying separate arrangements for cautioning juvenile and adult offenders (Home Office, 1985) and establishing national standards for cautioning procedures (Home Office, 1990).

ACPO subsequently devised a gravity factor matrix to guide police forces on the offences for which a simple caution is appropriate and additionally forces may seek the advice of the CPS as to whether a caution is appropriate to the nature of the offence or the offender. Only the CPS is empowered to authorize the use of a caution in connection with an indictable-only offence (Home Office, 2008: para 29).

The 2003 Criminal Justice Act introduced the conditional caution which facilitates the involvement of agencies other than the police service in formulating responses to offending behaviour for those aged 18 or over. One consequence of this was that in order to differentiate this innovation from the existing system of formal cautions, the latter were renamed 'simple cautions'. A simple caution is a mechanism to dispose of a criminal offence and should not be confused with the caution that the police administer to a suspect following his or her arrest.

The old system of cautioning for juvenile offenders was replaced by a system of reprimands and warnings for those aged 10–17 in the 1998 Crime and Disorder Act. Reprimands were similar to the old-style formal cautions (so that a record was kept which could be used if the youth committed a further offence) and provide an instant response to a minor instance of juvenile offending in cases where a reprimand or warning had not been given in the previous two years.

A warning is issued if a further offence is committed by someone who has been reprimanded, provided that the offender admitted the offence and it was not sufficiently serious to be referred to the courts. If a young person had received a warning in the previous two years he or she would have to be referred to the courts if a further offence was committed, thus ending the old system of repeat cautioning which had been viewed as an ineffective approach to juvenile crime. A warning may also be given as an initial intervention in connection with a serious offence without a reprimand being first issued.

The decision to issue a reprimand or warning is made by the police whose decisions are based on a gravity factor matrix developed by ACPO that takes into account the seriousness of the crime and the offending history of the youth. However, although the police remain responsible for determining what course of action should be taken against a young offender, they are required to refer the youth issued with a warning to the Youth Offending Team which may decide to intervene, although they will not do so in all cases.

See also: criminal record, Crown Prosecution Service, detection rates, discretion, Home Office Circular, out of court disposals, youth justice system

References and further reading

Home Office (1985) *The Cautioning of Offenders*. London: Home Office, circular 14/85.

Home Office (1990) *The Cautioning of Offenders*. London: Home Office, circular 59/90.

Home Office (2008) *Simple Cautioning – Adult Offenders*. London: Home Office, circular 016/2008.

charge reduction ('downgrading')

See **plea bargaining**

Civil Justice Council

See **Law Commission**

cognitive behavioural programmes

Cognitive behavioural programmes seek to identify the attitudes and thinking patterns that underpin offending behaviour and to replace these with alternative values which exert a positive influence on an individual's awareness, thought processes and judgement and thus reduce the likelihood of criminal behaviour.

Cognitive behavioural programmes are based upon cognitive behavioural therapy and are used to treat a range of clinical and non-clinical disorders that include personality disorders, various forms of substance abuse and sex offending. These programmes may be delivered within the community or in prisons where therapeutic treatment is available.

Historically, therapeutic treatment in prisons was available to a limited number of violent psychiatric offen-ders in specialist institutions such as Grendon or in therapeutic units in prisons such as Hull, where the traditional emphasis on work, education and physical exercise is replaced by therapeutic groupwork in which prisoners are challenged to face up to their offending behaviour within a supportive environment in which doctors play a key role.

These therepeutic regimes were costly but achieved success in terms of subsequent reconvictions of those with violent and sexual offences (Genders and Player, 1995) although there was a need for inmates to spend at least 18 months to achieve positive results that were evidenced by reconviction rates of around one-fifth to one-quarter (Marshall, 1997: 1).

Subsequently, accredited sex offender, anger control and drug rehabilitation programmes have been introduced in prisons to address the offending behaviour of inmates. These include the Sex Offender Treatment Programme (SOTP), designed to challenge the excuses and justifications that underpin such offending behaviour and to provide offenders with an understanding of the impact of their crimes on the victim, and Controlling Anger and Learning how to Manage it (CALM) that seeks to teach skills and manage anger and emotions.

However, cognitive behavioural programmes to address all forms of offending behaviour are not universally available within the prison service which means that a number of prisoners are not able to benefit from them to aid their reform. Programmes of this nature to combat alcohol abuse, for example, are, in general, poorly provided in prisons. Substance abuse is frequently treated through detoxification and psychiatric disorders have traditionally been responded to by a heavy reliance being placed on drugs.

See also: non-custodial sentences, prisons

References and further reading

Genders, E. and Player, E. (1995) *Grendon: Study of a Therapeutic Prison.* Oxford: Clarendon Press.
Marshall, P. (1997) *A Reconviction Study of HMP Grendon Therapeutic Community.* London: Home Office Research and Statistics Directorate, Research Findings Number 53.

cold case review

See **National DNA Database (NDNAD)**

committal proceedings

See **criminal court system England and Wales**

Common Law

See **law (sources of)**

Community Order

See **non-custodial sentences, sentences of the criminal courts**

community safety

See **crime prevention**

Comprehensive Area Assessments

See **joined-up government**

Comprehensive Spending Review

See **Police Service England and Wales**

concurrent sentence

See **sentences of the criminal courts**

conditional caution

See **out of court disposals**

conditional discharge

See **sentences of the criminal courts**

consecutive sentence

See **sentences of the criminal courts**

constabulary independence

Constabulary independence refers to the concept that police officers should be immune from control, especially political control, in respect of the performance of their law enforcement responsibilities.

This concept is based upon the common law derivation of the office whose holders are required to uphold the law using the powers granted to them by law. It follows from this that constables exercise 'original' jurisdiction derived from the office and in performing their duties are accountable only to the law which defines their powers. Legal accountability and constabulary independence are thus closely related doctrines.

This principle of constabulary independence developed during the course of the nineteenth century and was affirmed in the case of Fisher v. Oldham Corporation [1930] which ruled that in executing the office of constable according to the law, the decisions of a constable could not be overruled by a watch committee (Jefferson and Grimshaw, 1984: 52). Although this concept applied to all police officers, an important consequence related to the power of chief constables in relation to law enforcement.

Decisions made by chief constables regarding law enforcement were often based on their ability to determine priorities for their forces – it was impossible to enforce all laws and a judgement had to be made as to what was most important for the locality. Constabulary independence suggested that no outside body could give the chief constable directions regarding the exercise of this form of discretion.

This situation was affirmed in connection with cases brought against the Metropolitan Commissioner of Police in 1968 and 1973 in connection with legislation concerned with illegal gambling and the distribution of obscene material. It appeared that the Commissioner was deliberately failing to enforce these laws.

In the former of these cases Lord Denning provided an important statement of constabulary independence when he argued, in connection with the duties of the Metropolitan Commissioner of Police, that 'No Minister of the crown can tell him that he must, or must not, keep observation on this place or that; or that he must, or must not, prosecute this man or that one. Nor can any police authority tell him so. The responsibility for law enforcement lies on him. He is answerable to the law and to the law alone'.

The ability of chief officers to determine priorities for their force was considerably constrained by the 1994 Police and Magistrates' Courts Act which enabled the Home Secretary to set key priorities for the entire police service in England and Wales. This considerably undermined the historic concept of constabulary independence.

Subsequently the police service has been subjected to a wide range of initiatives imposed upon it by central government and has effectively become politicized in the sense that a key role has become that of implementing government programmes.

See also: law (sources of), discretion, judges

References and further reading

Fisher v. Oldham Corporation [1930] 2 K.B. 364.

R v. Metropolitan Police Commissioner ex parte Blackburn [1968] All E.R. 769.

Jefferson, T. and Grimshaw, R. (1984) *Controlling the Constable: Police Accountability in England and Wales.* London: Cobden Trust.

Marshall, G. (1965) *Police and Government.* London: Methuen.

consultation

Consultation entails a procedure whereby members of the general public are able to express their opinions regarding the manner in which a service is delivered. The views they put forward are not binding on the service providers whose only obligation is to listen to what is being said and offer explanations of their current practices.

Consultation is an important aspect of contemporary criminal justice policy. The 1984 Police and Criminal Evidence Act, for example, initiated a procedure (which is now governed by the 1996 Police Act) whereby the police service was required to consult with local communities regarding the policing of an area. The 1996 Police Act also introduced a requirement that police authorities had to make arrangements to secure the views of the public which would inform the policing plan. The 2009 Crime and Policing legislation built upon this provision by requiring police authorities to take the views of people in a police authority area into account.

The objective of community safety also requires consultation. The 1998 Crime and Disorder legislation provided for the creation of Crime and Disorder Reduction Partnerships, one of whose processes involved a local crime audit, whose operations enabled local people to influence the local crime-fighting agenda. Subsequently the three-year Partnership Plan has to embrace engagement with local communities.

Although consultation may be regarded as compatible with the operations of a liberal democratic system of government and an approach that is compatible with enabling the specific '"interests and needs of diverse communities" to be recognized and addressed' (Hirst, 2000) in criminal justice policy, it raises problems in particular in connection with the extent to which those who turn up to meetings are representative of the community from which they derive, whose views (if acted upon) may serve to further exclude those who are already marginalized.

Further, unlike participation in which policy-making becomes a joint exercise between citizens and service providers, consultation does not alter the power relationship between service provider and citizen. At its worst it may provide for 'a form of "explanatory" accountability without teeth' (Newburn and Jones, 1996: 124) since the consultees have no sanctions available to them if explanations offered by service providers are deemed to be inadequate or when the views they express are not acted upon.

Nonetheless, it does present the possibility that the public can influence policy-making. For this reason it is compatible with the empowerment agenda. However, the relationship that may be forged between agencies and the general public through consultative mechanisms may be used as a way for professionals to 'sell' a policy initiative to the local public, thereby enhancing its legitimacy within the community. In cases such as this, consultation becomes a method to manipulate the public rather than to empower them.

See also: accountability, Crime and Disorder Reduction Partnerships, empowerment, self-policing society

References and further reading

Hirst, P. (2000) 'Statism Pluralism and Social Control' in D. Garland and R. Sparks (eds) *Criminology and Social Theory*. Oxford: Oxford University Press.

Newburn, T. and Jones, T. (1996) 'Police Accountability' in W. Saulsbury, J. Mott and T. Newburn (eds) *Themes in Contemporary Policing*. London: Independent Committee of Inquiry into the Role and Responsibilities of the Police.

contestability

See **new public management**

control orders

See **internment**

coroners

Coroners are independent judicial officers whose role is to ascertain the medical cause of death where this is not known and to investigate whether this arose from violence or other unnatural causes.

Coroners are usually lawyers but in some cases are doctors. The office of coroner dates from 1194 and the basis of the modern office was created by the 1887 Coroners' Act. The 1887 measure was consolidated by the 1988 Coroners' Act.

Coroners are appointed by local authorities, although the Lord Chancellor or High Court has the power to remove them in certain circumstances. They hold office under the Crown. England and Wales is divided into a number of districts (or coroners' jurisdictions) to which coroners are assigned. There are approximately 110 coroners in England and Wales, of which 32 work in a full-time capacity. All coroners, deputy and deputy assistant coroners are members of the Coroners' Society of England and Wales.

The coroner has the duty to investigate the circumstances of sudden, unnatural or uncertified deaths that are reported to him, usually by the police, a doctor or a local registrar of deaths. If the coroner decides that a medical examination of the deceased is required, a pathologist will carry out a post-mortem examination.

An inquest in a coroner's court is held in circumstances where the post-mortem examination suggests that there was reasonable cause to suspect that the dead person suffered a violent or unnatural death or in cases where a sudden death occurred and the cause is not known, or where a death occurred in prison or in police custody. Inquests may con-cern individual or mass deaths, an example of the latter being the Coroner's Inquest in 1991 into the death of 95 football supporters at Hillsborough in 1989. Approximately 29,000 inquests are held in England and Wales each year.

A coroner's inquest is an inquiry to determine how, when and why the deceased person died but not to determine who was to blame for the death. In theory the proceedings are inquisitorial, although it has been alleged that inquests involving controversial deaths often tend to become adversarial in character (Hartley, 2001: 186–7).Witnesses are not compelled to answer questions at an inquest and a refusal to answer is not held against them as it would be in a normal criminal trial (where under the provisions of the 1994 Criminal Justice and Public Order Act juries may draw inferences from a witness's silence).

The 1988 Coroners' Act provided for juries of between seven to eleven persons to be used. When used, juries make the final decision as to whether death arose from a number of categories that include lawful killing, unlawful killing, accidental killing, misadventure or natural causes. The coroner will usually direct the jury as to which verdicts are available to them (and, as was the case in the inquest held into the death of Jean Charles de Menezes in 2008, may indicate what verdicts are not available to them). Until 1977, inquest juries were able to declare that one person had been murdered by another, which led to the accused person being automatically tried for murder. This power was last used in 1975 when Lord Lucan was declared to be the murderer of his children's nanny (although his subsequent disappearance prevented him from being tried for that offence). It was then abolished, for reasons that included the fairness of a future trial after such an emotive verdict had been delivered. In 2004 coroners were permitted to issue a narrative verdict in which the circumstances of a death are recorded without attributing the cause to a named individual.

The independence of coroners provides them with the ability to criticize actions undertaken by the state or its agents. Historically the independence of the coroners made for critical scrutiny of police actions. This was displayed early in the life of the Metropolitan Police when a police baton charge at a political rally organized by the National Union of the Working Classes resulted in an officer, PC Culley, being fatally stabbed. The Inquest Jury returned a verdict of justifiable homicide (Bunyan, 1977: 63).

Although it has been alleged that in more recent years bias has been displayed towards the police service (Howarth and Leaman, 2001: 119) there have been exceptions to this. The verdict of an Inquest Jury in

1997 into the murder of Stephen Lawrence that he had been 'unlawfully killed in a completely unprovoked racist attack by five white youths' emphasized the shortcomings of the police investigation into his murder. Additionally, some coroners who have held inquests into the deaths of British soldiers killed in Iraq or Afghanistan have criticized the Ministry of Defence in connection with issues that include deficiencies in equipment.

Important changes were introduced by the 2009 Coroners and Justice Act which created a new national coroner's service headed by a chief coroner, established a new system of secondary certification which did not require the involvement of a coroner and provided for a judicial inquiry to be held in secret under the provisions of the 2005 Inquiries Act rather than an inquest where there was sensitive evidence (which was likely to consist of intercept evidence).

See also: criminal court system England and Wales

References and further reading

Bunyan, T. (1977) *The History and Practice of the Political Police in Britain*. London: Quartet Books.

Hartley, H. (2001) *Exploring Sport and Leisure Disasters: A*

Socio-legal Perspective. London: Cavendish.

Howarth, G. and Leaman, O. (ed.) (2001) *Encyclopedia of Death and Dying.* London: Routledge.

Matthews, P. (2006) *Jervis on the Office and Duties of Coroners.* London, Routledge, twelfth edition.

Crime and Disorder Reduction Partnerships (CDRPs)

Crime and Disorder Reduction Partnerships (termed Community Safety Partnerships in Wales) have the same boundaries as English and Welsh district councils or unitary local authorities. They were established by the 1998 Crime and Disorder Act and provide a mechanism whereby a number of agencies that operate within the local authority can pool their efforts to tackle local crime and public disorder problems and attain the goal of community safety.

The 1998 Act placed a statutory duty on police forces and local authorities (termed 'responsible authorities') to cooperate with police authorities, health authorities and probation committees in multi-agency bodies which became known as Crime and Disorder Reduction Partnerships (although this designation did not appear in the legislation).

The 2002 Police Reform Act made police and fire authorities responsible authorities as defined by the 1998 legislation and in the following year were joined by Primary Care Trusts in England (and health authorities in Wales). The 2002 measure required CDRPs to work closely with drug action teams in areas with a two-tier structure of local government and to integrate their work with drug action teams in areas which had a unitary structure of local government by April 2004. The 2002 Act also enabled CDRPs to merge where this course of action seemed appropriate to tackle issues involving a number of related local authority areas. The powers of CDRPs in connection with drug misuse and anti-social behaviour were amended by the 2002 Police Reform Act, the 2003 Anti-social Behaviour Act and the 2006 Police and Justice Act. The latter legislation expanded the role of CDRPs to include alcohol and other substances in addition to drugs.

The starting point of the process to reduce crime and disorder in each locality was the preparation of a local crime audit (conducted by the local authority) that formed the basis of the local crime reduction strategy. The audit had to take into account the views of the public who lived and worked in the local authority area concerning crime and disorder. Following the audit, the CDRP formulated priorities, and a three-year strategy to tackle crime and disorder was published.

Subsequently, a new procedure was introduced whereby CDRPs were required to produce a three-year rolling Partnership Plan (the first of which was for 2008–11) in place of a three-year year strategy based on an audit of crime. The Partnership Plan contains the objectives required to be implemented, how these will be delivered (in particular specifying the contribution of partners to support the delivery of the priorities), the manner through which performance against priorities would be assessed and the way in which the partnership would engage with their communities. Progress in attaining these objectives is monitored (through the mechanism of a strategic assessment produced every year) so that adjustments can be made as required.

CDRPs were initially given little central guidance as to how they should perform their work. The 2006 Police and Justice Act introduced national standards (in the form of Hallmarks of Effective Partnerships) as minimum statutory requirements. Hallmarks of Effective Partnerships were identified to consist of empowered and effective leadership; visible and constructive accountability; intelligence-led business processes; effective and responsive delivery structures; engaged communities and appropriate skills and knowledge (Home Office, 2007a: 4).

Initially the performance of CDRPs was assessed through a number of mechanisms which included the Policing Performance Assessment Framework through which police performance in relation to crime and community safety was assessed. This was replaced in 2008 by the Assessments of Policing and Community Safety (APACS) which enabled the performance of agencies operating in partnership to be more easily assessed by the ability to align indicators used by these separate bodies thereby providing a 'common language for the discussion of performance' (Home Office, 2007a: 17).

The work of CDRPs is superintended by the nine Government Offices for the Regions. These were established in 1994 and are headed by a Regional Director and since 2007 by a Regional Office Minister.

CDRPs had to overcome a number of difficulties that included the dispersed leadership which undermined attempts by CDRP managers to achieve targets, the disinclination of partnership agencies to share information with each other and the degree of central control that was exerted over their operations that was evidenced in the setting of targets for CDRPs in connection with vehicle crime, domestic burglary and robbery and the introduction of performance indicators for CDRPs.

Some attempt to ameliorate problems of this nature have included changes introduced by the 2006 Police and Justice Act to the governance structure of each partnership, requiring the creation of a 'strategy group' to exercise ultimate responsibility for the implementation of the Partnership Plan and the 2008–11 Crime Strategy which promised to reduce the number of specific targets set for CDRPs within the safer communities Public Service Agreement (PSA) to ensure that the attainment of priorities felt to be important by local communities were placed at the forefront of agency action (Home Office, 2007b: 43).

See also: joined-up government

References and further reading

Crawford, A. (1999) *The Local Governance of Crime: Appeals to Community Partnerships.* Oxford: Oxford University Press.

Home Office (2007a) *Delivering Safer Communities: A Guide to Effective Partnership Working: Guidance for Crime and Disorder Reduction Partnerships and Community Safety Partnerships.* London: Home Office, Police and Crime Standards Directorate.

Home Office (2007b) *Cutting Crime: A New Partnership 2008–2011.* London: Home Office.

Loveday, B. (2005) 'Police and Community Justice in Partnership' in J. Winstone and F. Pakes (eds) *Community Justice: Issues for Probation and Criminal Justice.* Cullompton, Devon: Willan Publishing.

crime prevention

Crime prevention embraces a wide range of measures which seek to prevent crime from taking place.

There are three broad approaches to crime prevention (Brantingham and Faust, 1976). Primary prevention focuses on the environment within which crime occurs and suggests that crime can be prevented by reducing the opportunities conducive to its commission. Secondary prevention targets those deemed to be most likely to embark on criminal activities, and may embrace activities such as early childhood intervention in the lives of those deemed most at risk of committing crime (Farrington, 2002). A third approach, tertiary prevention, is directed at known offenders, and seeks to prevent crime by stopping them from re-offending. These approaches underpin specific crime prevention initiatives.

A number of contemporary crime prevention policies entail situational methods. This approach typically entails a pre-emptive approach which is pursued by '(1) measures directed at highly specific forms of crime; (2) that involve the measurement, design or manipulation of the immediate environment in as systematic and permanent a way as possible; (3) so as to increase the effort and risks of crime and reduce the rewards as perceived by a wide range of offenders' (Clarke, 1992: 4). The aim of situational methods of crime prevention is to introduce 'specific changes to influence the offender's *decision* or ability to commit these crimes at *particular* places and times. . . . it sought to make criminal actions less attractive to offenders rather than relying on detection, sanctions or reducing criminality through . . . improvements in society or its institutions' (Ekblom, 1998: 23).

Situational methods of crime prevention originated in America and provide an example of policy transfer. Typically they are focused on the target of crime and seek to prevent its occurrence by methods that include target removal, target hardening (using physical approaches to crime prevention such as burglar alarms, car steering locks or property marking) or target devaluation (which seeks to ensure that only authorized owners can make use of a particular product).

Additionally this approach includes enhanced mechanisms of surveillance (which may be achieved through closed-circuit television (CCTV)) or the redesigning of the physical environment. The latter approach was based upon the concept of defensible space (Newman, 1972) which highlighted the relationship between the physical environment and crime. The solution was to reconstruct residential environments to foster territoriality, facilitate natural surveillance and re-establish access control. This approach is frequently referred to as 'designing out crime'.

There are, however, problems associated with the use of situational crime prevention methods. Situational crime prevention may not prevent crime but instead may merely alter the pattern of offending behaviour. This is referred to as displacement which may take four forms: temporal (in which the crime is committed at a different time than had been intended), spatial (in which the crime is committed in a different place to that originally intended), tactical (in which the methods used to commit a crime are adjusted to take account of initiatives such as target hardening) or target/functional (in which a different crime from that originally intended is carried out) (Barr and Pease, 1992; Pease, 1997: 977).

Additionally, although the situational approach may help to gel communities and reinforce social controls within areas protected by the use of these methods, they may result in the creation of 'gated communities' in which 'access is restricted to residents in the hope of keeping out offenders who cruise neighbourhoods looking for crime opportunities' (Clarke, 2005: 59). This may heighten the sense of social exclusion of those who feel targeted by initiatives of this nature.

Situational crime prevention has also been accused of victim-blaming (Walklate, 1996: 300). Individuals and communities that have failed to protect themselves adequately against crime might be held partly to blame for its occurrence which shifts blame away from the perpetrator.

An alternative approach to crime prevention entails social approaches to combat crime. This embraces measures that seek to improve social conditions, strengthen community institutions and enhance recreational, educational and employment opportunities. Unlike situational methods of crime prevention (which tend to focus on opportunity reduction), social approaches seek to tackle crime 'at its roots'. Social crime prevention has been pursued through a number of initiatives that are often delivered through locally oriented multi-agency approaches. However, there are problems associated with this approach.

One difficulty associated with social crime prevention is that evaluation (a key feature of situational approaches which are often funded and evaluated by central government) has not always been rigorously conducted. This tends to mean, therefore, that perceptions that youth clubs help to divert young persons from crime are based upon faith rather than empirical evidence. Second, it is not always clear why particular initiatives seem to work effectively. Social crime prevention typically embraces a range of actions which are pursued simultaneously and it is thus difficult to analyse the effectiveness of individual measures within the overall programme.

In the United Kingdom, crime prevention initiatives in recent years have been pursued within the context of community safety. This term emphasizes that combating local crime and disorder issues cannot be left solely to the police but instead requires a multi-agency or partnership approach involving a wide range of local agencies using situational and social methods of crime prevention together with law enforcement approaches. These pursue measures whose aims include tackling the fear of crime and alleviating signs of neighbourhood neglect. Local government performs an important role in coordinating community safety policies which also involve local people identifying problems that have an adverse impact on their everyday lives and who may participate in delivering solutions to them.

See also: 'broken windows', empowerment, neighbourhood management, neighbourhood policing, policy transfer, reassurance policing, self-policing society, surveillance, What works?

References and further reading

Barr, R. and Pease, K. (1992) 'The Problem of Displacement' in D. Evans, N. Fyfe and D. Herbert (eds) *Crime, Policing and Place: Essays in Environmental Criminology*. London: Routledge and Kegan Paul.

Brantingham, P. and Faust, F. (1976) 'A Conceptual Model of Crime Prevention' in *Crime and Delinquency*, 22: 130–46.

Clarke, R. (1992) *Situational Crime Prevention: Successful Case Studies*. New York: Harrow and Heston.

Clarke, R. (2005) 'Seven Misconceptions of Situational Crime Prevention' in N. Tilley (ed.) *Handbook of Crime Prevention and Community Safety*. Cullompton, Devon: Willan Publishing.

Ekblom, P. (1998) 'Situational Crime Prevention: Effectiveness and Local Initiatives' in P. Goldblatt and C. Lewis (eds) *Reducing Offending: An Assessment of Research Evidence on Ways of Dealing with Offending Behaviour*. London: Home Office, Research Study 187.

Farrington, D. (2002) 'Developmental Criminology and Risk-Focused Prevention' in M. Maguire *et al.* (eds) *The Oxford Handbook of Criminology*. Oxford: Oxford University Press.

Newman, O. (1972) *Defensible Space: Crime Prevention Through Urban Design*. London: Architectural Press.

Pease, K. (1997) 'Crime Prevention' in M. Maguire, R. Morgan and R. Reiner (eds) *Oxford Handbook of Criminology*. Oxford: Clarendon Press, second edition.

Walklate, S. (1996) 'Community and Crime Prevention' in E. McLaughlin and J. Muncie (eds) *Controlling Crime*. London: Sage.

crime statistics

Crime statistics provide an indication of the volume of crime committed in society and the offences that have been carried out within a designated period of time.

Official Crime Statistics are published on a regular basis by the Home Office and since April 2008 they have been produced under the auspices of the Statistics Authority. Official crime statistics rely on information that is provided by police forces relating to the crime that has occurred within their area. However, these figures do not provide a completely accurate picture regarding crime. There is a gap between the amount of crime which is actually committed and that which enters into official crime statistics. This is referred to as the 'dark figure' of crime and is caused by a number of factors that relate to the procedures that are involved in crime reporting and crime recording. These procedures entail a number of stages, each of which serves as a filtering process in which crimes that have been committed are removed from the official record. It is in this sense that official crime statistics can be said to be socially constructed, reflecting the reporting preferences of the public and the recording practices of the police service – both of which are subject to change across historical time periods.

Initially, in order to report a crime, the victim must be aware that he or she has experienced a criminal act. However, this may not always be obvious – a missing wallet, for example, may be explained by personal carelessness rather than another's criminal actions.

If a victim is aware that a crime has occurred, the next stage is to report the matter to the police. However, this does not always happen. The victim may believe the crime too trivial to warrant police intervention or that the police would be unable (or perhaps unwilling) to do much about the incident were it reported. Alternatively, the victim may feel intimidated and not report a crime as they fear that they will suffer reprisals if they do so. This has been identified as a particular problem on high-crime housing estates (Maynard, 1994: 5).

Embarrassment may also be a reason why crimes such as thefts from their clients by prostitutes or their accomplices are not reported. Finally, victims may believe that the criminal justice system will not handle the complaint justly. The treatment by criminal justice agencies of female victims of serious sexual attacks is one reason why official statistics have traditionally underestimated crime of this nature.

The final stage of the process whereby crime is entered into official statistics is the recording of the offence by the police service. The gap between offences reported to the police and what is actually recorded is called the 'grey area' of crime (Bottomley and Pease, 1986). Decisions concerning whether to record a crime officially that has been reported are dependent on a range of factors that include the seriousness of the matter (which might lend itself to an informal intervention perhaps by warning a person who has behaved incorrectly).

One way whereby crimes reported to the police fail to be recorded is through the process of 'cuffing'. This entails either not recording a crime which has been reported, or downgrading a reported crime to an incident which can be excluded from official statistics. The decision to do this was initially motivated by a desire to avoid the time-consuming practice of filling out a crime report for minor incidents, although this problem was ameliorated by the introduction of computerized crime recording systems.

However, the introduction of performance indicators for the police service in 1992 intensified pressures on the police to avoid recording all offences notified to them. Crime statistics were a key source of evidence of police performance, so increased levels of reported crimes could imply inefficiency.

There are further factors that affect the accuracy of official crime statistics as a guide to the total volume of crime in society. Some crimes are deliberately missed off. The police are required to pass to the Home Office only details of 'notifiable offences'. Since 1999 these have included all crimes which are triable on indictment in a Crown Court, many which are triable 'either way' and some summary offences. Thus many crimes (including the great majority of motoring offences) are not notifiable and are therefore excluded from crime statistics.

Additionally, the manner in which a crime with several victims is recorded will influence statistics relating to the total volume of crime within a specified period. What are termed 'Home Office Counting Rules' give guidance on matters that include how these issues (for example, theft from several cars in a car park) should be handled. Changes to these rules (the most recent version of which was published in 2008) requiring the number of victims rather than

criminal acts to be recorded may result in an apparent increase in the total volume of crime which is not based on any actual increase in criminal activity.

One difficulty with the role performed by police forces in recording crime concerned the variations in practices adopted by different forces. This undermined attempts to use crime statistics as a mechanism to assess the comparative efficiency of forces. In 2002 ACPO, with the support of the Home Office, sought to address this issue by introducing the National Crime Recording Standard (NCRS). This sought to promote 'greater reliability and consistency in collecting and recording crime data. It requires police services to take an approach that focuses on the victims' perspective and requires all forces to record crimes according to a clear set of principles' (Audit Commission, 2004: 2).

The problems that are associated with the accuracy of official crime statistics might be remedied by the use of alternative methods to gather information on crime. The main alternatives are victimization surveys (which are employed by the British Crime Survey), self-report studies and field research.

See also: attrition, criminal court system England and Wales, detection rates, field research, Police Service England and Wales, victimization surveys

References and further reading

Audit Commission (2004) *Crime Recording: Improving the Quality of Crime Records in Police Authorities and Forces in England and Wales*. London: Audit Commission.

Bottomley, K. and Pease, K. (1986) *Crime and Punishment: Interpreting the Data*. Buckingham: Open University Press.

Coleman, C. and Moynihan, J. (1996) *Understanding Crime Data: Haunted by the Dark Figure*. Buckingham: Open University Press.

Maynard, W. (1994) *Witness Intimidation: Strategies of Prevention*. London: Home Office, Police Policy Directorate, Crime, Detection and Prevention Series, Paper 55.

Smith, A. (2006) *Crime Statistics: An Independent Review*. London: Home Office.

criminal court system England and Wales

The criminal court system in England and Wales consists of a hierarchy of tribunals that are responsible for trying those charged with committing criminal acts. The court system additionally provides for procedures whereby persons convicted of a crime by one court can appeal to a higher (or appellate) court against either their sentence or conviction. Since 2005 all courts save the House of Lords have been administered by Her Majesty's Courts Service.

The lowest tier in the hierarchy of criminal courts is a Magistrates' Court. Trials are usually heard by three lay magistrates (who are termed a 'bench'), although a small number of Magistrates' Courts are presided over by a full-time official initially termed a 'stipendiary magistrate' but now referred to as a District Judge (Magistrates' Courts). Juries are not used in Magistrates' Courts. Around 95 per cent of criminal trials take place in Magistrates' Courts (Sanders, 2001).

A person who has been formally charged with an offence by the police is either delivered directly to a Magistrates' Court from police custody or is freed on bail from police custody and summonsed to appear at a Magistrates' Court at a later date.

The least serious criminal charges (termed 'summary offences') will be tried in this court. These are offences that carry a short term of imprisonment and/or a fine (which was historically a maximum of six months/£5,000). The 2003 Criminal Justice Act intended to enable magistrates to impose prison sentences of 12 months and to place severe restrictions on their ability to hand out prison sentences of less than this period but this reform has not yet been implemented. Historically, cases were prosecuted by the police (hence Magistrates' Courts were commonly referred to as 'police courts') but are now handled by the Crown Prosecution Service.

In addition to trying summary offences, a defendant may opt to be tried in a Magistrates' Court if charged with an offence which is 'triable either way' (that is, it may be heard in either a Magistrates' Court or a Crown Court). Theft and burglary are examples of offences that can be tried in either court. Typically a defendant in a case of this nature will plead guilty and hope that he or she will benefit from the reduced sentencing powers of the magistrates, although under the provisions of the 2000 Powers of Criminal Courts (Sentencing) Act, magistrates have the right to try a case and then submit it to a Crown Court for sentencing if they feel their powers are inadequate to deal with the seriousness of the matter.

Persons charged with the more serious criminal charges (those which are triable on indictment, in a Crown Court) also initially appear at a Magistrates' Court. Unless a voluntary bill of indictment procedure is used (whereby a High Court judge can authorize a defendant to be committed to a Crown Court for trial without first appearing in a Magistrates' Court), magistrates traditionally held preliminary hearings (termed 'committal proceedings') which enabled the strength of the evidence against the defendant to be tested. In performing this task magistrates performed the function of 'examining justices'. At the completion of committal hearings the magistrates decided whether there was sufficient evidence to warrant the defendant standing trial in a Crown Court. If they decided that the evidence was insufficient to warrant this course of action, the defendant was discharged.

Committal hearings have been subject to a number of recent changes. The 1998 Crime and Disorder Act effectively abolished them for indictable offences, seeking to provide for a speedier transfer of these cases to Crown Court. The 2003 Criminal Justice Act provided for the abolition of committal proceedings for offences that were triable either way but only limited progress (in connection with juvenile offenders) has been made in implementing this reform.

In the case of indictable offences or offences that are triable either way that proceed to a Crown Court trial, magistrates decide whether to remand the suspect in custody or to free him or her on bail (to which conditions may be attached) until the Crown Court trial is held.

The more serious criminal charges (those which are termed 'indictable offences') have to be tried in a Crown Court. These were established by the 1971 Crown

Courts Act. They are presided over by judges consisting of around 1,300 recorders and 650 circuit judges. Juries are used to determine the guilt or innocence of the offender and to convict it is necessary for the prosecution to prove their case 'beyond a reasonable doubt'. If the jury determines that a defendant is guilty the judge will then hand out a sentence.

The High Court of Justice mainly deals with the more serious civil law cases, standing in hierarchy above the County Courts. It is divided into three divisions: the Queen's Bench, Chancery and Family divisions and its work is performed by 110 High Court judges (termed *puisne* [junior] judges) and around 450 deputy High Court judges. They may be aided by Circuit judges, District judges and (occasionally) Recorders. The Queen's Bench Division has some responsibilities for criminal matters such as hearing appeals for writs of habeas corpus. Civil claims seeking damages against a police force for actions that include assault or false imprisonment may also be heard in the High Court or County Court.

The Crown Court, High Court and the Court of Appeal were collectively referred to as the supreme court. This term originated in the Judicature Acts of the 1970s. The intention of the 2005 Constitutional Reform Act to create a Supreme Court in place of the Judicial Committee of the House of Lords resulted in these three

courts being renamed as the 'Senior Courts of England and Wales'.

Decisions reached by Magistrates' Courts, Crown Courts and the High Court are subject to challenge and may be reviewed by an appellate court. An appellate court is one that may hear appeals against decisions that have been made by lower courts or tribunals. This responsibility is mainly exercised by the Court of Appeal and historically by the House of Lords, although Crown Courts also act in an appellate capacity in connection with conviction or sentencing decisions reached by a Magistrates' Court or a youth court. The Judicial Committee of the Privy Council also exercises a limited range of appeal functions.

The Court of Criminal Appeal was established in 1908, and was renamed the Court of Appeal in 1966. The court is staffed by 38 Lord Justices of Appeal and High Court and Deputy High Court judges (whose work is concerned with civil law) may also serve.

This court hears appeals related to criminal trials from the Crown Courts and also hears appeals related to decisions in civil cases that have been made by County Courts and the High Court. The Appeal Court provides a forum in which mistakes committed by junior judges can be overturned by their senior colleagues. These errors may relate to conviction or to the sentence that has been imposed and the Criminal Cases Review Commission is one avenue through which alleged errors of this nature may be referred to the Court of Appeal.

The 1988 Criminal Justice Act gave the Attorney General the ability to refer sentences related to serious crimes to this court, when these sentences were felt to be too lenient.

The crimes to which this provision applies were extended in the Criminal Justice Act 1988 (Review of Sentencing) Order 2006 to cover all indictable offences and a number that were triable either way. The Appeal Court reviews the sentence and has the power to quash it and impose a new sentence that it feels to be appropriate.

The final court of appeal for both criminal and civil cases which derive from decisions initially made by the Court of Appeal in England and Wales and the Court of Appeal in Northern Ireland was the Judicial Committee of the House of Lords. This court also heard civil, but not criminal, appeals from Scotland. It was staffed by 12 judges termed 'Lords of Appeal in Ordinary'). Cases were normally heard by a panel of five judges, and the outcome of a case could be determined by a 3:2 majority vote. The small size of this panel gave individual judges considerable influence over particular decisions.

The 2001 Labour government proposed the creation of a Supreme Court to take over the judicial functions of the House of Lords. It would constitute the ultimate court of appeal for all matters connected with civil and criminal law under English law, Northern Irish Law and Welsh law save that made by the Welsh Assembly. It would exercise no authority over criminal cases in Scotland but would retain the existing powers of the House of Lords regarding appeals from the Scottish Civil Court of Session.

Its initial members would be the existing Law Lords but new members would be chosen through a process involving the establishment of an *ad hoc* selection commission when vacancies arose. This would consist of the President and Deputy President of the Supreme Court and members of the Judicial Appointments Commission for England and Wales, the Judicial Appointments Board of Scotland and the Northern Ireland Judicial Appointments Commission. The consequence of this reform would be that those sitting on the Supreme Court would only exercise judicial functions and would no longer automatically be members of the House of Lords.

The new court was not modelled on the American Supreme Court. Although it would assume the powers currently exercised by the Judicial Committee of the Privy Council in connection with devolution issues, it would not constitute a specific constitutional court, and would not be given the power to overturn legislation. Neither would its main role be that of giving preliminary rulings on difficult points of law (Department for Constitutional Affairs, 2003: 9). This new body was created by the 2005 Constitutional Reform Act and began sitting at the end of 2009.

The Judicial Committee of the Privy Council also exercises certain appellate functions. It was established the 1833 Judicial Committee Act and is composed of a diverse group of people who include the Law Lords, retired Law Lords below the age of 75, privy councillors who are or were senior judges, past and present members of the Court of Appeal of England, Wales and Northern Ireland or of the Inner Court of Session in Scotland and privy councillors who are judges of certain superior courts in countries of the Commonwealth (Department for Constitutional Affairs, 2003: 18).

This body is the final court of appeal regarding both civil and criminal matters from UK overseas territories and Crown Dependencies and for Commonwealth countries that have retained the right to appeal to the Privy Council. Its decisions are reached on the basis of the law of the countries from which each appeal comes. It also hears appeals from Guernsey, Jersey, the Isle of Man and exercises technical jurisdiction in areas which include appeals

against pastoral schemes of the Church Commissioners and from the Disciplinary Committee of the Royal College of Veterinary Surgeons.

The role of the Judicial Committee of the Privy Council was expanded by devolution legislation (consisting of the 1998 Scotland Act, the 1998 Northern Ireland Act, and the 1998 Government of Wales Act) that made it responsible for adjudicating on constitutional matters derived from this legislation. The 2005 Constitutional Reform Act provided for the transfer of these powers to the Supreme Court.

See also: bail, coroners, criminal court system Scotland, Crown Prosecution Service, habeas corpus, judges, jury system, magistrates, miscarriage of justice, political oversight of the criminal justice system, sentences of the criminal courts

References and further reading

Department for Constitutional Affairs (2003) *Constitutional reform: A Supreme Court for the United Kingdom, A Consultation Paper Prepared by the Department for Constitutional Affairs.* London: Department for Constitutional Affairs, Consultation Paper CP 11/03, July.

Malleson, K. (2007) *The Legal System.* Oxford: Oxford University Press, third edition.

Sanders, A. (2001) *Community Justice: Modernising the Magistracy in England and Wales.* London: Central Books.

Slapper, G. and Kelly, D. (2004) *The English Legal System.* London: Cavendish, seventh edition.

criminal court system Scotland

As is the case in England and Wales, the criminal court system in Scotland consists of a hierarchy of tribunals that are responsible for trying those charged with committing criminal acts. The Scottish court system additionally provides for procedures whereby persons convicted of a crime by one court appeal to a higher (or appellate) court against either their sentence or conviction.

Under the provisions of the 1998 Scotland Act, criminal justice affairs constitute a devolved function of government in Scotland. The Justice Department of the Scottish Government is responsible for criminal and civil law and is headed by the Minister of Justice.

The 1995 Criminal Procedure (Scotland) Act distinguished between summary and solemn procedure for disposing of criminal cases. The decision as to which procedure should be used is made by the Crown Office and Procurator Fiscal Service which is headed by the Lord Advocate and is Scotland's equivalent to the Crown Prosecution Service in England and Wales. Unlike in England and Wales, the defendant has no ability to determine this decision. In 2005/6 around 96 per cent of criminal cases were heard under summary procedure (McCallum *et al.*, 2007).

Summary procedure is used for the less serious criminal offences which are heard either in a Sheriff's Court or before one or more lay magistrates in a District Court. Stipendiary Magistrates are used in the Glasgow District Court.

District Courts were established by the 1975 District Courts (Scotland) Act. They were administered by local authorities and were divided into 30 Commission Areas. The sentencing power of these courts was up to 60 days imprisonment or a fine of up to £2,500 (although Stipendiary Magistrates possess the same powers as Sheriff's Courts when acting as a court of summary jurisdiction). Prosecutions in District Courts were conducted by the local Procurator Fiscal or by a Procurator Fiscal Depute.

The 2007 Criminal Proceedings etc. (Reform) (Scotland) Act provided for the replacement of District Courts by Justice of the Peace Courts presided over by a lay magistrate (or, in the case of Glasgow, a stipendiary magistrate). It is intended that this process will be complete by early 2010.

Sheriff's Courts dispose of the bulk of Scotland's criminal offences heard under summary procedure (and they also exercise jurisdiction over civil cases). There are 49 Sheriff's Courts throughout Scotland divided into six Sheriff's Courts Districts. Prosecutions in these courts are conducted by the local Procurator Fiscal or by a Procurator Fiscal Depute. When sitting as a court of summary jurisdiction, the sentencing powers of Sheriff's Courts were limited to three months imprisonment (or six months in connection with a second offence relating to dishonesty or personal violence) or a fine of £5,000. The 2007 Criminal Proceedings etc. (Reform) (Scotland) Act provided for increased powers of 12 months imprisonment and a fine of £10,000.

The most serious criminal cases – those heard on indictment – are held under solemn procedure before either a judge of the High Court of Justiciary or before a Sheriff in a Sheriff's Court. Some serious criminal matters including murder and rape can be heard only in the High Court of Justiciary where the prosecution is conducted by Advocates Depute.

Juries consisting of 15 persons are used in all trials held under solemn procedure (whether in the Sheriff's or High Court of Justiciary) whose verdicts may be 'guilty', 'not guilty' or 'not proven'. A simple majority (8:7) is sufficient to establish a defendant's innocence or guilt (Pakes, 2004: 10–11). When sitting as a court of solemn procedure the maximum sentencing powers of a Sheriff's Court are five years' imprisonment or an unlimited fine. Cases which the Sheriff feels deserve a higher penalty may be referred to the High Court of Justiciary for sentence.

Appeals against decisions made by Sheriff's Courts, District Courts or by the High Court of Justiciary when it hears a case in the first instance are heard by the High Court of Justiciary. This was established in 1672 and is staffed by judges of the two Scottish Supreme Courts – the High Court of Justiciary [criminal] and the Court of Session [civil]. The High Court of Justiciary is Scotland's supreme criminal court and (unlike civil cases heard in the Court of Session) there is no appeal to the Supreme Court against its verdicts.

The High Court of Justiciary, Sheriff's Courts and Justice of the Peace Courts are administered by the Scottish Courts Service which is an executive agency of the Scottish Government. District Courts are administered by local authorities.

See also: criminal court system England and Wales, Crown Prosecution Service, jury system

References and further reading

Apex Scotland (2008) *An Overview of the Criminal Justice System in Scotland.* [Online] http://www.apexscotland.org.uk/docs/oview_scot_crim_just.pdf

McCallum, F., Ross, G. and Oag, D. (2007) *The Scottish Criminal Justice System: The Criminal Courts.* [Online] http://www.scottish.parliament.uk/business/research/pdf_subj_maps/SMDA07–04.pdf#4

Pakes, F. (2004) *Comparative Criminal Justice.* Cullompton, Devon, Willan Publishing.

criminal record

A criminal record is an official document that provides details of crimes that an individual has previously committed. These include all crimes which received a court sentence and cautions (which do not count as a conviction).

All persons convicted of a crime possess a criminal record (even if the sentence of the court was an absolute discharge). However, under the provisions of the 1974 Rehabilitation of Offenders Act a criminal record may be ignored after what is termed a 'rehabilitation period' has been completed, at the end of which the conviction is regarded as being 'spent' and does not have to be declared on job application forms although specific forms of employment are exempt from this procedure.

The length of the rehabilitation varies according to the severity of the offence (for example it is six months for an absolute discharge and ten years for a person aged over 18 who received a prison sentence of between 6 months and 2.5 years). Crimes involving a prison sentence of more than 2.5 years can never become spent. Criminal records, even if spent, will be retained on the Police National Computer in some cases (for example, when a custodial sentence was given) for life.

Some employers (who are required to register with the Criminal Records Bureau (CRB)) may seek information of a job applicant's criminal record from the CRB. This is an executive agency of the Home Office which was provided for in the 1997 Police Act and became operational in 2002. It is designed to aid informed recruitment decisions by helping registered employers in the public, private and voluntary sectors to identify candidates who may be unsuitable for certain work, especially that which entails contact with children or involves the job applicant in a position of trust. Registered organizations are those entitled to ask exempted questions under the 1975 Exceptions Order to the Rehabilitation of Offenders Act 1974 or those which may countersign applications on behalf of people or organizations who themselves are entitled to ask exempted questions.

Disclosure may be of two types. Standard disclosure provides details of all previous convictions whether spent or not and information derived from the Police National Computer in connection with cautions, reprimands or warnings. Enhanced disclosure additionally provides information sourced from police intelligence derived from where the applicant has lived for the previous five years (National Audit Office, 2004: 5).

Each year the CRB completes more than 3.5m checks against criminal records with 50 per cent of applications coming from just 265 organizations. In 2009 the CRB introduced an e-application system (e-bulk) to enable organizations to apply for bulk criminal records checks (Kablenet, 2009).

A new procedure related to CRB checks is the Vetting and Barring Scheme (VBS) which seeks to prevent people who pose a known risk of harm from working with children and vulnerable adults. The scheme is administered by the Independent Safeguarding Authority (ISA) which assesses all relevant information including data held on the Police National Computer, disciplinary action taken by employers, and social services records. Anyone deemed unsuitable will be placed on one of two (ISA) barred lists relating to children or to vulnerable adults.

From October 2009, any individual who is working or volunteering, or seeking to work or volunteer, with children or vulnerable adults on a frequent or intensive basis (known as regulated activity) must apply to join the scheme. Only applicants who are judged not to pose a known risk to vulnerable people can be ISA-registered.

From July 2010, standard CRB checks will be based on information derived from the Police National Computer. Enhanced CRB checks will derive from information contained in the two ISA barred lists.

See also: cautioning (formal), sentences of the criminal courts

References and further reading

Kablenet (2009) 'Criminal Records Bureau launches e-disclosure service' [Online] http://www. theregister.co.uk/public_sector/ policing/earlier.html

National Audit Office (2004) *Criminal Records Bureau: Delivering Safer Recruitment?* London: TSO, House of Commons Paper 266, Session 2003–4.

Crown Prosecution Service (CPS)

The CPS is an independent authority that conducts criminal prosecutions on behalf of the state. It was created by the 1985 Prosecution of Offences Act and is headed by the

Director of Public Prosecutions. The Attorney General is responsible to Parliament for its conduct.

The introduction of new policing arrangements in England and Wales in the early decades of the nineteenth century was not accompanied by the establishment of a prosecution authority as was the case in other European countries. Accordingly, all prosecutions were conducted by private persons or the police. The establishment of the office of the Director of Public Prosecutions in 1879 introduced a new element into prosecution policy, but its powers were limited and the police (advised by lawyers but whose advice was neither independent or binding) conducted the great majority of prosecutions.

The possibility that the involvement of the police in prosecutions might contribute to miscarriages of justice (since they had a vested interest in securing a positive outcome and might thus be tempted to apply undue pressure on a suspect to admit guilt) was one factor that led to the creation of the CPS. Its work is performed by salaried lawyers (mainly solicitors) whose main task is to review files submitted to them by the police arising from an investigation and to determine whether to proceed with (or to discontinue) a criminal prosecution. They also determine what charge should be preferred. In performing this task, their conduct is governed by the Code for Crown Prosecutors.

CPS lawyers also prosecute cases. Initially this role was confined to solicitors conducting cases in Magistrates' Courts, but the 1990 Courts and Legal Services Act as amended by the 1999 Access to Justice Act resulted in the agency directly employing barristers to prosecute cases in the higher courts.

Initially the CPS suffered from problems that included remoteness (especially an unwillingness to explain its decisions) and suspicion on the part of the police that its insistence of there being a reasonable chance that prosecution would lead to a conviction was responsible for the release without charge of persons they believed to be criminals or was encouraging negotiation with the defence to secure a guilty plea to a less serious offence than the one the accused was initially charged with. These problems were aggravated by the different organizational boundaries used by police forces and the CPS.

A number of reforms have been put in place to ameliorate these problems. Following the Glidewell Report (1998), the organizational boundaries of both agencies were aligned. Proposals put forward by Lord Justice Auld (2001) were incorporated into the 2003 Criminal Justice Act which created the legal framework to transfer the responsibility of charging from the police to the CPS. This system of what is termed 'statutory charging' (whereby the CPS decided what offence, if any, an individual should be charged with) resulted in developments that included CPS staff being placed in police stations to advise the police at the outset regarding the most appropriate course of action.

One benefit of statutory charging was the reduction in the discontinuance rate but a problem was the delay that sometimes occurred when the police felt ready to charge but had to wait for a decision from the CPS. This situation could increase the length of time between arrest and the disposal of the case. One solution to this was to enhance the role performed by CPS Direct (a CPS unit that provided charging decisions by telephone out of hours).

The CPS is not the only agency responsible for prosecuting those who are accused of breaking the law. It exists alongside others that include the Serious Fraud Office, the Health and Safety Executive, local authorities and the Royal Society for the Prevention of Cruelty to Animals.

See also: criminal court system England and Wales, legal profession England and Wales, magistrates, plea bargaining

References and further reading

Auld, Rt Hon Lord Justice (2001) *Review of the Criminal Courts of England and Wales*. London: TSO.

Glidewell, Sir I. (1998) *Review of the Crown Prosecution Service: A Report*. London: TSO, Cm 3960.

House of Commons Justice Committee (2009) *The Crown Prosecution service: Gatekeeper of the Criminal Justice System*. London: TSO, 9th Report of Session 2008–9, HC 186.

Smartt, U. (2009) *Law for Criminologists: A Practical Guide*. London: Sage.

cuffing

See **crime statistics**

custodial sentence

See **sentences of the criminal courts**, and also **prisons**

D

dark figure of crime

See **crime statistics**

deferred sentence

See **sentences of the criminal courts**

delegated legislation

Delegated legislation enables Ministers to make law without the need to engage in the normal law-making process. Delegated legislation is typically written by civil servants acting on behalf of a Minister and the main rationale for using this procedure is to prevent Parliament being overloaded with work (House of Lords, 2008).

An Act of Parliament (termed 'primary legislation') may impose broad principles and leave civil servants to fill in the details through what is termed 'delegated legisla-tion' or 'secondary legislation'. This takes a number of forms that include Statutory Instruments. These are the most common form of delegated legislation, around 3,000 of which are issued each year (Smartt, 2009: 20). Some Statutory Instruments are subject to Parliamentary procedure (perhaps requiring an affirmative resolution to be passed before they become law) but others are not. The requirement of Parliamentary involvement is determined in the primary legislation.

There are other types of delegated legislation. The 1998 Human Rights Act empowered judges to draw Parliament's attention to any incompatibility between existing legislation and the European Convention on Human Rights. In these cases the primary legislation can be amended by a Remedial Order in order to secure compatability.

A further form of delegated legislation is Regulatory Reform Orders which enable ministers to reform primary legislation without having to secure the passage of a new Act of Parliament. This procedure is provided for in the 2001 Regulatory Reform Act and the 2006 Legislative and Regulatory Reform Act. Other forms of delegated legislation include Orders in Council (issued by the monarch following consultation with the Privy Council) and by-laws made by local authorities.

Codes of Practice constitute a further form of delegated legislation. Typically codes provide guidance to a public body regarding its operations in specified aspects of its work, the breach of which does not constitute a criminal offence. An important example of these are the Codes of Practice related to issues such as arrest, detention and stop and search that are derived from the 1984 Police and Criminal Evidence Act. The benefit of rule-making in this fashion is that the codes can be constantly updated without the time-consuming process of securing the enactment of a new Act of Parliament.

In addition to consideration by the process of a Parliamentary debate, both Houses have delegated legislation committees to consider these items. These included the Joint Committee on Statutory Instruments, the House of Lords Delegated Powers Scrutiny Committee and the House of Commons Regulatory Reform Committee.

See also: judicial review, law-making process, PACE Codes of Practice

References and further reading

House of Lords (2008) *Looking at the Small Print: Delegated Legislation.* Parliamentary website [Online]: http://www.parliament.uk/documents/upload/HofLBp Delegated.pdf

Pond, C. (2002) *Delegated Legislation: The Procedure Committee Report and Proposals for Change.* Parliamentary website [Online] http://www.parliament.uk/commons/lib/research/briefings/snpc-00469.pdf

Smartt, U. (2009) *Law for Criminologists: A Practical Guide.* London: Sage.

derogation

See **European Convention on Human Rights**

desistance

Desistance refers to the cessation of offending behaviour – an offender who voluntarily chooses not to re-offend. Criminal justice policy seeks to identify factors that influence this behaviour with a view to incorporating them into programmes that are addressed to offenders.

Traditionally, criminological study focused on the factors that caused offending behaviour to occur (such as Farrington, 1992: 129) as opposed to seeking to explain why an event (*re*-offending) failed to take place.

Accredited programmes constitute one approach that is designed to prevent re-offending. However, the extent to which programmes of this nature prevent recidivism has been questioned. It has been argued that 'some programmes *do* work and the best may reduce re-offending by around 25 per cent'. But to achieve this, programmes have to be clearly targeted on offending behaviour, consistently delivered by well trained staff, relevant to offenders' problems and needs, and equally relevant to the participants' learning styles (Whitfield, 1998: 16).

Accredited programmes offer a generalized approach to addressing offending behaviour and will not produce standardized responses from their participants. Accordingly individualized initiatives (in particular mentoring whether by probation officers or from third sector providers) may be required in order to achieve desistance. This suggests that desistance consists of a gradual process of turning away from crime as opposed to an abrupt decision to end behaviour of this nature (Laub and Sampson, 2001: 11) which requires case workers to address mental factors that influ-ence an offender's propensity to desist from further crime.

Literature that deals with an individual's transition from prison to the community (such as Zamble and Quinsey, 1997 and Immarigeon and Maruna, 2004) emphasize the importance of factors such as motivation and argue that this needs to be sustained (often in the face of setbacks) in order to turn an offender away from crime and secure his or her successful resettlement in the community.

This is compatible with discussions alluding to primary and secondary desistance (Maruna and Farrall, 2004 cited in Gelsthorpe and Morgan, 2007: 360–1) in which a respite from criminal activity ('primary desistance') is maintained by the ex-offender acquiring new values that leads to the permanent cessation of re-offending ('secondary desistance'). The decision to turn away from crime may also be reinforced by other factors external to the individual that include finding employment, acquiring accommodation, terminating contacts with peer groups that were associated with crime (perhaps by moving to another area) and the formation of new personal relationships.

The need to tackle desistance is an important concern in contemporary UK criminal justice policy and was a key reason for the formation of the National Offender Management Service.

See also: accredited programmes, National Offender Management Service, new public management, Probation Service, recidivism

References and further reading

Farrington, D. (1992) 'Juvenile Delinquency' in J. Coleman (ed.) *The School Years.* London: Routledge.

Immarigeon, R. and Maruna, S. (eds) (2004) *After Crime and Punishment: Ex-Offenders' Reintegration and Desistance from Crime.* Cullompton, Devon: Willan Publishing.

Laub, J. and Sampson, R. (2001) 'Understanding Desistance from Crime' in M. Tonry (ed.) *Crime and Justice: An Annual Review of Research,* Vol 26. Chicago, IL: University of Chicago Press.

Maruna, S. and Farrall, S. (2004) 'Desistance from Crime: A Theoretical Reformulation' cited in L. Gelsthorpe, and R. Morgan (2007) *Handbook of Probation.* Cullompton, Devon: Willan Publishing.

Whitfield, D. (1998) *Introduction to the Probation Service.* Winchester: Waterside Press, second edition.

Zamble, E. and Quinsey, V. (1997) *The Criminal Recidivism Process.* Cambridge, MA: Cambridge University Press.

detection rates

Detection rates are official statistics that indicate the amount of crime that has been detected (or 'cleared up') by the police service.

Detection or 'clear up' rates are not the same as conviction rates. The circumstances under which a crime is deemed to be detected or 'cleared up' are laid down by the Home Office. There are two methods whereby this can be determined – sanction and non-sanction detections.

A sanction detection relates to a situation in which a person receives some form of punishment for the act they have committed – this can range from a fixed penalty notice, a caution, a charge, a summons or an offence that is 'taken into consideration' (TIC).

TICs (otherwise known as 'secondary detections') arise when a person convicted of an offence asks the court to take similar crimes into consideration. In the 12 months ending in March 2009, there were 101,653 notifiable offences resolved by the TIC procedure (National Criminal Justice Board, 2009). Those who ask for offences to be 'taken into consideration' do so for reasons that include the hope that cooperation with the police will help secure a lighter sentence. This procedure enables the police to record crimes as 'cleared up' even though there is often little evidence to associate them with the person who admits to carrying them out.

Non-sanction (or administrative) detections occur when the police possess sufficient evidence to charge a person with an offence but choose not to do so. Historically (Home Office, 1991) this was for a number of reasons that included the existence of practical hindrances to a prosecution (including the absence of witnesses willing to give evidence), the offender or key witness had died or was too ill to proceed, the offender, having admitted an offence, was under the age of criminal responsibility, or the police or Crown Prosecution Service considered that the public interest would not be served by proceeding with a charge. From 2007, the scope of non-sanction detections was reduced to cover only those situations when the CPS declined to prosecute an indictable offence or where the accused person died.

The detection rates for all recorded crime in England and Wales was 28 per cent in 1997 and 27 per cent for both 2005/6 and 2006/7. In 2006/7, the most successful forces were in Wales – North Wales with a 48 per cent detection rate and Dyfed-Powys with a 45 per cent rate. The lowest was the Metropolitan Police Service with 21 per cent (McNulty, 2007).

There were wide discrepancies within the overall figure of 27 per cent for 2006/7 which ranged from a 95 per cent detection rate for drug offences (94 per cent sanctioned), to 11 per cent for offences against vehicles (10 per cent sanctioned) and 14 per cent for burglary (also 14 per cent sanctioned). The figure for criminal damage was 15 per cent (13 per cent sanctioned) (McNulty, 2008).

Detection rates have constituted an important aspect of the 'narrowing the justice gap agenda' which seeks to increase public confidence in the criminal justice system by ensuring that an increased proportion of crimes recorded by the police as notifiable offences were 'brought to justice' in the sense of the offender receiving a formal caution, a conviction or having an offence taken into consideration The use of out of court disposals to combat minor crime and public order issues offences is a further development that is compatible with this approach. The Attorney General acts as Ministerial champion for this initiative for which a Justice Gap Task Force has been established.

See also: attrition, Crown Prosecution Service, out of court disposals, political oversight of the criminal justice system, re-balancing the criminal justice system

References and further reading

Home Office, (1991) *Criminal Statistics, Volume IV, Annual &*

Miscellaneous Returns. London: Home Office.

McNulty, T. (2007) *House of Commons Debates*, Vol. 468, Col. 769W.

McNulty (2008) *House of Commons Debates*, Vol. 471, Col. 512W.

National Criminal Justice Board (2009), Offences Taken into Consideration, [Online] http://lcjb.cjsonline.gov.uk/ncjb/perfStats/tics.html

deterrence

See **Punishment (aims of)**

Diplock Courts

Diplock Courts were set up in Northern Ireland in 1973 to try 'scheduled offences'. These were crimes associated with politically motivated violence that emerged during the late 1960s and the main feature of these courts was the absence of a jury. The trial judge presided over the case, delivered a verdict of 'guilty' or 'not guilty' and if the former then pronounced sentence.

These courts derived from a recommendation contained in a report written by Lord Diplock (1972). They were designed to remedy jury intimidation and were a key component of the process of 'criminalization' that sought to restore normality to the Northern Ireland criminal justice process by replacing internment with a procedure whereby a person accused of an offence associated with terrorism could be tried in a court.

Diplock Courts were subjected to a number of criticisms. The list of scheduled offences specified in the 1973 Northern Ireland (Emergency Provisions) Act went beyond crimes specifically associated with terrorism (such as bombing) to embrace other serious crimes such as murder. The absence of a jury to determine guilt or innocence was viewed as unfair to those accused of scheduled offences. Judges were accused of 'case hardening' (Walsh, 1983: 94) which implied a bias to convict those who came before them. These problems undermined the legitimacy of the courts, especially within the nationalist community.

Other intrusions into civil liberties arose in conjunction with the introduction of the Diplock Courts. These included the circumstances under which confessions were viewed as valid evidence and the manner in which uncorroborated evidence of an accomplice to a crime was treated. These changes underpinned some of the more controversial tactics used by the security forces to combat politically motivated violence that included interrogation and the supergrass system.

One consequence of the normalization of the criminal justice process that was associated with the Diplock Courts was the abolition in 1976 of the special category status that had been applied to convicted paramilitary prisoners since 1972 whereby they were effectively treated as political prisoners. The ending of the differential treatment given to those whose crimes were politically motivated led to the 'blanket protest' in 1976 which transformed into the 'dirty protest' in 1978 and the hunger strikes of 1980–81.

The 1998 Belfast Agreement instigated the ending of the 'Troubles' and in 2007 the Justice and Security (Northern Ireland) Act was enacted which abolished the Diplock Courts. However, the Northern Ireland Director of Public Prosecutions retains the option to authorize a trial without a jury in cases where this is felt to be an appropriate course of action.

See also: informants, internment, jury system

References and further reading

Diplock, Lord (1972) *Report of the Commission to Consider Legal Procedures to deal with Terrorist Activity in Northern Ireland.* London: HMSO, Cm 5185.

Jackson, J. and Doran, S. (1995) *Trial without Jury: Diplock Trials in the Adversary System.* Oxford: Clarendon.

Walsh, D. (1983) *The Use and Abuse of Emergency Legislation in Northern Ireland.* London: Cobden Trust.

discretion

Discretion is exercised by professionals in the criminal justice system when they apply their independent judgement in a situation rather than follow the strict letter of the law.

It has been argued that discretion 'refers to the freedom, power, authority, decision or leeway of an official, organization or individual to decide, discern or determine to make a judgement, choice or decision, about alternative courses of action or inaction' (Gelsthorpe and Padfield, 2003: 1). The term conjures up a variety of images which include 'rule-bending' or the application of 'tact', 'sympathy', 'understanding' and 'common sense'.

Discretion is exercised by all criminal justice practitioners. It may be utilized in the context of an encounter between an individual and a police officer in which the latter applies his or her independent judgement to provide what the officer believes to be a just outcome. Magistrates and judges may also exercise discretion in their sentencing decisions in particular by taking the circumstances of the offender into account.

There are several factors that influence how discretion is exercised. These include 'process' (whereby practitioners are provided with the ability to screen out or divert cases from the criminal justice system based on legal or practical considerations), 'environment' (which suggests that actions undertaken by practitioners will be influenced by community views concerning appropriate courses of action) and 'context' (in which a practitioner's decisions are influenced by 'internal' organizational and occupational factors). What are termed 'illicit considerations' (whereby factors such as class, race and gender underpin a professional's actions) may also influence the manner in which discretion is utilized (Gelsthorpe and Padfield, 2003: 6–9).

Discretion can be used in both negative and positive ways. It has been concluded that discretion 'is a force for ill when it leads to unjustifiable decisions (negative discrimination) and inconsistency (disparity) whereby similar crimes are treated differently, but it can be a good thing in that it provides a mechanism to show mercy which, even if defying precise definition, many would recognise as being necessary to the conception and delivery of justice' (Gelsthorpe and Padfield, 2003: 6).

Classicist criminologists were opposed to the use of discretion since this 'diminishes the possibility of accurately predicting sentence outcome'(Easton and Piper, 2008: 41) so that a person was not able to make a rational choice regarding the benefits and disadvantages that would derive from committing a criminal act. In recent years the exercise of discretion by criminal justice practitioners has been eroded. The 1994 Police and Magistrates' Courts Act enabled the Home Secretary rather than chief constables to establish priorities for their forces and the discretion enjoyed by magistrates and judges has been eroded by the mandatory sentencing provisions contained in the 1997 Crime (Sentences) Act and the 2000 Powers of Criminal Courts (Sentencing) Act and also by the directions issued by the Sentencing Guidelines Council.

See also: judges, magistrates, Sentencing Guidelines Council

References and further reading

Easton, S. and Piper, C. (2008) *Sentencing and Punishment: The Quest for Justice.* Oxford: Oxford University Press, second edition.

Gelsthorpe, L. and Padfield, N. (2003) *Exercising Discretion: Decision-Making in the Criminal Justice System and Beyond.* Cullompton, Devon: Willan Publishing.

displacement of crime

See **crime prevention**

District Policing Partnership (Northern Ireland)

See **Police Service Northern Ireland**

Dixon of Dock Green

Dixon of Dock Green was the leading character in a television programme, and his style of policing epitomized the home beat method.

The character of PC George Dixon initially appeared in the film *The Blue Lamp* (1950). The television programme, *Dixon of Dock Green* was first shown on BBC television in 1955 and the last (367th) episode was screened in 1976. It was written by Ted Willis and the character of George Dixon was played by actor Jack Warner.

The programme put forward the image of George Dixon as a friendly neighbourhood bobby who was a trusted member of the working-class community in which he both lived and worked and who was respected by all residents, law-abiding and criminal alike. The task of policing was depicted as responding to a wide range of problems which members of the local public brought to the attention of the police, many of which were not crime-related.

Subsequent styles of policing (especially the move away from foot patrol), changes to the nature of crime (which became less local and more organized), alterations to the structure of society (which was characterized by the absence of community cohesion) and the erosion of the post-war consensus that underpinned the 'Golden Age' of policing rendered the image of police work portrayed in the programme as outdated. Although a fictional account of policing and police work which reflected a particular image of police officers as 'carers' as opposed to 'controllers' (Reiner, 1994: 18, 22), it nonetheless depicted an ideal as to how policing by consent could operate, emphasizing the importance of popular support for the police function in society.

Although nostalgia may underpin this perception both of policing and the communities in which it operated (whereby 'Dixonian' is 'evoked as a form of shorthand to define the traditional values of English policing and society') (McLaughlin, 2007: 23), George Dixon remains important to contemporary policing and his image is frequently evoked by politicians and practitioners alike. Community and neighbourhood policing have sought to cultivate the nature of police–public relationships portrayed in the programme.

See also: fire brigade policing, neighbourhood policing

References and further reading

McLaughlin, E. (2007) *The New Police*. London. Sage.

Reiner, R. (1994) 'The Changing Image of the TV Cop' in M. Stephens and S. Becker, *Police Force, Police Service – Care and Control in Britain*. Basingstoke: Macmillan.

doli incapax

See **youth justice system**

domestic violence

Domestic violence refers to abusive behaviour that is exhibited by one or both partners in an intimate relationship present or past (such as marriage or cohabitation) that typically occurs within the confines of a home. It is not a specific statutory offence, but covers a wide range of actions that include physical, sexual and emotional abuse, controlling, domineering or threatening behaviour, economic deprivation of a dependant partner by the other or psychological intimidation through means such as stalking.

Domestic violence is narrower in scope than family violence which includes child abuse. Women are frequently the victims of domestic violence and are likely to experience repeat victimization. In 1995 it was estimated that there had been 3.29 million incidents of domestic violence against women, 1.86 million of which resulted in physical injury. Additionally, women were estimated to have received over five million frightening threats in that year.

Traditionally domestic violence was not regarded as a high priority for police intervention. However, official attitudes began to change in the 1980s. The need for effective training to foster a greater level of understanding of the needs of victims and to develop the skills and sensitivities necessary to encourage the confidence and cooperation of victims of domestic violence was emphasized (Home Office, 1986) and it was later argued that 'domestic violence . . . is a crime and it is important that the police should play an effective and positive role in protecting the victim' (Home Office, 1990: 2). Chief constables were also advised to liaise with other agencies and voluntary bodies to set up arrangements to refer victims of such attacks to long-term support (Home Office, 1990: 9).

Domestic Violence Units became an important aspect of the police's response to crime of this nature. The first of these had been set up by the Metropolitan Police in Tottenham in 1987. The 1990 circular urged chief officers to consider establishing dedicated domestic violence units (Home Office, 1990: 9) and by the end of

1992, 62 of the Metropolitan Police's 69 divisions had set up such units, which were also found in 20 of the remaining 42 police forces (Home Affairs Committee, 1993: para. 23). Officers from these units were responsible for co-operating with other agencies such as Women's Aid and reflected the need for the police service to become victim-oriented.

Pressure on the police service to act robustly with regard to domestic violence was subsequently exerted by external actions (such as the 1993 Declaration on the Elimination of Violence Against Women) and by government programmes such as the 1998 Crime Reduction Programme. This included the Reducing Violence Against Women Initiative which focused on domestic violence, rape and sexual assault by perpetrators known to their victims.

The 1990 Home Office Circular on domestic violence was subsequently revised. The new guidance stated domestic violence was 'a serious crime which is not acceptable, and should be treated as seriously as any other such crime' (Home Office, 2000: 1). A force policy on domestic violence was to be drawn up to give guidance to officers regarding how the force prioritized the issue, what standards of investigation were expected and the procedures that should be followed. Further changes occurred

in 2002 when all forces were required to review their facilities for examining victims.

Specific legislation related to domestic violence included the 1997 Protection from Violence Act which was concerned with behaviour that caused alarm or distress (such as stalking) and was enforced by imprisonment and a range of civil remedies such as restraining orders.

Subsequently, the 2004 Domestic Violence, Crime and Victims Act included measures to make breach of a non-molestation order punishable by up to five years' imprisonment. The powers of the court were increased to impose restraining orders which could be made on conviction or acquittal for any offence in order to protect the victim from harassment, and established multi-agency domestic homicide reviews in order to learn the lessons from deaths associated with domestic violence. Improved mechanisms to respond to crimes of violence against women have included the piloting of domestic violence courts.

See also: hate crime, Police Service England and Wales, victimology

References and further reading

Home Affairs Committee (1993) *Domestic Violence.* London: House of Commons, Session

1992–93, Third Report, House of Commons Paper 245.

Home Office (1986) *Violence Against Women: Treatment of Victims of Rape and Domestic Violence.* London: Home Office, circular 69/86.

Home Office (1990) *Domestic Violence.* London: Home Office, circular 60/90.

Home Office (2000) *Domestic Violence.* London: Home Office, circular 19/2000.

Mirrlees Black, C. (1999) *Domestic Violence.* London: Home Office, Research, Development and Statistics Directorate Report, Home Office Research Study 191.

double jeopardy

Double jeopardy is a rule that prevents a person being tried a second time for an offence for which they have previously been acquitted by a court.

This rule is designed to prevent the unfairness and harassment that may arise if the state repeatedly and relentlessly pursued a person whom they wish to see convicted. It formed an important aspect of the 'procedural protections and civil liberties' possessed by citizens in England and Wales (Tonry, 2004: 21).

There are, however, imperfections with this rule, in particular that guilty persons may escape rightful punishment if new evidence subsequently emerges. The enhanced use of DNA profiling and the process of cold case review has increased the possibility of this situation arising.

The weakness of double jeopardy was highlighted following the breakdown of a private prosecution brought by the parents of the murdered teenager, Stephen Lawrence, against three of those whom they alleged had killed him. The technical acquittal of two of these persons in 1996 meant that they could not be re-tried for this offence should new evidence subsequently emerge even though they were judged to be 'prime suspects' (Macpherson, 1999: para 2.18).

Reforms to the double jeopardy rule have been introduced to deal with problems of this nature. The 1996 Criminal Procedure and Investigation Act made it possible for the prosecution to appeal for a retrial under a limited range of circumstances that included evidence of jury tampering. This procedure has never been successfully used.

The 2003 Criminal Justice Act made it possible for a person to be re-tried for a range of offences that include murder, rape, kidnapping and armed robbery if 'new and compelling evidence' emerged following the first trial. The procedure entails the Director of Public

Prosecutions (DPP) referring the matter to the Court of Appeal who must overturn the original acquittal in order for a new trial to be authorized. A re-trial will only take place if the Court of Appeal believes that this is in the interests of justice.

In 2006 Billy Dunlop became the first person to be convicted under this procedure for the murder of Julie Hogg, having previously been acquitted of the crime.

See also: criminal court system England and Wales, National DNA Database

References and further reading

Ingman, T. (2006) *The English Legal Process.* Oxford: Oxford University Press, eleventh edition.

Macpherson, Sir W. (1999) *The Stephen Lawrence Inquiry: Report of an Inquiry by Sir William Macpherson of Cluny.* London: TSO, Cm 4262.

Tonry, M. (2004) *Punishment and Politics: Evidence and Emulation in the Making of English Crime Control Policy.* Cullompton, Devon: Willan Publishing.

E

electronic monitoring ('tagging')

Electronic monitoring (or 'tagging') is a method of exercising supervision over offenders without the need for them to physically contact a supervisor such as a probation officer. It enables their whereabouts to be monitored through the use of electronic tracking equipment and is used to ensure compliance with conditions imposed by curfew orders.

Electronic monitoring was proposed in a Green Paper (Home Office, 1988) and tagging as a condition of bail was introduced on a trial basis in 1989/90. The 1991 Criminal Justice Act (as amended by the 1994 Criminal Justice and Public Order Act) introduced a new sentence of a curfew order enforced by tagging available for offenders aged 16 years and above. The 1997 Crime (Sentencing) Act extended the use of electronically monitored curfew orders to offenders aged 10–15. Curfews could be used in conjunction with other community sentences or as a stand-alone penalty.

Electronic monitoring was extended in 1999 with the introduction of the Home Detention Curfew (HDC). This entailed the early release of short-term prisoners serving sentences between three months and less than four years for the last two months of their sentence provided that they stayed at an approved address and agreed to a curfew (usually from 7 p.m. to 7 a.m.) which would be monitored by an electronic tag. This would last for a minimum of 14 days and a maximum of 90 days. Those who breached the conditions of their curfew (including attempting to remove the tag) or who committed another offence whilst on curfew were returned to prison. This form of early release was subject to a risk assessment which involved prison, probation and police services. In 2003 HDC was extended to young offenders serving custodial sentences.

The use of electronically monitored curfews rose from 9,000 in 1999/2000 to 53,000 in 2004/5. One reason for this was cost – a 90-day HDC cost £1,300 to administer, an adult curfew order for the same period cost £1,400 while a 90-day custodial sentence cost £6,500 (National Audit Office, 2006: para 5).

While it is possible that offenders who are compelled to spend longer periods of times with their families may come to lead more structured lives, there are problems associated with the scheme, in particular confusion over its objectives. HDC could be viewed as an alternative to custody, a substitute for other forms of community punishment (in the expectation that an offender whose movements are monitored will modify their behaviour) or merely a device to remedy prison overcrowding.

Early evidence suggested that the failure rate of the scheme was low partly because prison governors exercised considerable caution as to whom they released. However, subsequent research indicated that the numbers who re-offended whilst wearing a tag had increased to one in nine in 2006 (Shapps, 2007: 3), a situation that was in part attributed to prison governors being less selective in their decisions because of the need to reduce overcrowding.

See also: non-custodial sentences, prisons, youth justice system

References and further reading

Home Office (1988) *Punishment, Custody and the Community.* London: Home Office.

National Audit Office (2006) *The Electronic Monitoring of Adult Offenders,* Session 2005–6, House of Commons Paper 800: London: TSO.

Shapps, G. (2007) *The Tagging Game.* [Online] http://www.shapps. com/reports/The-Tagging-Game. pdf

empowerment

Empowerment entails an adjustment of the power relationship between the state and its citizens enabling them to become collectively able to take decisions affecting their everyday lives.

Empowerment has a prominent place in the contemporary criminal justice agenda. The 2005 Labour government promoted increased opportunities for the public to participate in national decision-making through a number of 'engagement mechanisms'. These included citizens' summits and juries and a strengthened procedure to petition Parliament and were designed to ensure that national policy development is a 'collaborative venture' between people and the state (Ministry of Justice, 2008: 11).

The empowerment of communities has also received considerable attention in the early years of the twenty-first century. Here the key objective is 'to give communities much more power to say what matters most to them and to ensure that local agencies focus on delivering the services and improvements their communities want. Power should lie with the people, not with institutions' (Casey, 2008: 84). It also requires effective mechanisms of communication so that communities can be made aware as to what action has been taken in relation to the concerns they have raised and to enable them to provide feedback as to whether intervention has been effective.

The principle of community empowerment in criminal justice matters (entailing developments that include neighbourhood policing and the policing pledge) has been developed within the context of increased public involvement in a wide range of local affairs. This principle was promoted in the 2000 Local Government Act (which – as amended by the 2007 Sustainable Communities Act – extended the role of local authorities to promote or improve the economic, social or environmental well-being of their areas through the mechanism of a sustainable community strategy) and the 2007 Local Government and Public Involvement in Health Act.

Subsequent initiatives to achieve community empowerment were put forward in a White Paper which proposed to place a new duty upon local councils to promote democracy through the provision of clearer information, better trained staff and more visible councillors in the community. The government intended that the 'duty to involve' local people in key decisions – introduced in the 2007 Local Government and Public Involvement in Health Act – would be complemented by a duty placed on local authorities to promote democracy. Additionally, the duty to involve would be extended to additional organizations that included chief constables and police authorities.

The White Paper also expressed support for neighbourhood management and the use of community justice whereby local people were given the chance to decide issues such as what tasks offenders on work orders should undertake (Department of Communities and Local Government, 2008: 75–6). Legislation to promote local democracy and economic development and to devolve greater power to local government and communities was subsequently introduced in the 2009 Local Democracy, Economic Development and Construction legislation.

Although community empowerment might be viewed as a principle to promote a greater level of citizen involvement in local services, in connection with criminal justice policy it has alternatively been depicted as an attempt to manipulate localities into pursuing law and order goals. The pursuance of the strategy of 'responsibilization' which encourages widespread popular involvement in combating crime (Garland, 1996: 445; Hughes, 1998: 128) might herald the advent of the disciplinary society, with neighbourhoods rather than the central state as the locus of power (Cohen, 1979).

See also: consultation, law-making process, neighbourhood management, new public management, reassurance policing

References and further reading

Casey, L. (2008) *Engaging Communities in Fighting Crime – A Review by Louise Casey.* London: The Cabinet Office.

Cohen, S. (1979) 'The Punitive City: Notes on the Dispersal of Social Control', *Contemporary Crises* 3: 339–63.

Department of Communities and Local Government (2008) *Communities in Control: Real People, Real Power.* London: TSO, Cm 7427.

Garland, D. (1996) 'The Limits of the Sovereign State', *British Journal of Criminology,* 36(4): 445–71.

Hughes, G. (1998) *Understanding Crime Prevention: Social Control, Risk and Late Modernity.* Buckingham: Open University Press.

Ministry of Justice (2008) *A National Framework for Greater Citizen Engagement.* London: Ministry of Justice.

equity

See **law (sources of)**

Eurojust

Eurojust is the European Union's judicial cooperation unit whose role is to enhance cooperation between national judicial authorities, particularly in connection with serious cross-border and organized crime.

The 1997 Treaty of Amsterdam promoted the objective of 'an Area of Freedom and Justice' which was taken one step further at the meeting of the European Council in Tampere, Finland, to establish a judicial cooperation unit to co-ordinate the activities of national prosecuting authorities and to support criminal investigations into serious cross-border and organized crime. This new body was referred to as Eurojust and was set up in 2002.

Eurojust is composed of a College of 25 members, one member being drawn from each EU country, each of whom is an experienced judge or prosecutor. It operates through a number of functional committees. Its key virtue is that as a permanent body it provides 'a platform for a permanent dialogue' that helps to 'point out and rub down some points of friction between different legal systems, thus gradually building confidence in member states' respective legal systems' (Guild and Geyer, 2008: 39).

Eurojust constitutes a permanent network of judicial authorities whose role is to secure improved coordination and enhanced co-operation between EU states in connection with criminal justice matters. It may also aid investigations and prosecutions between a member and a non-member state or between member states and the European Commission in connection with criminal offences that affect the financial interests of the EU. Although unable to commence or conduct criminal investigations, Eurojust can make formal requests to national authorities to initiate an investigation or a prosecution (Bantekas and Nash, 2003: 280).

These functions are performed through a range of activities that include providing a forum for *ad hoc* meetings between investigators and prosecutors of states whose cooperation is needed to deal with a specific case, and acting as a mechanism through which legal assistance between member states can be facilitated and information exchanged and through which European Arrest Warrants are implemented. Eurojust also receives information from Europol and works closely with the European Judicial Network.

See also: European Arrest Warrant, Europol, Justice and Home Affairs Council

References and further reading

Bantekas, I. and Nash, S. (2003) *International Criminal Law.* London: Cavendish, second edition.

Guild, E. and Geyer, F. (ed.) (2008) *Security versus Justice? Police and Judicial Cooperation in the EU.* Aldershot: Ashgate.

European Arrest Warrant

The European Arrest Warrant was designed to speed up extradition procedures between member states and is based upon the principle of mutual recognition of member states' national criminal laws and procedures (House of Lords European Union Committee, 2003: para 2). It was introduced in 2004.

The European Arrest Warrant 'operates on the principle of mutual recognition of court judgments and is the enforced transfer of a person from one member state to another' (Bentekas and Nash, 2003: 282). It provides for the arrest and surrendering of a national of one EU state for an action defined as a crime in another EU state in whose borders it was committed. It assumes 'a high level of trust between both judicial and law enforcement authorities of member states' (Bentekas and Nash, 2003: 283).

In the UK, applications for extradition from the UK to member states are processed by the Fugitives Unit of the Serious Organized Crime Agency (SOCA). Between January 2004 and August 2006 the Crown Prosecution Service issued a total of 307 EAWs in the UK on behalf of EU partners which resulted in the arrest of 172 suspects (House of Lords European Union Committee, 2007: para 77).

See also: Eurojust, Europol, Schengen initiatives, Serious Organized Crime Agency

References and further reading

Bantekas, I. and Nash, S. (2003) *International Criminal Law*. London: Cavendish, second edition.

House of Lords European Union Committee (2003) *Europol's Role in Fighting Crime,* Session 2002–3, 5th Report. House of Lords Paper 43. London: TSO.

House of Lords European Union Committee (2007) *Schengen Information System, II (SIS II)* Session 2006–7, 9th Report. House of Lords Paper 49. London: TSO.

European Convention on Human Rights

The European Convention on Human Rights (properly referred to as the European Convention for the Protection of Human Rights and Fundamental Freedoms) was adopted by the European Council in 1950 which imposes on member states a body of legal principles to which they are obliged to conform (Drzemczewski, 1983: 22).

The Convention identified a number of basic rights which are:

- the right to life (Article 2)
- the prohibition of torture (Article 3)
- the prohibition of slavery and forced labour (Article 4)
- the right to life and security (Article 5)
- the right to a fair trial (Article 6)
- the right not to be punished save in accordance with the law (Article 7)
- the right to respect for private and family life (Article 8)
- freedom of thought, conscience and religion (Article 9)
- freedom of expression (Article 10)

- freedom of assembly and association (Article 11)
- the right to marry (Article 12)
- the prohibition of discrimination (Article 14).

However, these rights are not of equal standing. Article 3 is absolute and can never be contravened.

Articles 2, 4, 5, 6 and 7 are fundamental but may be temporarily set aside for specific reasons identified in the Convention under the procedure known as 'derogation' (Article 15). The circumstances under which derogation is permissible relate to a time of 'war or other public emergency threatening the life of the nation' and it is also necessary to demonstrate that this course of action is 'strictly required by the exigency of the situation'.

Articles 8, 9, 10 and 11 are qualified rights that may be subject to qualifications provided that certain circumstances or conditions that are laid down in the Convention are met and also that the interference is legitimated in the nation's domestic law.

The Convention also has a number of protocols some of which add to the rights protected by the Convention. These cover issues such as the protection of property, the right to education and the right to free elections (Protocol 1), discrimination (Protocol 13) and the total abolition of the death penalty (Protocol 13) and come into force if member states choose to ratify them.

The Convention is ultimately enforced by the European Court of Human Rights. In 1998 the Labour government enacted the Human Rights Act which incorporated the European Convention on Human Rights into British Law. Henceforth allegations by aggrieved citizens in the UK that public authorities had denied them their basic rights (either by interfering with them or by failing to take measures to ensure that they could exercise them) could be heard in British courts rather than complainants having to take their grievances to the European Court of Human Rights.

The 1998 Human Rights Act had significant consequences for the power of the judiciary since it was enabled to use this legislation as a yardstick with which to judge other Acts passed by Parliament. This judgment could be made retrospectively in connection with old legislation as well as with new Acts.

However, in order to uphold the concept of the sovereignty of Parliament, judges could not directly overturn an Act of Parliament that they felt contravened the principles of the Human Rights legislation. Instead, they were empowered to issue a certificate that declared a law passed by Parliament to be 'incompatible with the convention'. It was assumed that such declarations by the courts would induce the government and Parliament to introduce corrective measures (through the use of delegated legislation in the form of a Remedial Order) to bring such complained-of legislation into line with the Convention on Human Rights. However, they cannot be compelled to do so, which would result in an aggrieved person referring the matter to the European Court of Human Rights whose decisions are binding on the UK as international treaty obligations (Jackson, 1997: 9).

Alternatively, judicial criticism of legislation may induce the government to bring forward a new measure that is designed to correct the abuse of human rights highlighted by the courts. The introduction of control orders to restrict the movements of terrorist suspects in the 2005 Prevention of Terrorism Act was prompted by the judiciary's condemnation in December 2004 of internment without trial which had been introduced in connection with foreign nationals suspected of terrorist involvement by the 2001 Anti-terrorism, Crime and Security Act.

See also: delegated legislation, European Court of Human Rights, human rights, judicial review, law (sources of)

References and further reading

Drzemczewski, A. (1983) *European Human Rights Convention in Domestic Law: A Comparative Study*. Oxford: Oxford University Press.

Jackson, D. (1997) *The United Kingdom Confronts the European Declaration of Human Rights*. Florida: University of Florida Press.

European Court of Human Rights (ECHR)

The European Court of Human Rights is ultimately responsible for enforcing the European Convention on Human Rights. It is based in Strasbourg.

In 1950 the Council of Europe (whose membership is wider than that of the EU with which it should not be confused) drew up the European Convention on Human Rights (whose formal title is the Convention for the Protection of Human Rights and Fundamental Freedoms). The ECHR acts as the 'judicial arm' of the Convention (Merrills, 1993: 4) and was reorganized in 1998, replacing the previous European Court of Human Rights and the European Commission of Human Rights, both of which were established during the 1950s.

The role of the ECHR is to investigate complaints concerning breaches of human rights by a nation that is a signatory to the European Convention on Human Rights. Complaints may be made by states or individuals.

Each country that is a party to the European Convention on Human Rights nominates three candidates for the ECHR. The Parliamentary Assembly of the Council of Europe elects one of these who serves for a six-year term of office. The ECHR is divided into five sections, each of which selects a chamber of seven justices. The ECHR also possesses a grand chamber of 17 justices.

Complaints to the ECHR were formerly investigated by the European Commission of Human Rights which was also based in Strasbourg. Its findings were then considered by the European Court of Human Rights. Currently, complaints are referred to a Section and a committee of three judges may throw out those regarded as 'unmeritorious'. Those judged to be meritorious are subsequently examined by a Chamber. Decisions of significance may be appealed to the Grand Chamber.

Decisions of the ECHR are binding on member states (unless the Court's opinion is an advisory one related to the interpretation of the Convention or Protocols). The Committee of Ministers of the Council of Europe supervises the implementation of ECHR decisions, although the only penalty it can exact for failure to comply is expulsion from the Council of Europe.

An example of how the operations of the European Court of Human Rights can affect criminal justice policy in the UK occurred in 1998. This body ruled (in the Osman case) that when the police were aware of a physical threat to a person they were under a legal obligation to protect that person. This ruling effectively ended the police immunity from legal action in cases alleging negligence, and could be applied by victims of a wide range of hate crimes. A second example concerned the storage of DNA samples of innocent people on the National DNA Database. This was ruled by the ECHR to be unlawful in the Marper judgment in 2008.

The 1998 Human Rights Act enabled domestic courts in the UK to enforce the Convention on Human Rights. However, those dissatisfied with the outcome of this procedure remain able to refer their complaint to the ECHR.

See also: hate crime, human rights, National DNA Database

References and further reading

Osman *v* UK (28 October 1998) (Application number 23452/94).

S and Marper *v* UK (December 4, 2008) (Application numbers 30562/04 and 30566/04).

Merrills, J. (1993) *The Development of International Law by the European Court of Human Rights.* Manchester: Manchester University Press.

European Court of Justice (ECJ)

The European Court of Justice (whose official title is 'Court of Justice of the European Communities') is an example of an international court that has jurisdiction in the UK. It was set up in 1952 and its main purpose is to interpret EU law and ensure that it is applied by all member countries. It is based in Luxembourg.

The ECJ has competence to determine a wide range of issues – it functions as 'an administrative court, a constitutional court, and a tribunal which deals with many specialized and technical aspects of law' (de Burca, 2001: 6). Its work embraces disputes between member states, between the EU and member states, between individuals and the EU, or between the institutions of the EU. Specific actions that are brought before it include applications regarding an EU institution's failure to act and applications to annul a measure that has been adopted by an EU institution. It has the power to declare unlawful any national law that contravenes EU law and also has the power to fine companies in breach of EU legislation.

The ECJ may also hear requests submitted by the domestic courts of member states for a preliminary ruling regarding the interpretation of EU law or the legality of EU law. This process entails a petition being presented to the Court of Justice. The outcome constitutes a decision with which the national court making the application (and all other national courts) are required to comply.

The ECJ acts as an important constraint on the autonomy of member states and its role in securing integration has been especially important since the passage of the 1986 Single European Act (Dehousse, 1993: 2).

The structure of the ECJ embraces two subordinate courts: the Court of First Instance (which was set up in 1988 and has the authority to determine direct actions brought by natural and legal persons) and the Civil Service Tribunal (which adjudicates on cases brought by employees of the institutions of the EU). Appeals against decisions made by the Court of First Instance are heard by the ECJ.

This court is staffed by 25 judges and 8 advocates general drawn from member countries of the European Union (EU) who serve for six years. The ECJ may sit as a full court (with a quorum of 15 judges), in a Grand Chamber (consisting of 11 judges) or in chambers of 3–5 judges. The advocates general conduct research on cases that are referred to the ECJ and present conclusions to the court.

The 2009 Treaty of Lisbon officially changed the name of the ECJ to that of the 'Court of Justice' and the

Court of First Instance to that of the 'General Court'.

See also: European Court of Human Rights, criminal court system England and Wales

References and further reading

de Burca, G. (2001) 'Introduction' in G. de Burca and J. Weiler (eds) *The European Court of Justice.* Oxford: Oxford University Press.

Craig, P. and de Burca, G. (2003) *EU Law, Text, Cases and Materials.* Oxford: Oxford University Press.

Dehousse, R. (1993) *The European Court of Justice.* Basingstoke: Macmillan.

Europol (the European Police Office)

Europol is an agency whose role is to facilitate the gathering and exchange of information regarding serious crime within the countries that comprise the European Union.

The 1993 Maastricht Treaty provided for the possibility of an enhanced degree of police cooperation within the formal EU structure to be developed under the auspices of its 'third pillar' of justice and home affairs. The establishment of Europol became the responsibility of the Council which drafted a Convention for member states to ratify. This – the Convention on the Establishment of a European Police Office – was drawn up in July 1995 and the organization formally came into being towards the end of 1998 and became operational from its headquarters in The Hague in July 1999.

Europol is funded by the member states and has around 250 members drawn from them (House of Lords European Union Committee, 2003: para 3). Its work is performed by liaison officers drawn from the police organizations of member countries who are seconded to work in Europol's Liaison Bureau.

The 1995 Convention gave Europol the role of improving 'the effectiveness and cooperation of the competent authorities in the Member States in preventing and combating terrorism, unlawful drug trafficking and other serious forms of international crime where there are factual indications that an organized criminal structure is involved and two or more Member States are affected by the forms of crime in question in such a way as to require a common approach by the Member States owing to the scale, significance and consequence of the offences concerned' (1995 Convention Article 2 (1), quoted in House of Lords European Union Committee, 2003: para 2).

The role of Europol is to act as an intelligence agency, a central organization to facilitate the gathering and exchange of information among the national policing units of member states and to analyse information received from them in connection with trans-national criminal activities. It does not conduct criminal investigations and possesses no operational powers such as the ability to detain or to search.

In order to accomplish its functions, Europol utilizes a computerized system of collected information which is discharged through two programmes: the Europol Information System (EIS) and the Overall Analysis System for Intelligence and Support (OASIS) whose work is stored in analysis work files (AWFs). Member states may participate in as many, or few, AWFs as they wish. These two programmes are, however, 'separate and independent' (House of Lords European Union Committee, 2008: para 86).

The orientation of Europol is primarily forward-looking and is based upon an intelligence-led model of policing implemented through Organized Crime Threat Assessments (OCTAs) rather than reacting to past events (House of Lords European Union Committee, 2008: para 68–9). These are published by Europol on an annual basis and are designed to inform the Justice and Home Affairs Council of the main threats that face the EU and to facilitate Europol-led responses to these threats by the member states (House of Lords European Union Committee, 2008: para 77).

Europol was established by a Convention between the member states rather than a Treaty. This has impeded making changes to matters that include the role, powers and governance of Europol and prompted moves initiated by the Justice and Home Affairs Council in 2006 to establish Europol on the basis of a Council Decision (based on the third pillar of the Maastricht Treaty) rather than a Convention. This was agreed in 2008 and will come into force in 2010, making Europol an EU agency. The remit of Europol will remain focused on organized crime, although this term is defined broadly to cover serious crimes that affect two or more member states and which requires these states adopt a common approach (House of Lords European Union Committee, 2008: para 35).

The 2009 Treaty of Lisbon merged the existing first and third pillars of the Maastricht Treaty. It established the role of Europol and the manner whereby the European Parliament and Council can determine its structure, operation, field of action and tasks and the way in which European and national Parliaments can scrutinize its work.

See also: Eurojust, Justice and Home Affairs Council, Schengen initiatives

References and further reading

House of Lords European Union Committee (2003) *Europol's Role in Fighting Crime,* Session

2002–3, 5th Report. House of Lords Paper 43. London: TSO.

House of Lords European Union Committee (2008) *Europol: Coordinating the Fight against Serious and Organised Crime.* Session 2007–8, 29th Report. House of Lords Paper 183. London: TSO.

Walker, N. (2003) 'The Pattern of Trans-national Policing' in T. Newburn (ed.) *Handbook of Policing.* Cullompton, Devon: Willan Publishing.

evaluation

See **What works?**

examining magistrates

See **inquisitorial justice**

expert witness

An expert witness assists the court by providing an independent opinion on specialist or technical matters about which judges, juries or magistrates would be unlikely to possess first-hand knowledge or experience. The knowledge possessed by expert witnesses is derived from their professional experience, qualifications or expertise relevant to the case before the court.

The role of expert witnesses originated in the thirteenth century and is used in both civil and criminal cases and in other legal forums such as tribunals. They prepare reports and may be required to attend a trial to answer questions regarding the evidence they have submitted. The duty of expert witnesses is to the court and not to the party which is instructing or paying them which emphasizes the duty of the expert witness to act independently. The decision as to whether a person can be regarded as an expert witness rests with the trial judge.

Although expert witnesses may enable judges, juries or magistrates to more readily understand the evidence that is presented in a case before them, problems have arisen with regard to the partisanship displayed by expert witnesses to those who have instructed them and to the delays and additional costs which their use may pose to cases before the courts. Dangers may also arise if the views put forward in their evidence are regarded as facts that cannot be disputed.

Problems of this latter nature arose in connection with several cases related to cot deaths in which mothers were convicted of killing their children on the testimony of a paediatrician, Sir Roy Meadows, who held that more than one child death in a family was unlikely to be a natural event. These cases included the wrongful convictions of Sally Clark and Angela Cannings (whose convictions for killing two of their children were overturned by the Court of Appeal in 2003).

This situation led the chair of the Criminal Cases Review Commission, Professor Graham Zellick, to call for an overhaul of the rules governing expert testimony whereby 'areas of expertise would be clearly defined and experts registered, judges should be able to throw out expert evidence they considered unreliable, it should be made clear to juries to what degree such testimony is a matter of opinion rather than undisputed fact, and different views should be offered where appropriate' (Zellick, 2004).

The conduct of expert witnesses is regulated in a number of ways. Professional bodies that include the General Medical Council provide guidelines for doctors who act in this capacity and the Society of Expert Witnesses seeks to promote excellence in the work they perform.

Organizations such as the Forensic Expert Witness Association also serve to guarantee standards.

See also: jury system, criminal court system England and Wales, miscarriage of justice

References and further reading

Dempsey, M. (2004) *The Use of Expert Witness Testimony in the Prosecution of Domestic Violence.* London: Crown Prosecution Service.

Luke, G. (2009) *The Expert Witness: An Occupational Therapist's Perspective.* Bury St Edmunds, Suffolk: Arima Publishing.

Zellick, G. (2004) quoted in R. Cowan, 'Call for Overhaul of Expert Testimony', *The Guardian*, 30 November.

F

field research

Field research entails researchers conducting first-hand investigations into particular forms of criminal activity. This is conducted 'in the field' rather than in a library or laboratory setting and 'offers the advantage of probing social life in its natural habitat' (Babbie, 2009: 299).

Field research entails a researcher engaging in a prolonged period of face-to-face contact with a person(s) being studied in order to obtain an understanding of the meaning which the subjects who are being observed attach to their actions. This approach 'stresses the importance of the subjective experience of individuals in the creation of the social world' (Cohen *et al.*, 2000: 7). The participant's perspective is centre-stage of the research and the aim of the researcher is to observe – or enter into – the social world of the subject(s) in order to investigate how they make sense of the social situation within which they exist. The researcher writes up an account of his or her observations either at the conclusion of the study or on a more regular basis as events unfold.

Field research can be conducted in various ways. The researcher may become a member of the community which he or she is studying and participate in all of its activities. In this case the research is likely to be covert with the subjects being unaware of the motives of the researcher. This is referred to as participant observation.

Alternatively, the researcher may attach him or herself to the community and make detailed observations of its actions and activities without joining in any of them. He or she becomes a 'fly on the wall'. Research of this nature can be either overt (where the researcher provides the true reasons for his or her attachment to the group) or covert (where the researcher gives false reasons for wishing to associate with it). This is referred to as non-participant observation.

Field research is an important tool of qualitative methodology and is especially useful for obtaining information on groups and organizations whose activities are conducted in a relatively closed environment, out of the gaze or scrutiny of the general public. These methods do, however, pose a number of problems which include the possibility of personal danger, especially if 'the cover is blown' of a researcher engaged in covert participant or non-participant observation, and reliability since the researcher may lose his or her objectivity by becoming too closely involved and sympathetic to the group with which he or she becomes associated.

Other problems affecting field research into crime and criminals is that in order to retain credibility with the group being studied, the researcher may engage in activities that are criminal, thus becoming an accessory to criminal actions. There are also ethical issues affecting covert research where this entails data being gathered from subjects without their knowledge or consent.

See also: crime statistics, self-report studies, victimization surveys

References and further reading

Babbie, E. (2009) *The Practice of Social Research.* Belmont, California: Wadsworth Cengage Learning, twelfth edition.

Cohen, L., Manion, L. and Morrison, K. (2000) *Research Methods in Education.* London: Routledge.

fines

See **sentences of the criminal courts**

fire brigade policing

Fire brigade (or reactive) policing involved redirecting patrol work to respond to events after they had taken place rather than seeking to prevent them from occurring.

Historically, the main orientation of police work had been the prevention of crime which was delivered by officers on foot patrol – the home beat method of policing that was epitomized by the 'bobby on the beat'. Problems in recruiting officers into the police service meant there were insufficient to discharge policing in this traditional way.

During the 1960s the preventive orientation of patrol work began to be replaced by a reactive focus. This change was actively promoted by the Home Office (Home Office, 1967) which led to forces reducing the number of officers who patrolled on foot or on bicycles in favour of the use of motorized vehicles. This was dubbed 'fire brigade policing' by Sir Robert Mark (Metropolitan Police Commissioner 1972–77).

This form of policing was implemented by the 'unit beat' method which was intimately associated with the use of cars and two-way radios, supplemented by technological developments such as the Police National Computer and the computer-aided dispatch of officers to incidents. It was also associated with the introduction of force-wide units which conducted high-profile operations to combat a particular form of criminal activity which had reached a level deemed too high by police commanders.

It was envisaged that officers would be able to devote some of their time to foot patrol when not responding to incidents and could thus gather local intelligence that would be coordinated by a collator. However, this ideal was undermined by increased public demand on police resources which meant that officers effectively spent their time driving from one incident to another. Accordingly, the rise of the 'technological cops' (Alderson, 1979: 41–2) meant that random foot patrol increasingly assumed a low status and priority within police forces with patrol work being performed mainly by officers driving from one incident to another.

There were a number of advantages associated with this new style of policing. In particular, it enabled the police to make use of technology to combat crime that was increasingly becoming less localized and more organized.

However there were several problems with fire brigade policing, in particular the way in which the police service failed to cultivate intimate relationships with the communities in which they operated. This posed particular problems in multi-racial, inner-city areas where lack of local knowledge was perceived to result in the use of powers such as stop and search on a random basis based on stereotypical assumptions.

Arguments that attributed the cause of the 1981 inner-city disturbances to a reaction against fire brigade policing methods by those on the receiving end of them (Kettle and Hodge, 1982) resulted in a shift away from reactive methods in favour of community policing.

See also: Dixon of Dock Green, neighbourhood policing, zero tolerance

References and further reading

Alderson, J. (1979) *Policing Freedom*. Plymouth: Macdonald and Evans.

Cowell, D., Jones, T. and Young, J. (eds) (1982) *Policing the Riots*. London: Junction Books.

Home Office (1967) *Police Manpower, Equipment and Efficiency.* London: Home Office.

Kettle, M. and Hodges, L. (1982) *Uprising! The Police, The People and the Riots in Britain's Cities.* London: Pan Books.

Lord Scarman (1981) *The Brixton Disorders, 10–12 April 1981 – Report of an Inquiry by the Rt Hon the Lord Scarman, OBE.* Cmnd 8427. London: HMSO.

G

General Council of the Bar (Bar Council)

See **legal profession England and Wales**

Green Paper

See **law-making process**

H

habeas corpus

Habeas corpus 'is the name for the procedure by which a court inquires into the legality of a citizen's detention' (Freedman, 2001: 1). It provides an important safeguard against arbitrary actions undertaken by the state.

In the UK, habeas corpus historically provided a pre-trial remedy for persons who were detained on the orders of the King (Federman, 2006: 4). It dated from the Anglo-Saxon period and was developed in the Magna Carta (1215) which allowed appeals against unlawful imprisonment. It was placed on a statutory basis in the 1679 Habeas Corpus Act (or in Scotland the 1701 Wrongous Imprisonment Act). It consists of a writ (a written instruction issued by a court) that compels the authorities who are holding a person in custody to present him or her to the courts in order to ascertain the validity of the detention.

However, this procedure failed to provide totally effective protection to a citizen's civil liberties, a key weakness being that a person who was being detained by the police was usually unlikely to be able to communicate his or her whereabouts to others who could initiate the habeas corpus procedure. This could result in lengthy periods of detention which might lead to miscarriages of justice. These might arise when a person who was detained for a relatively long period without access to legal representation felt pressurized to confess to a crime that he or she had not committed.

To address problems of this nature the 1984 Police and Criminal Evidence Act imposed restrictions on the period of detention. Under the legislation, detention in custody would normally last for a period of

24 hours, although an officer of the rank of Superintendent could add a further 12 hours. If a further extension was required, it had to be granted by a magistrate, and could extend to a total period of 96 hours. At that stage a person should either be charged with an offence or released.

The Habeas Corpus Act was occasionally suspended in times of national emergency (such as 1817) and in more recent times its underlying principles have been undermined by anti-terrorist legislation. The 2001 Anti-terrorism, Crime and Security Act permitted detention without trial for a person whose presence in Britain was deemed to be a risk to security and who was suspected of being concerned with international terrorism. The 2006 Terrorism Act provided for an elongated period of detention (termed 'pre-charge detention') for a period of 28 days for those suspected of having committed terrorist offences. The government had wanted a period of 90 days and has subsequently attempted to increase the 28 day limit.

See also: miscarriage of justice, PACE Codes of Practice

References and further reading

Federman, C. (2006) *The Body and the State: Habeas Corpus and American Jurisprudence.*

Albany, New York: State University of New York Press.

Freedman, A. (2001) *Habeas Corpus: Rethinking the Great Writ of Liberty.* New York: New York University Press.

hate crime

Hate crime is defined as a criminal offence that is motivated by hostility or prejudice towards a group of which the individual victim is – or is presumed to be – a member. Victims are targeted.

Hate crime is targeted at groups defined in terms of disability, race, religion or belief, sexual orientation or transgender and violence may extend towards property with which they are associated (such as the desecration of cemeteries).

Hate crime covers a wide range of offences that range from 'name-calling' and other forms of incivility to harassment, assault and murder. It is, however, different to other forms of crime since it constitutes a form of discrimination that infringes human rights and prevents people from enjoying the full benefits of society; it is the cause of greater psychological harm than similar crimes lacking such a motivation and it causes fear among victims, groups and communities that are on the receiving end of such actions (Home Office, 2009). It thus justified a specific response from criminal justice agencies, one aspect of which is to relate punishment to the motives of offenders.

Initially racially motivated violence was a key manifestation of hate crime and historically criminal justice agencies were accused of insufficient vigour in tackling problems of this nature despite the ability of such actions 'to corrode the fabric of our tolerant society' (Home Affairs Committee, 1994).

However, the need to take effective action against racial violence was forcibly expressed by the inquiry conducted by Sir William Macpherson into the investigation conducted by the Metropolitan Police Service into the murder of Stephen Lawrence, one aspect of which was the inability of investigating officers to discern a racial motive for the attack (Home Office, 1999: 23). This resulted in reforms to tackle institutional racism within the criminal justice agencies which was identified as a key issue in the Macpherson Report (Home Office, 1999: 28). The definition of what constituted an act of racial violence was also redefined for the police service in an attempt to make them become more victim-oriented in their response to such actions.

Subsequently, existing legislation to combat racial violence (that included the 1986 Public Order Act, the 1991 Football Offences Act and the 1998 Crime and Disorder Act which was subsequently amended by the 2001 Anti-terrorism, Crime and Security Act), was augmented by other measures designed to combat other forms of hate crime. These measures included the 2003 Criminal Justice Act, the 2006 Racial and Religious Hatred Act and the 2008 Criminal Justice and Immigration Act.

See also: human rights, institutional racism

References and further reading

Hall, N. (2005) *Hate Crime.* Cullompton, Devon: Willan Publishing.

Home Affairs Committee (1994) *Racial Attacks and Harassment,* Session 1993–94, House of Common Paper 71. London: HMSO.

Home Office (1999) *The Stephen Lawrence Enquiry: Report of an Inquiry by Sir William Macpherson of Cluny.* Cm 4262. London: TSO.

Home Office (2009) *Crime and Victims.* [Online] http://www.homeoffice.gov.uk/crime-victims/reducing-crime/hate-crime/

Her Majesty's Courts Service

See **political oversight of the criminal justice system**

Home Detention Curfew (HDC)

See **electronic monitoring ('tagging')**

Home Office

See **political oversight of the criminal justice system**

Home Office Circular

A Home Office Circular consists of guidance issued by this government department to agencies for which it has responsibility regarding the performance of their functions.

Circulars perform a number of functions that include clarifying the law, indicating the impact of new legislation (including that promoted through delegated legislation) on the subsequent practices of practitioners and putting forward suggestions regarding the future direction of policy that an agency should pursue, including standards of service delivery. They are addressed to key officials that include chief constables, clerks to police authorities, ACPO and the Association of Police Authorities.

Home Office Circulars are not legally binding on their recipients, but they possess considerable authority over subsequent actions and have on occasions exerted a considerable impact on criminal justice policy. The imposition of the principles of new public management on the police service derived from a circular (Home Office, 1983) and a circular on crime prevention (Home Office, 1984) was responsible for shifting the focus of crime prevention to a partnership approach involving the police, local government and other agencies.

Other government departments concerned with the operations of the criminal justice system (such as the Ministry of Justice) also issue circulars.

See also: crime prevention, delegated legislation, new public management, police authority, Police Staff Associations, political oversight of the criminal justice system

References and further reading

Home Office (1983) *Manpower, Effectiveness and Efficiency in the Police Service.* London: Home Office, Circular 114/1983.

Home Office (1984) *Crime Prevention.* London: Home Office, Circular 8/1984.

Home Office Circulars from 2003 are to be located on the Home Office Website [Online] http://www.homeoffice.gov.uk/about-us/publications/home-office-circulars/

human rights

Human rights are basic entitlements that all persons should be permitted to enjoy wherever they live and which no government should be entitled to take away. The designation of rights as '*human*' implies that they should be universal in application and constitute 'important instruments for protecting human beings against cruelty, oppression and degradation' (Ignatieff *et al.*, 2001: xi).

The concept of human rights developed from the tradition of natural rights that sought to establish boundaries to protect individuals from unwarranted interference either by another individual or by the government. Human rights were thus closely associated with the political ideology of liberalism that wished government to be limited in its scope and sought to impose restraints on the actions that others might undertake. The English political philosopher John Locke (1632–1704) defined human rights as embracing 'life, liberty and property', while the American Declaration of Independence referred to them in 1776 as including 'life, liberty and the pursuit of happiness'.

In the contemporary period, human rights embrace a wider range of civil and political liberties. These are often provided for in a codified constitution (such as the first ten amendments to the American Constitution which were inserted in 1791, collectively referred to as the 'Bill of Rights'). In countries such as the United Kingdom that lacked a codified constitution, the rights of the citizen were historically derived from common law. The most recent declarations of human rights are to be found in the United Nations Declaration of Human Rights (1948) and the European Convention for the Protection of Human Rights and Fundamental Freedoms (1950).

The concept of rights as universal in application implies that their enforcement may go beyond the jurisdiction of individual states and require states to answer to the international community with regard to their treatment of individuals (Forsythe, 2000: 4). Accordingly, international machinery has been developed to enforce their application throughout the world. The United Nations Human Rights Council was set up in 2005 with a mandate to investigate violations of human rights. This is a subsidiary body of the UN General Assembly and can call upon the UN Security Council to act in response to violations of human rights, for example by imposing sanctions against errant countries. The Security Council may also refer violations to the International Criminal Court.

International organizations such as Amnesty International and Human Rights First also campaign to promote the concept of human rights across the globe by highlighting injustices, and in the UK Liberty is an example of a national organization that seeks to protect civil liberties and promote human rights.

See also: European Convention on Human Rights, law (sources of), International Criminal Court

References and further reading

Forsythe, D. (2000) *Human Rights in International Relations.* Cambridge: Cambridge University Press.

Ignatieff, M., Appiah, K. and Gutmann, A. (2001) *Human Rights as Politics and Idolatry.* Princeton, NJ: Princeton University Press.

I

incapacitation

See **punishment (aims of)**

indictable offence

See **criminal court system England and Wales**

informants (grasses/supergrasses)

An informant (sometimes known as a 'grass' or – depending on the scale of activity – a 'supergrass') is either a criminal or a person who associates with criminals who passes on to the police information relating to the criminal activities of others.

A person may become an inform-ant for a variety of reasons (Morton, 2002: xiii) but arrest or conviction for a serious crime may prompt this action. A criminal may provide the police with information regarding his or her accomplices in order to secure immunity from prosecution or a reduced sentence. This process is also known as 'turning Queen's evidence'. It is used relatively infrequently. Problems with it include the perceived juries' sus-picion of the character of the cooperating defendant and the incentives to him or her not being seen as sufficiently clear or sub-stantial (Home Office, 2004: 48).

Those who have taken this path include the bank robber Bertie Smalls in 1971 who was given immunity from prosecution in return for information that led to the arrest of 27 of his former criminal colleagues (Morton, 2002: 56). Informants (or supergrasses) were also used in Northern Ireland in the early 1980s to combat politically motivated violence. One estimate suggested that between 1981 (when Christopher Black turned supergrass) and 1984 at least 446 people were charged on the basis of supergrass information (Gifford, 1984: 10).

The justification for the use of informants and the lenient treatment they subsequently received is that they may be the only available source of evidence against some forms of criminal activity whose capacity to conduct crime may be crippled by the informant's testimony. The Audit Commission viewed them as one way of improving detection rates (alongside other methods that included crime pattern analysis) (Audit Commission, 1993). However, there have also been a number of problems associated with the use of informants.

These include the spectre of serious, hardened criminals not being adequately brought to justice for the crimes they have committed and perhaps being rewarded in return for the information they have provided. Informants may go beyond providing the police with information on a crime that has already been planned and may incite persons to commit an offence that would not have occurred but for the informant's involvement. It has also been alleged that police officers may turn a blind eye (or be asked to turn a blind eye by the informant's detective 'minder') to other crimes committed by an informant in order to keep him 'onside'. This situation may mean that informants are able to act as powerful criminals in their own right, furnished with a degree of police protection.

Much of this type of work was historically conducted on a personal basis between a detective and his/her 'snitch', although some informants were registered on the authority of a senior officer in a police force. In more recent years police forces have established central source handling units to exercise supervision over the use of informants and the information that they provide, and other forces have developed IT to manage the information obtained from informants. The 2000 Regulation of Investigatory Powers Act provided a statutory basis for the authorization and use of covert surveillance, informants and undercover officers.

See also: plea bargaining, thief takers

References and further reading

Audit Commission (1993) *Helping With Enquiries.* Abingdon: Audit Commission.

Gifford, T. (1984) *Supergrasses: The Use of Accomplice Evidence in Northern Ireland.* London: The Cobden Trust.

Home Office (2004) *One Step Ahead: A 21st Century Strategy to Defeat Organised Crime.* London: TSO, Cm 6167.

Morton, J. (2002) *Gangland.* London: Time Warner, omnibus edition.

inquisitorial justice

Inquisitorial justice underpins a legal system which is based upon an inquiry conducted by judges to determine the facts relating to an accusation of criminal wrongdoing.

Inquisitorial justice is found in countries with a Roman Law tradition or those whose legal procedures are based upon the Napoleonic Code. A person who is accused of committing a crime has his or her case examined by a judge or judges who seek to establish the truth of the allegations that have been made. Evidence is frequently presented in documentary form (although the oral presentation of evidence does occur) and the judge(s) play a key role in proceedings by possessing the power to 'determine the examination, collection and evaluation of evidence' (Adler and Laufer, 1999: 18). In exercising these functions they may question witnesses that the defence and prosecution produce and act proactively by summoning and questioning witnesses that they bring forward.

In conducting the inquiry, the judges(s) have considerable discretion to consider any evidence that is felt to be relevant to the case. There is no strict adherence to rules of evidence that is a feature of adversarial justice and these rules may be minimal in inquisitorial justice systems.

This system is used in France where an allegation of wrongdoing is investigated by an examining magistrate (*juge d'instruction*). This official is independent of the executive branch of government and also of the prosecution and seeks to ascertain the facts of the case. The authority of examining magistrates to initiate an inquiry is given by the prosecutor's office and they may not unilaterally initiate proceedings. Defendants are not required to enter a plea of guilty or not guilty but commonly play a part in proceedings that take place (Pakes, 2004: 780–1).

These procedures are used for the more serious criminal and are not used for the majority of criminal cases which are alternatively investigated by law enforcement agencies under the supervision of state prosecutors (*procureurs*). There are around 560 examining magistrates throughout France who conduct approximately 60,000 investigations each year (Lichfield, 2002).

In France there are two stages to the criminal process. The first is the investigation, which may be lengthy. If, as the result of the investigation, the examining magistrate feels there is a case to answer, it will be referred to a court for trial.

The term 'non-adversarial' justice is sometimes used in place of 'inquisitorial justice'. This term embraces a range of methods that seek to resolve conflicts outside of a court or tribunal. It is associated with developments such as arbitration, ombudsman and restorative justice some of which operate in countries whose legal system is underpinned by adversarial justice principles.

See also: adversarial justice, judges, jury system, rules of evidence, restorative justice

References and further reading

Adler, F. and Laufer, W. (eds) (1999) *The Criminology of Criminal Justice.* New Brunswick, NJ: Transaction Publishers.

Lichfield, J. (2002) 'Why the French are Growing Envious of Britain's Justice System', *The Independent*, 15 March.

Pakes, F. (2004) *Comparative Criminal Justice.* Cullompton, Devon: Willan Publishing.

institutional racism

Institutional racism refers to a situation in which an agency's organizational culture and the working practices that derive from it discriminate against persons from minority ethnic communities.

An important distinction exists between institutionalized racism (which refers to beliefs and attitudes which are prevalent in society) and institutional racism which affects the conduct of particular organizations which can be reformed in order to eliminate racist practices.

The concept of institutional racism was developed in the struggles of Black Americans for civil rights. Despite court-room victories and the enactment of legislation such as the 1965 Civil Rights Act and 1965 Voting Act, the condition of most Black Americans failed to change for the better. This situation was explained by institutional racism which suggested that racism should be analysed not only from the perspective of an individual act of prejudice but at the level of a racist power structure within society.

It was argued that institutional racism was akin to a system of internal colonialism in which black people stood as colonial subjects in relation to white society (Carmichael and Hamilton, 1967). This term was subsequently defined to embrace established laws, customs and practices that systematically reflected and produced racial inequalities and the interactions of various spheres of social life to maintain an overall pattern of oppression (Blauner, 1972).

Problems that affected the relationship of minority ethnic communities with the criminal justice system and in particular the police service led to considerations as to whether institutional racism was the root cause of these difficulties. This was considered by Lord Scarman in his inquiry into the 1981 riots

(Home Office, 1981: 64). However, he rejected this explanation and instead endorsed the 'bad apple' explanation of racism (Crowther, 2000: 98) which attributed racism to personal attitudes which were held by a minority of officers who knowingly and intentionally discriminated against persons from minority ethnic groups.

However, the inquiry conducted by Sir William Macpherson into the investigation mounted by the Metropolitan Police Service (MPS) into the murder of Stephen Lawrence came to a different conclusion. Macpherson argued that racism existed throughout the Metropolitan Police and that the problem was organizational rather than one that affected a small number of individuals. Macpherson concluded that the MPS was institutionally racist, a term which was defined in his report as

> the collective failure of an organisation to provide an appropriate and professional service to people because of their colour, culture or ethnic origin. It can be seen or detected in processes, attitudes and behaviour which amount to discrimination through unwitting prejudice, ignorance, thoughtlessness and racist stereotyping which disadvantage minority ethnic people.
>
> (Home Office, 1999: 28)

Although this term has been criticized for being 'almost incoherent' (Tonry, 2004: 76), for sidestepping questions of causality and for asserting racism to be the sole or primary cause of black disadvantage (thus ignoring other processes relating to class and gender), it is useful as it directed attention to how 'racist discourses can be embodied within the structures and organisations of society' (Singh, 2000: 29, 38). Further, the emphasis that was placed on organizational practices and procedures as the root cause of the problem implied that racism was an unwitting or unintended consequence of the actions undertaken by individual members of staff.

Following the publication of the Macpherson Report, numerous reforms were undertaken by criminal justice agencies in an attempt to rid them of institutional racism. These embraced issues such as recruitment, promotion and retention, training and operational practices that included the response to racial violence and monitoring the use made by the police of stop and search procedures.

See also: hate crime, Police Service England and Wales

References and further reading

Blauner, R. (1972) *Racial Oppression in America*. New York: Harper and Row.

Carmichael, S. and Hamilton, C. (1967) *Black Power*. New York: Vintage.

Crowther, C. (2000) *Policing Urban Poverty*. Basingstoke: Macmillan.

Home Office (1981) *The Brixton Disorders, 10–12 April 1981: Report of an Inquiry by the Rt Hon Lord Scarman OBE*. London: HMSO.

Home Office (1999) *The Stephen Lawrence Inquiry: Report of an Inquiry by Sir William Macpherson of Cluny*. London: TSO Cm 4262, chaired by Sir Willam Macpherson of Cluny.

Singh, G. (2000) 'The Concept and Content of Institutional Racism' in A. Marlow and B. Loveday (eds) *After Macpherson*. Dorset: Russell House Publishing.

Tonry, M. (2004) *Punishment and Politics: Evidence and Emulation in the Making of English Crime Control Policy*. Cullompton, Devon: Willan Publishing.

International Court of Justice (ICJ)

The International Court of Justice (also known as the World Court) is the principal judicial organ of the United Nations whose role is to settle legal disputes to which states are a party (termed 'contentious issues'), against which no appeal is possible, and to give advisory opinions on legal issues submitted by the United Nations General Assembly or Security Council and also by other organizations authorized by the UN General Assembly to seek legal advice from the ICJ on matters arising within the scope of their activities. It is located at The Hague, Netherlands.

The ICJ was established by the 1945 United Nations Charter to succeed the Permanent Court of International Justice that was created by the League of Nations in 1920 which had itself superseded the Permanent Court of Arbitration established in 1899. Its operations are regulated by the Statute of the International Court of Justice. It consists of 15 judges elected by the UN General Assembly and Security Council from lists nominated by national groups sitting in the Permanent Court for Arbitration. They serve for nine years. Additionally, *ad hoc* judges may also serve. These are typically appointed by states that are party to a contentious issue.

The UN Security Council is technically authorized to enforce decisions of the ICJ, but the five permanent members possess a veto power.

The role of the ICJ in adjudicating on contentious issues and providing advisory opinions make it an important instrument for developing international law (Lissitzyn, 2006: 13). However, this potential has not been fully realized since neither the ICJ nor its predecessor, the Permanent Court of Arbitration, have been widely used and 'a remarkable and disappointing consistence in the quantity of work handled by the International Court' has been observed. This situation has been explained by a reluctance of states and international organizations to use this form of international adjudication and it has been suggested that 'opening the jurisdiction of the ICJ to individuals is probably the best and perhaps the only means for ensuring its effective utilization' (Janis, 1997: 208–9).

See also: European Court of Human Rights, European Court of Justice, International Criminal Court

References and further reading

Janis, M. (1997) 'Individuals and the International Court' in S. Muller, D. Raic and J. Thuranszky (eds) *The International Court of Justice: Its Future Role After Fifty Years.* The Hague, Netherlands: Kluwer Law International.

Lissitzyn, O. (2006) *The International Criminal Court: Its Role in the Maintenance of International Peace and Security.* Clark, NJ: Lawbook Exchange.

International Criminal Court (ICC)

The International Criminal Court was established in 2002 under the provisions of the Rome Statute of the International Criminal Court. It is a permanent tribunal whose role is to prosecute individuals suspected of having committed genocide, crimes against humanity and war crimes. It is based in The Hague, Netherlands.

The driving force behind creating the ICC was 'to drive a crack into the wall of sovereignty behind which individuals aligned with the state can shield their misdeeds' (Glasius, 2006: 17). It is functionally independent of the United Nations and has 110 members (termed 'state parties'). However, a number of nations (including the United States, Russia, China and India) are not state parties. Its governing body is an Assembly of States Parties, one of whose functions is to elect a bench of judges. The first election of 18 judges took place in 2003. They are organized into three divisions: pretrial, trial and appeals.

Investigations and prosecutions are conducted by the Office of the Prosecutor. The Prosecutor may open an investigation when a matter is referred by a state party or by the United Nations Security Council or where the Pre-Trial Division authorizes an investigation. The Prosecutor has 'significant discretionary powers' to determine whether to initiate an investigation and as the result of this to determine whether there is sufficient basis to mount a prosecution (Lee, 1999: 229).

The proceedings of the ISS provide accused persons with a number of rights that include the presumption of innocence, the right to legal representation and the right to silence. It is necessary to prove a case beyond reasonable doubt in order to obtain a conviction. The ICC's Rules and Procedure and Evidence also guarantee rights to victims who may play a part in all stages of the ICC's proceedings.

The Court is a court of last resort which supplements the criminal justice systems of nations that are party to it and these have the initial responsibility to investigate and prosecute cases that fall under the remit of the Court which will intervene only when national courts are unable or unwilling to mount investigations.

Additionally, the Court may only deal with cases where the person accused of crime is a national of a state that has ratified the Rome Statute, where the alleged crime occurred in the territory of a state that has ratified the Rome Statute or where the issue is referred to the Court by the United Nations Security Council.

See also: European Court of Human Rights, European Court of Justice, International Court of Justice

References and further reading

Glasius, M. (2006) *The International Criminal Court: A Global Civil Society Achievement*. Abingdon, London: Routledge.

Lee, R. (ed.) (1999) *The International Criminal Court: The Making of the Rome Statute: Issues: Negotiations: Results*. Cambridge, MA: Kluwer Law International.

International Law Commission

See **Law Commission**

internment

Interment entails arresting and placing a person in custody for an indefinite period without presenting a formal charge against him or her. This means that the courts are unable to determine the legality or otherwise of the detention.

Internment may be resorted to when the state believes (on the basis of intelligence gathered by its security agencies) that a person is guilty of a serious crime but lacks the hard evidence necessary to secure a court conviction. Internment may be used to remove the suspect from the community pending a decision as to a future course of action (which may be release when the relevant emergency has died down, a trial if evidence materializes or deportation in the case of persons who are not UK nationals).

Internment departs from the rule of law and is resorted to in liberal democracies in times of crisis. In the United Kingdom it was used in Northern Ireland in 1971 under the provisions of the 1922 Civil Authorities (Special Powers) Act in an attempt to counter politically motivated violence.

This legislation had historically been directed at dissident republicans (Catholics) and those interned in 1971 in what was termed 'operation Demetrius' were exclusively from the nationalist community. In the original sweep conducted by the army on 9 August 1971, 342 men were arrested, of whom 226 were detained (McGuffin, 1973: 86). However, interment failed to prevent violence. The intelligence on which this action was based was obsolete (Kennedy-Pipe, 1997: 55) and many of those who were rounded up were not active members of paramilitary groups. The unfairness of the procedure tended to fuel violence rather than halt it. This was aggravated by the treatment those detained received during and after arrest where allegations of brutality were made, especially in connection with the interrogation of detainees (McGuffin, 1973: 118). Internment was abandoned in 1975 by which time around 2,000 persons had been detained.

The procedure was latterly employed in the UK following terrorist attacks in New York and Washington on 11 September 2001 associated with Islamist fundamentalism. The 2001 Anti-terrorism, Crime and Security Act enabled the Secretary of State to issue a certificate in connection with a person whose presence in Britain was deemed to be a risk to security and who was suspected of being concerned with international terrorism. This person could then be detained without a trial pending deportation.

However, in December 2004 the Law Lords ruled that the right to impose indefinite detention on a person was not justified since there was no 'state of public emergency' warranting an opt-out from Article 5 of the Convention on Human Rights. The government's position was ruled 'disproportionate' to the threat facing the nation from terrorism. Accordingly, the 2005 Prevention of Terrorism Act replaced internment with control orders. These imposed obligations on a person that might include residence, movement or possession of items. They are tailored to the individual and based on the risk that that individual posed.

See also: habeas corpus, rule of law

References and further reading

A (FC) and others (FC) (Appellants) *v.* Secretary of State for the Home Department (Respondent) [2004] UKHL 56.

Kennedy-Pipe, C. (1997) *The Origins of the Present Troubles in Northern Ireland.* Harlow: Longman.

McGuffin, J. (1973) *Internment.* Tralee, County Kerry: Anvil Books.

Interpol (International Criminal Police Organization)

Interpol is an example of an organization that seeks to facilitate police cooperation on an international scale. It was established in 1923 to further assistance between police forces and related agencies whose role was to combat international crime.

Interpol primarily fulfils its responsibilities by collecting and circulating information about individuals. This is stored on databases that provide information such as criminal names, fingerprints, DNA profiles, travel documents and stolen property such as passports and vehicles. A communications system referred to as I-24/7 provides direct access to these databases.

It may additionally provide emergency practical help to law enforcement agencies by dispatching response teams of officers to help deal with episodes such as disasters (for example the Indian Ocean tsunami in 2004 in connection with victim identification) and major crime. A 24-hour Command and Co-ordination Centre has been set up within Interpol which monitors events around the world in order to respond to requests for assistance concerning investigations or major crises.

Its work overlaps with that performed by Europol in areas that include terrorism, drugs, organized crime and people trafficking, although its orientation is on crime that has already occurred rather than Europol's concern to respond to its future manifestations (House of Lords European Union Committee, 2005: para 69, 2008: para 191).

Interpol is also involved in international responses to terrorism. In 2002 this organization set up the Fusion Task Force whose main role was to identify members of criminal groups who were engaged in terrorist activity. Interpol's importance in this area of activity especially rests on the fact that it is the only police organization with worldwide coverage (House of Lords European Union Committee, 2005: para 69 and 74).

Interpol's General Secretariat is housed in Lyon and this liaises with the National Central Bureaus of each member country, of which there are now 187 (House of Lords European Union Committee, 2008: para 28). Its broadening membership has moved it away from its original European orientation to that of a worldwide body, although Interpol has a liaison officer stationed at Europol and the two bodies signed a Joint Initiative in 2001.

See also: Europol, National DNA Database

References and further reading

Fooner, M. (1989) *Interpol: Issues in World Crime and International Criminal Justice.* New York: Plenum Press.

House of Lords European Union Committee (2005) *After Madrid: the EU's Response to Terrorism,* Session 2004–5, 5th Report. London: TSO, House of Lords Paper 53.

House of Lords European Union Committee (2008) *Europol: Co-ordinating the Fight against Serious and Organised Crime.* Session 2007–8, 29th Report. London: TSO, House of Lords Paper 183.

J

joined-up government

As applied to the criminal justice system, the term 'joined-up government' refers to measures that have been pursued by post-1997 Labour governments to ensure the greater coordination of a number of public sector organizations whose work might contribute towards combating crime, whether these were mainstream criminal justice agencies (such as the police and probation service) or bodies such as education and social services that had not traditionally viewed crime-fighting as one of their functions.

Initially reforms to achieve a joined-up approach in criminal justice policy were based on the multi-agency or partnership approach that was formalized in the fields of youth justice and community safety through the development of Youth Offending Teams and Crime and Disorder Reduction Partnerships.

This approach was developed through a number of other initiatives including multi-agency performance targets. An early example of this was Public Service Agreements, introduced in the 1998 Comprehensive Spending Review. These sought to coordinate the work of a number of government departments behind a common theme (the PSA) whose attainment was measured by a number of performance indicators. These themes embraced a wide range of government activity, including criminal justice affairs.

A further aspect of joined-up government sought to coordinate the work of individual criminal justice agencies. An important example of this was the National Offender Management Service (NOMS) that was set up in 2004 to bring together the operations of the probation and prison services. The formation of Her Majesty's Courts Service in 2005 aimed to secure the unified organization and administration of the civil, family and criminal courts in England and Wales.

A key reform to promote a joined-up approach at national level involving the three criminal justice agencies was the creation of the Office for Criminal Justice Reform (OCJR). The OCJR consists of a cross-departmental team designed to aid criminal justice agencies to work together which is responsible to the Home Secretary, Lord Chancellor/Secretary of State for Justice and the Attorney General. It is located within the Ministry of Justice's Criminal Justice Business Group. One mechanism through which the OCJR achieves joined-up government is the production of strategic plans that shape the future operations of criminal justice agencies into which the strategic plans of individual government departments are fitted.

One example of this was the CJRS strategic plan, *Working Together to Cut Crime and Deliver Justice* (Office for Criminal Justice Reform, 2007) that set out the approach whereby the key criminal justice agencies (police, prosecution, probation, prisons and youth justice system) could cooperate in order to more effectively combat crime, bring more offenders to justice and help to tackle crime and reduce re-offending. The objectives contained in this strategy document were closely aligned with the Home Office Crime Reduction Strategy for 2008–11 (Home Office, 2007a) which set out a number of key areas that should be focused on (serious violence, anti-social behaviour, young people, designing out crime, reducing re-offending, partnership and building public confidence) (Home Office, 2007a: 3–5).

The broad objectives contained in strategic and national policy documents are translated into more specific objectives and targets by the National Criminal Justice Board whose role is to define 'the vision and targets and for the high level policy framework' within which the criminal justice system operates (Office for Criminal Justice Reform, 2007: 49). The NCJB works closely with the OCJR, the National Crime Reduction Board and the National Policing Board and reports to the Criminal Justice System Cabinet Committee which is also responsible for monitoring the delivery of Criminal Justice System PSA targets.

The objectives put forward by the NCJB are incorporated into local programmes by the Local Criminal Justice Boards which are key delivery mechanisms to achieve NCJB strategic objectives. LCJBs were established in 2003. There are 42 of these and are composed of the chief officers of each of the criminal justice agencies and exist to secure close working relationships between the police, CPS, probation, prison and youth services at a local level. LCJBs have been given an enhanced role to deliver services and the ability to tailor service improvement to local needs and priorities (Office for Criminal Justice Reform, 2007: 17 and 49).

LCJBs seek to coordinate the operations of criminal justice agencies at local level. However, joined-up government seeks to incorporate agencies outside of the criminal justice sector in the fight against crime, some of which work together in alternative partnership structures such as CDRPs. The work performed by a wide range of partnership bodies is joined-up through the mechanism of a community strategy.

The 2000 Local Government Act imposed a statutory duty on local authorities to prepare community strategies,and Local Strategic Partnerships (LSPs) were developed to drive these strategies forward. This approach was further developed in the 2007 Local Government and Public Involvement in Health Act which provided for LSPs to become the main vehicle through which the government's Sustainable Community Strategy would be advanced.

An LSP is a non-statutory, multi-agency, non-executive body whose boundaries are coterminous with those of a local authority (either a district or county council or a unitary authority). Their role is to bring together the public, private, voluntary and community sectors in

order to tackle problems such as crime that require a response from a range of different bodies acting in an integrated manner. They are not a single organization 'but a "family" of partnerships and/or themed sub-groups' (Home Office, 2007b: 130). Typically, the LSP develops themes to advance the local authority's community strategy. The delivery mechanisms of these themes are multi-agency bodies such as CDRPs.

The link between local strategic planning and national objectives is fashioned by Local Area Agreements (LAAs) whose content is informed by Public Service Agreements (PSAs) and the priorities contained in CDRP partnership plans. LSPs negotiate and deliver LAAs which is the main delivery agreement between central government and its partners. LAAs establish the priorities for a local area which are agreed between central government and the local authority, LSP and other local-level partners. Their aim is to join up local public services (entailing the sharing of information and pooling of resources) thereby tailoring service delivery to local needs.

LAAs are structured around four policy areas: children and young people, safer and stronger communities, healthier communities and older people, and economic development and enterprise. They operate over a three-year planning cycle. In two-tier areas, LAAs are negotiated at county level which are required to involve districts when formulating them.

The extent of joined-up government at a local level is now subject to an annual inspection regime known as the Comprehensive Area Assessment (CAA). It is being delivered jointly by six inspectorates (the Audit Commission, Ofsted, the Care Quality Commission, Her Majesty's Inspectorate of Constabulary, Her Majesty's Inspectorate of Probation and Her Majesty's Inspectorate of Prisons), and will examine the workings of the LSP, the delivery of the community strategy and LAAs.

The CAA will have two main elements, an area assessment that looks at how well local public services are delivering better results for local people in local priorities such as health, economic prospects and crime and safety and how likely they are to improve in the future. There will also be organizational assessments of individual public bodies including performance against targets and use of resources. The new CAA framework commenced in 2009 and provides an independent assessment of the work of partner agencies in improving outcomes and the quality of life for people living in local communities.

Information technology has important implications for joined-up government both within individual agencies and also between them. The Bichard Inquiry (2004) that followed the Soham murders drew particular attention to the absence of information-sharing within the police service. This gave rise to a number of developments to facilitate this objective including the IMPACT Nominal Index (INI) that enables individual police forces to share information they have gathered locally. The INI provided pointers to the location where those looking for information could find it. It was intended to develop this to provide direct access to material of this nature through the mechanism of a Police National Database. However, problems with the nature of data stored by individual forces have impeded the progress of this reform.

Technology also potentially enables one criminal justice agency to share the information it has collected with another. Traditionally agencies did not share their data with others but sharing information at an offender's point of entry into the criminal justice system is crucial to ensure appropriate responses and to avoid harm both to the offender and to others.

Developments to achieve joined-up information-sharing across criminal justice agencies have been implemented. XHIBIT is a computer system used in Crown Courts which provides information relating to court hearings and case details to a range of key stakeholders that include the police, Crown prosecutors and witnesses.

A further development affected the probation and prison services. It was initially intended that a development termed C-NOMIS would promote joined-up data-sharing across the prison and probation services' databases. However, spiralling costs required this project to be scaled down and what is now termed NOMIS has been rolled out only within the public sector prison service.

See also: Crime and Disorder Reduction Partnerships, National Offender Management Service, political oversight of the criminal justice system, prisons, Probation Service, youth justice system

References and further reading

Audit Commission (2009) *What is CAA?* [Online] http://www.auditcommission.gov.uk/localgov/audit/caa/pages/whatiscaa.aspx

Bichard, Sir M. (2004) *The Bichard Enquiry Report.* London: TSO, House of Commons Paper 653.

Home Office (2007a) *Cutting Crime: A New Partnership 2008–11.* London: Home Office.

Home Office (2007b) *Delivering Safer Communities: A Guide to Effective Partnership Working: Guidance for Crime and Disorder Reduction Partnerships and Community Safety Partnerships.* London: Home Office,

Police and Crime Standards Directorate.

Office for Criminal Justice Reform (2007) *Working Together to Cut Crime and Deliver Justice: A Strategic Plan for Criminal Justice 2008–11.* London: TSO.

judges

Judges are members of the legal profession who preside over trials dealing with the more serious criminal offences. They also serve in civil courts.

The main role performed by a judge is to preside over a trial which involves making important legal rulings related to its conduct that include the admissibility of evidence and what law governs the case before the court. Judges may also intervene during trials to question witnesses and their role may require them to interpret the law as opposed to merely enforcing it. At the conclusion of a Crown Court trial, judges sum up the proceedings of a trial for the benefit of the jury and they pass sentence on those found guilty of committing a crime.

In order to become a judge it is first necessary for a candidate to be eligible, as initially defined in the 1990 Courts and Legal Services Act. This legislation stipulated the number of years' right of audience required in the type of court over which the applicant would preside. Historically, if eligibility was satisfied, selection was governed by three guiding principles: merit, proof of competence and suitability and 'soundings' (Memorandum from the Lord Chancellor's Department cited in evidence to Home Affairs Committee, 1996).

'Soundings' enabled serving members of the judiciary who had knowledge of the performance of a potential candidate to express their opinions on a candidate's suitability for appointment. This provided the potential for judges to effectively become a self-perpetuating elite and was regarded as an important reason to explain why judges were socially unrepresentative of the population as a whole. This process was secretive and flawed – 'it was unclear who was consulted, those who gave opinions were untrained in assessment, much was hearsay. . . . There was agreement that women, ethnic minorities and solicitors, because of lack of visibility, could be disadvantaged' (quoted in Peach, 1999: 6–7).

In order to address criticisms of this nature, a number of reforms have been made to the appointments procedure. In 2001 a Commission for Judicial Appointments was established to oversee the process used to appoint judges and Queen's Counsel and to make recommendations for reforms to the system.

Subsequently the 2005 Constitutional Reform Act transferred the appointment of judges from the executive branch of government to an independent body, the Judicial Appointments Commission for England and Wales (JAC). Henceforth judges were appointed on the basis of open competition and selected according to merit. The JAC's role is that of a recommending commission, generally putting forward only one name to the Lord Chancellor who is empowered to reject it and require another to be put forward (Department for Constitutional Affairs, 2003: 13 and 17).

The 2005 legislation also provided for the role performed by the Commission for Judicial Appointments to be transferred to a Judicial Appointments and Conduct Ombudsman who would investigate complaints from dissatisfied applicants to judicial office. A subsequent measure, the 2007 Tribunals, Courts and Enforcement Act, reduced the eligibility period for appointment to judicial office as specified in the 1990 Act, one rationale for this reform being to broaden the composition of the judiciary.

Once appointed, judges enjoy considerable autonomy and hold office subject to good behaviour. Although this situation may be justified by the separation of powers (ensuring that judges are free from political pressure) it may mean that they are insufficiently accountable for their actions. The Lord Chancellor has the ability to discipline judges of the rank of Circuit Judge and below but judges of the High Court and above are immune from pressures of this nature and may only be removed by an address from both Houses of Parliament to the monarch.

See also: criminal court system England and Wales, discretion, legal profession England and Wales, Sentencing Guidelines Council, separation of powers

References and further reading

Department for Constitutional Affairs (2003) *Constitutional Reform: A New Way of Appointing Judges*. London: Department for Constitutional Affairs, Consultation Paper.

Home Affairs Committee (1996) *Judicial Appointments Procedures*, Third Report, Session 1995–96, House of Commons Paper 52–1.

Peach, Sir L. (1999) *An Independent Scrutiny of the Appointment Processes of Judges and Queen's Counsel in England and Wales*. London: Lord Chancellor's Department.

Judges' Rules

Judges' Rules constituted a code of practice to guide the conduct of the police when questioning a suspect.

The process of police questioning persons suspected of having committed a crime developed slowly during the nineteenth century. The police would record any information or statements that were voluntarily given by suspects but questioning them was not a routine procedure.

In 1912 Judges of the King's Bench division formulated four rules to give guidance to the police on the questioning of persons in their custody. A further five rules were added in 1918 and in 1930 a statement was produced to clear up ambiguities arising from these new rules (St Johnston, 1966: 85). The need for judicial intervention arose from the Common Law requirement that a confession was admissible at a trial only 'if it was made without inducements, threats or force'.

Judges' Rules established norms of behaviour which if breached might cause a trial judge to exercise discretion to exclude evidence. The heavier reliance on confessions derived from police interrogation prompted their revision by Judges of the Queen's Bench in 1964 (published by Home Office, 1964) which gave a 'cautious recognition' to the interrogation of persons in police custody as a legitimate aspect of a criminal investigation (Thomas, 1964: 383).

Judges' Rules included provisions that the police should charge a suspect as soon as there was sufficient evidence to warrant this course of action and should cease any further questioning in relation to that offence. A caution should be given before the charge was made.

There were, however, short-comings with Judges' Rules. They did not possess the force of law and were sometimes flouted by the police who used aggressive methods against those held in custody in order to obtain a confession. Interviews did not require the presence of a solicitor and the frequent absence of detailed notes sometimes gave rise to the fabrica-tion of confessions (a procedure known as 'verballing'). This could result in miscarriages of justice. Abuses of this nature became public knowledge during the 1970s in connection with episodes that included the report into the murder investigation of Maxwell Confait (Fisher, 1977).

In 1988, Judges' Rules were replaced by Code of Practice C issued under the provisions of the 1984 Police and Criminal Evidence Act.

See also: discretion, judges, crim-inal court system England and Wales, miscarriage of justice

References and further reading

Fisher, Sir H. (1977) *Report of an Inquiry into the Circumstances Leading to the Trial of Three Persons Arising out of the Death of Maxwell Confait and the Fire at 27 Doggett Road, London, SE6*. London: House of Commons, House of Commons Paper 80.

Home Office (1964) 'Judges' Rules and Administrative Directions to the Police'. London: Home Office, circular 31/64.

St Johnston, T. (1966) 'The Judges' Rules and Police Interrogation in England and Wales', *Journal of Criminal Law, Criminology and Police Science*, 57(1): 85–92.

Thomas, D. (1964) 'The Revised Judges' Rules', *British Journal of Criminology*, 4: 383–6.

Judicial Committee of the Privy Council

See **criminal court system England and Wales**

judicial review

Judicial review in the UK is a process whereby the judiciary is able to scrutinize actions under-taken by a wide range of public bodies to assess whether decisions have been properly reached.

Judicial review in the UK com-prises an assessment of a decision made by a public body (which includes government departments, local authorities, tribunals, or any other organization that exercises a public function such as the immi-gration authorities, regulatory bodies or the police and prisons services). It may also seek to ensure that non-statutory, self-regulatory bodies such as the Press Council act in accordance with recognized legal principles (Le Sueur *et al.*, 1999: 225).

The basis on which judicial intervention is founded is the doctrine of *ultra vires* which suggests that a public body has acted beyond its authorized limits. The contemporary grounds for judicial review were laid down by Lord Diplock in a decision delivered in 1985 in connection with the government's ban on trade unions at the Government Communications Headquarters (GCHQ). These embrace an assessment of whether the public body has acted illegally, irrationally (unreasonably), or has made an unfair decision by failing to observe procedures laid down in legislation (procedural impropriety or unfairness). Actions undertaken by governments based upon an exercise of the royal prerogative are also subject to judicial review. In doing so, the courts seek to 'reassert the dominance of the rule of law ideal' (Slapper and Kelly, 2006: 181).

In reviewing accusations of this nature, the judiciary focus on the procedures by which a decision was made and not the decision itself. Applications that such problems have arisen are made to the High Court or the Administrative Court (which is within the High Court's Queen's Bench Division). Legal aid is available for such submissions. The remedies available to a court are the three prerogative orders: quashing (formerly *certiorari*), mandatory (formerly *mandamus*) and prohibiting. Additionally a claimant may seek an injunction, a declaration or damages from the errant public body.

Judicial review may be a potent weapon to restrain the excesses of central government (Anthony, 2002: 23–4). In particular it provides an important safeguard whereby the courts can intervene in connection with the abuse of discretion by public bodies (Slapper and Kelly, 2006: 181).

In countries that possess codified constitutions, the judiciary are responsible for ensuring that the constitution is upheld. Senior courts (such as the American Supreme Court or the French *Conseil Constitutionnel*) perform this function. However, in countries such as the UK that lack a codified constitution, judicial review has traditionally assumed a more limited character because the law passed by the legislature is itself a source of the constitution.

However, the enactment of the 1998 Human Rights Act increased the scope of judicial review. Although adherence to the concept of the sovereignty of Parliament prevents the judiciary from directly overturning Acts of Parliament on the grounds that they contravene the 1998 measure, the judiciary may notify Parliament that provisions of an Act are contrary to the Human Rights Act. This is performed through the mechanism of a 'declaration of incompatibility' and makes Parliament and not the courts responsible for applying remedial action through a form of delegated legislation termed a 'remedial order'.

See also: administrative law, delegated legislation, European Convention on Human Rights, human rights, judges, law (sources of), law-making process, legal aid, criminal court system England and Wales, rule of law

References and further reading

Anthony, G. (2002) *UK Public Law and European Law: The Dynamics of Legal Integration.* Portland, OR: Hart Publishing.

Council of the Civil Service Unions *v* Minister for the Civil Service (1985) AC 374.

Le Sueur, A., Herberg, J. and English, R. (1999) *Principles of Public Law.* London: Cavendish.

Slapper, G. and Kelly, D. (2006) *The English Legal System.* London: Routledge, sixth edition.

jury system

Juries provide a trial by one's peers, and are composed of ordinary people selected at random from the electoral register. They are 'triers of fact' – their role is to listen to the evidence which is presented by the defence and prosecution in a trial and to determine on the guilt or innocence of the defendant based upon an objective consideration of the facts which emerge during the proceedings.

In England and Wales, juries are used in Crown Court trials and in some civil cases (although their use in civil matters has been greatly reduced since the implementation of the 1933 Administration of Justice Act). Historically a different form of jury, the Grand Jury, was used to determine if there were sufficient evidence to warrant a trial. This procedure was abandoned in England and Wales in 1933 in favour of committal proceedings.

Juries consist of 12 persons (8 in civil cases). Initially the universal agreement of all 12 members was required to reach a verdict but the 1967 Criminal Justice Act permitted the outcome of a trial to be determined by a majority verdict of 10:2.

Around 480,000 persons are summoned to sit as jurors each year (Falconer, 2003: 3), of which less than half actually serve. Approximately 4 per cent of criminal cases are heard in a Crown Court. Juries are randomly selected by computer from the electoral register. This was formerly the responsibility of the jury summoning officer of the Crown

Court until 2000 when a national Jury Central Summoning Bureau took over this function for England and Wales. Historically there were certain categories of persons who were not qualified for, or excused from, jury service. However, the 2003 Criminal Justice Act radically altered the eligibility for jury service by removing most of the categories of individuals who were disqualified, ineligible or entitled as of right to be excused from serving.

The jury system possesses a number of advantages. They enable popular involvement in the operations of the criminal justice process and take decisions that not only affect individual defendants but also the communities in which they live: 'few decisions made by members of the public have such an impact upon society as a jury's verdict' (Falconer, 2003: 3). There is also evidence that serving on a jury may promote civic engagement (Roberts and Hough, 2009: i).

When considering whether to convict or acquit a defendant, juries may take into account personal circumstances or motives for breaking the law in order in order to produce a verdict they consider to be just. This may result in a jury declaring a person to be not guilty even though s/he broke the law. Although this may enable the law to be kept in line with the prevailing public consensus by influencing legislators to change laws that lack

popular support, the ability of a jury to pronounce a verdict of not guilty in the face of overwhelming evidence to the contrary may bring the legal system into disrepute. In America, a jury's acquittal of Los Angeles police officers who had severely attacked a Black American, Rodney King, in 1992 resulted in riots against the obvious manifestation of racial bias in this verdict.

There are, however, a number of problems associated with trial by jury. It has been argued that the composition of juries often fails to mirror that of society resulting in age, class, gender and race biases imbalances (Devlin, 1956; Commission for Racial Equality, 1991). However, in connection with the participation of minority ethnic groups, it has been suggested that there was no significant underrepresentation of Black and Minority Ethnic Groups (BME) in almost all Crown Courts in England and Wales and that in most courts there was no significant difference between the proportion of BME jurors serving and the BME population levels in the local juror catchment area for each court (Thomas, 2007: i–ii).

A further problem associated with juries is that factors not related to the evidence presented in a trial may influence the outcome of jury deliberations. Jurors may be swayed by factors such as race, gender, accent, dress, occupation, level of articulation, body language, the performance of lawyers retained by the defence and prosecution or irrational considerations in which a juror's emotions form the basis of a decision. Jury decision-making may also be shaped by factors affecting group dynamics – the ability of one vocal member to dominate proceedings or polarization whereby decisions reflect the jurors' views of each other rather than their opinions of the evidence.

Recent reforms to the jury system in England and Wales include the 2003 Criminal Justice Act which enabled the prosecution to apply for certain fraud cases to be heard without a jury (although this reform has not so far been implemented) and also allowed the prosecution to apply for a trial to be heard without a jury if there was 'a real and present danger' of jury tampering (or 'nobbling'). This provision was used for the first time in 2009 in connection with the trial of four men accused of a robbery at Heathrow Airport in 2004.

A subsequent piece of legislation, the 2004 Domestic Violence, Crime and Victims Act, further permitted the trial of some, but not all, counts included on an indictment to be conducted without a jury.

See also: criminal court system England and Wales, criminal court system Scotland, Diplock Courts, domestic violence

References and further reading

Commission for Racial Equality (1991) *Evidence to the Royal Commission on Criminal Justice.* London: Commission for Racial Equality.

Devlin, Lord (1956) *Trial by Jury.* London: Stevens and Sons.

Falconer, Lord (2003) 'Foreword by the Secretary of State' in *Jury Summoning Guidance.* London: Department for Constitutional Affairs, Consultation Paper, December.

Roberts, J. and Hough, M. (2009) *Public Opinion and the Jury: An International Literature Review.* London: Ministry of Justice, Ministry of Justice Research Series 1/09.

Thomas, C. with Balmer, M. (2007) *Diversity and Fairness in the Jury System.* London: Ministry of Justice, Ministry of Justice Research Series 2/07.

Justice and Home Affairs (JHA) Council

The Justice and Home Affairs (JHA) Council brings together EU ministers with responsibilities for justice, home affairs and immigration. It meets around six times each year and seeks to secure the coordination of judicial, police, asylum and migration policies of member states, thereby advancing the creation of an area of freedom, security and justice within the EU as proposed by the 1993 Treaty of the European Union.

The cooperation of member states in justice and home affairs issues commenced in the mid-1970s. An important step to advance cooperation in these areas was provided by the Schengen Agreement which operated outside the EU's institutional framework. The involvement of the EU in justice and home affairs issues was subsequently advanced by the Maastricht Treaty (1993) whose Third Pillar embraced Justice and Home Affairs. This indicated that issues that concerned 'the crossing of external borders, immigration, asylum, drug addiction, fraud, judicial cooperation in civil and criminal matters, customs and police cooperation were matters of common interest for the member states' (Barnard, 2007: 502). The treaties of Amsterdam (1999), which incorporated the Schengen rules into the EU's institutional framework, and Nice (2003) further advanced this justice and home affairs cooperation. All three treaties constituted a significant departure from the original focus of the European Economic Community on the creation of a common market (Nugent, 2006: 55–6). Currently, the Hague Programme (adopted by the European Council in 2004) guides the work of the JHA Council in the development of EU justice and home affairs policies.

As the UK and Ireland are not party to the Schengen rules concerning the free movement of persons, external borders controls and visa policy, their ministers do not vote when these matters come before the JHA Council.

Discussions that take place in this forum usually originate from proposals put forward by the European Commission. Unanimity is usually required in order for the JHA Council to adopt policies, although some matters (that include asylum and visas) can be adopted by qualified majority voting.

See also: Europol, Schengen initiatives

References and further reading

Barnard, C. (2007) *The Substantive Law of the EU: The Four Freedoms*. Oxford: Oxford University Press.

Nugent, N. (2006) *The Government and Politics of the European Union*. Basingstoke: Palgrave/ Macmillan, sixth edition.

L

Law Commission

The Law Commission is an independent body whose role is to keep the criminal law under review and to make recommendations for reform. It was created by the 1965 Law Commissions Act and its chair is appointed by the Lord Chancellor.

The Law Commission is solely concerned with criminal law. The 1997 Civil Procedure Act established a Civil Justice Council whose role is to keep the civil justice system under review.

One specific task of the Law Commission is that of Statute Law Repeals which involves removing measures from the statute book when they are no longer of practical use. The need to delete anachronistic legislation may arise for several reasons that include: the law contains powers that have not been exercised for a period of many years, the law makes reference to bodies or organizations that no longer exist or the law has been superseded by more modern legislation that renders the measure obsolete. In order to carry out this process, the Law Commission conducts consultation exercises with relevant stakeholders including relevant government departments and agencies. Following consultation a report is prepared for the Lord Chancellor and repeal is usually achieved by Statute Law (Repeals) Bills. Eighteen such Bills have been enacted since 1965, repealing more than 2,000 whole Acts and achieving partial repeals in thousands of others (Law Commission, 2009: para 3).

The Law Commission may also initiate changes to the existing law when this need arises. It is not the only body that exercises this function – Royal Commissions, for example, may be set up to achieve this purpose (Slapper and Kelly, 2003: 100).

Proposals for law reform may be made to the Law Commission by government ministers (as was the case when Home Secretary Jack Straw referred the reform of the law of double jeopardy to the Law Commission in the wake of the Macpherson Report, 1999) or it may itself put forward suggestions. Changes to the law would normally be made through the normal law-making process.

The work of the Law Commission embraces criminal legislation affecting England and Wales; legislation specific to Scotland is dealt with by the Scottish Law Commission; and the Northern Ireland Law Commission is responsible for the reform of legislation that is specific to Northern Ireland.

The Law Commission is separate from a body with a similar name, the International Law Commission. This was set up by the United Nationals General Assembly in 1948 to secure the progressive development and codification of international law. Members of the Commission are nominated by member states of the United Nations and are formally elected by the UN General Assembly.

See also: law-making process

References and further reading

Law Commission (2009) *Statute Law Repeal: Consultation Paper.*

Poor Relief – Proposed Repeals. London: TSO, SLR 03/09.
Slapper, G. and Kelly, D. (2003) *The English Legal System.* London: Cavendish, sixth edition.

law-making process

There are a series of stages through which a proposal must progress within Parliament before it becomes the general law of the United Kingdom in the form of a Public General Act. These stages comprise the law-making process.

Suggestions which require legislation to be enacted by Parliament will often undergo a process which serves as an advance warning that legislation is being considered. This constitutes a pre-legislative stage in which proposals are put forward in documents termed 'Green' or 'White' papers.

In theory a Green Paper precedes a White Paper. The former is a consultation document in which legislative proposals are at a formative stage. White papers put forward specific proposals for legislative changes. However, there is no requirement that green or white papers should precede legislation and, additionally, a government may decide that a Green Paper is a sufficient basis on which legislation can be based and that a White Paper is unnecessary. This happened, for example, in connection with the 2009 Police and Crime legislation that was based on ideas put forward in a Green Paper (Home Office, 2008).

Legislative proposals are drawn up in a document termed a 'Bill' which is presented to Parliament. Between 30 and 40 per cent of the workload of the House of Commons is devoted to debating Bills (Jones *et al.*, 2001: 354). There are a number of stages through which this must pass before it becomes an Act whose provisions citizens are required to obey. A Bill is required to undergo similar stages in both Houses of Parliament, the House of Commons and the House of Lords. There is no requirement as to which of these should be given the first opportunity to consider a Bill.

A Bill that is initially introduced in the House of Commons will be given a formal introduction in what is termed a 'first reading'. This constitutes an announcement that legislation affecting a particular topic is to be introduced and there is no debate at this stage.

The next stage in the law-making process is the 'second reading'. This constitutes a full debate regarding the general principles that are contained in the Bill. At the end of the debate a vote may be taken (although this is not always necessary if there is a general agreement within the House of Commons that the measure is desirable), following which the Bill receives a detailed examination in a 'committee stage'. It is also quite common, following a Bill's second reading, that the government will put forward a Programme Order that provides a timetable for the Bill's subsequent progress through the House of Commons. This is designed to restrict unnecessary debate whose main purpose is to delay the Bill's progress.

Most Bills are considered by a standing committee that consists of a small number of MPs who are able to put forward amendments to specific proposals contained in the Bill. Following the committee stage the Bill, as amended, is referred back to the House of Commons in what is termed a 'report stage'. This gives all members the opportunity to endorse or vote down changes that have been made during the committee stage of the Bill. At the end of this stage, a general debate takes place in the House of Commons that is termed the 'third reading'. If required, a vote may be taken and if the Bill successfully receives its third reading it is taken to the House of Lords.

The stages that the Bill undergoes in the House of Lords are similar to those that have taken place in the House of Commons. However, the committee stages of Bills are usually heard before a Committee of the Whole House or a Grand Committee. Both are open to all members of the House of Lords, the main difference being that votes are not taken in Grand Committees. Select Committees are also occasionally used at committee stage in this House.

If the House of Lords amends a Bill that has been submitted to it by the House of Commons, it is necessary to resolve these differences. If the House of Commons is content with the changes put forward by the House of Lords, it may endorse them. However, the House of Commons has the ability to reject these changes by voting against them. If this happens, the Bill is passed back to the House of Lords for re-consideration. It is often the case that the House of Lords will bow to the wishes of the House of Commons since its members are elected. However, it has the ability to re-affirm its support for the amendments that it has proposed and pass the Bill back to the House of Commons for further discussion. This game of Parliamentary 'ping-pong' with the measure may last for some considerable time and is often used in an attempt by the House of Lords to exact concessions regarding the Bill from the House of Commons. When all outstanding disagreements are reconciled the Bill is submitted for Royal Assent. This is granted automatically by the monarch and is the process by which a 'Bill' becomes an 'Act'.

Should it prove impossible for both Houses to reconcile their differences, the Bill does not become law. Under the terms of the 1949 Parliament Act, it may be re-introduced in the following Session of Parliament and the House of Lords loses its ability to put forward amendments.

Historically it was necessary for a Bill to complete all of the above stages in both Houses within the period of a Parliamentary Session (which is typically around a year in length). However, since 2002 a carry-over procedure has been used whereby a Bill presented in one Parliamentary Session may be continued into the next, subject to certain constraints – namely it applies only to a Bill put forward by a government minister that usually originated in the House of Commons and all stages of the Bill have to be completed within a year of the Bill's original first reading.

Most Bills are promoted by the government although all MPs have the ability to put forward legislative proposals in the form of Private Members' Bills.

See also: Human rights, judges, political oversight of the criminal justice system

References and further reading

Acts of Parliament (Statutes) since 1996 are located on the Office of Public Sector Information website, *Acts of the UK Parliament and Explanatory Memoranda* [Online] www.opsi.gov.uk/acts

Home Office (2008) *From the Neighbourhood to the National: Policing Our Communities Together.* London: Home Office, Cm 7448.

Jones, B., Kavanagh, D., Moran, M. and Norton, P. (2001) *Politics UK*. Harlow: Pearson Education, fourth edition.

Law Society

See **legal profession England and Wales**

law (sources of)

Sources of law refers to the authorities on which the rules that govern a citizen's relationship with government and with each other are based.

There are four key sources to the law in England. A small amount of law (that usually applies to local or geographic rights) (Smartt, 2009: 17) is based on custom. Some common law (see below) may be based on custom but this also includes rules that were derived from specific local practices. There are a number of conditions that have to be fulfilled in order for custom to constitute a source of contemporary law: the custom must have existed from 'time immemorial' (defined as 1189), it must have been exercised continuously within that period without opposition and it needs to be reasonable in its operation (Slapper and Kelly, 2006: 4).

Common law (otherwise known as judge-made law or case law) entailed the nation-wide adoption of decisions made by judges when trying specific cases. These become a source of law through the doctrine of judicial precedent whereby the future decisions of sentencers when dealing with a similar case should result in the same outcome.

The origins of this process date to the Norman Conquest in 1066 and the principle that underpins it is known as *stare decisis* and was developed after the accession of Henry II to the throne in 1154. One benefit of common law is that precedent is not inflexibly followed which enables judges to reinterpret the law in accordance with changed circumstances without requiring Parliament to put forward new legislation. Although Parliament may overturn case law by enacting new legislation, this situation promotes the role of judges as law-makers.

Common law connotes all judge-made law and therefore includes equity (Slapper and Kelly, 2006: 1). Equity comprises a set of legal principles that derived from the ability of a litigant who felt that common law had failed to provide an effective remedy to seek further redress. This procedure originated in the fifteenth century and initially entailed a litigant petitioning the King for redress. Subsequently, the administration of these cases was devolved to the Lord Chancellor who presided over a specific court, the Court of Chancery, which operated in parallel with the common law courts. This Court dealt only with civil affairs and had achieved an influential position by the reign of Henry VIII.

The 1873 and 1875 Judicature Acts created a High Court of Justice (with five divisions) and a Court of Appeal in place of the Chancery, Common Pleas, Queen's Bench and Exchequer courts. Judges were henceforth required to administer whatever rules of law (common law or equity) were applicable to a case before them thus ending the previously independent application of common law and equity (Hepburn, 2001: 25). In the case of any conflict, equity was supreme.

Examples of equitable remedies include injunctions issued by the High Court that are designed to prevent a person or persons from performing a particular action, or writs that impose mandatory, prohibiting or quashing orders or which provide a remedy against unlawful detention. Although derived from equity, injunctions may be used to enforce common law claims. Additionally, injunctions may be derived from statute law as is the case with anti-harassment injunctions that are provided for in the 1997 Protection from Harassment Act.

A considerable proportion of law is to be found in Acts that are passed by Parliament. These may provide ministers with the ability to draw up further regulations in the form of delegated legislation.

The 1999 devolution legislation created a Scottish Parliament, a National Assembly for Wales and an Assembly for Northern Ireland. These Acts (and subsequent amendments that include the 2006 Government of Wales Act) provide these institutions of government with certain law-making powers regarding domestic affairs that have the same effect within their areas of jurisdiction as an Act of Parliament.

Law drawn up by the European Union constitutes a further source of law following Britain's membership of the European Economic Community in 1973. Primary legislation takes the form of Treaties of the EU which include the 1957 EEC Treaty of Rome and the 1993 Maastricht Treaty on European Union. Treaties take precedence over the national law of member states once their ratification process has been completed.

Additionally, secondary sources of legislation exist in the form of regulations, directives and decisions. These are issued by the European Parliament acting jointly with the Council of Ministers, by the Council of Ministers or by the European Commission.

Regulations take immediate effect without the need for member states to alter their domestic law, whereas directives require member states to amend their law in a manner they feel to be appropriate to achieve the objective contained in the directive. Decisions are typically directed at individuals or commercial concerns which require them to undertake (or desist from performing) a particular activity and do not require any action by member states' law-making procedures. Additionally, recommendations may be made and opinions delivered that constitute a suggested way that member states may act in connection with a specific activity without requiring them to do so.

Law in Scotland combines uncodified civil law with aspects of common law. A particular difference with English law concerns the use of precedent which is primarily concerned with investigating the principles that underpinned the law. Additionally, the principle of natural justice (which emphasizes the importance of procedural fairness to the operations of a legal system) is an important source of Scots law.

See also: delegated legislation, European Court of Justice, habeas corpus, judges, Law Commission, law-making process, criminal court system England and Wales

References and further reading

Hepburn, S. (2001) *Principles of Equity and Trust.* London: Cavendish, second edition.

Slapper, G. and Kelly, D. (2006) *The English Legal System.* Abingdon, Oxfordshire: Routledge-Cavendish, sixth edition.

Smartt, U. (2009) *Law for Criminologists.* London: Sage.

legal aid

Legal aid enables persons charged with a criminal offence or those wishing to defend or enforce their rights through civil litigation to be provided with the means to defend or promote their case through the state funding legal representation for those unable to afford it themselves.

An important aspect of equality before the law is equality of access to it. The 1949 Legal Aid and Advice Act gave defendants facing a serious criminal charge the right to proper legal representation in court. Additionally, aid was available to enable citizens to defend or to enforce their rights in civil litigation. The 1949 legislation was amended on a number of occasions (including the 1988 Legal Aid Act that repealed all previous legislation in this area).

The 1999 Access to Justice Act replaced the Legal Aid Board (which had been established by the 1988 legislation to take over the administration of legal aid from the Law Society) with a Legal Services Commission (LSC) to administer the legal aid system for England and Wales. The work of the LSC is overseen by the Ministry of Justice and it is responsible for operating two schemes: the Community Legal Service and the Criminal Defence Service. An important motivation for this reform was the cost of the legal aid budget which by 2004/5 amounted to £2.1 billion (Department for Constitutional Affairs, 2005: 11).

The role of the Community Legal Service is to offer information, advice and legal representation in civil and family cases (Liebmann, 2000: 33). The level of this aid is based upon the applicant's income and, in some cases, capital. Henceforth, the state's support for civil actions was restricted through the imposition of cash limits on legal aid for civil actions. Since April 2001, only legal firms with a contract with the LSC can provide advice or representation in civil cases funded by the LSC and are required to meet quality standards. State funding also became more difficult to obtain, being subject to a stringent funding code which involved calculating the chances of success against the likely award of damages and costs. Alternatives to litigation (such as mediation in divorce disputes) were encouraged.

Criminal legal aid was also subjected to reforms in the 1999 Access to Justice legislation. This Act set up the Criminal Defence Service that is also managed by the Legal Services Commission to provide advice and legal representation for persons facing criminal charges. The defendant's right to choose his or her own lawyer was ended, and henceforth state-funded defence work (including free advice and assistance to a person held for questioning at a police station) would be handled by firms which had secured a contract with the Legal Services Commission or by a salaried defender who was directly employed by this body. The latter development was compatible with American-style public defenders and was piloted in six areas in 2001.

One object of this reform was to reduce the costs of criminal legal aid, which had been bloated by the high fees paid to some 'fat cat' lawyers, so that 1 per cent of cases heard in Crown Courts consumed around 40 per cent of legal aid funding of cases heard in these courts. It is intended that the LSC will move onto a process of best value tendering during the period 2010–12.

See also: legal profession England and Wales

References and further reading

Department for Constitutional Affairs (2005) *A Fairer Deal for Legal Aid*. London: Department for Constitutional Affairs, Cm 6591.

Liebmann, M. (ed.) (2000) *Mediation in Context*. London: Jessica Kingsley Publishers.

legal profession England and Wales

The legal profession in England and Wales consists of persons whose qualifications and training equips them to carry out a wide range of legal services that includes providing advice, preparing cases that come before the courts, representing those who are involved in civil or criminal proceedings and prosecuting those accused of criminal activities.

In England and Wales there are two distinct categories of legal personnel: solicitors and barristers.

Solicitors deal directly with the general public who require legal advice on a wide range of problems and they prepare cases that are heard in the higher courts and prosecute (on behalf of the CPS) or defend cases in Magistrates' Courts.

In order to qualify, solicitors require either a degree in law or a non-law degree plus a one year's conversion course (officially termed the Common Professional Examination or the Graduate Diploma in Law) to provide entry to the post-graduate Legal Practice Course. This is followed by a training contract (which usually lasts for two years) in a solicitor's office or that of a relevant legal employer. This aspect of training was formerly termed 'articles'. During the training contract the trainee is required to complete the Professional Skills Course (PSC). Solicitors are equipped to deal with a wide range of legal issues, although there is an increasing tendency to specialize, especially in large practices. In 2008 there were around 112,000 solicitors in England and Wales with a practising certificate.

Barristers specialize in one area of the law and their key role is that of advocacy (representing their clients in court). There are far fewer barristers than solicitors, in 2008 numbering around 15,000 in England and Wales. The majority of these are in private practice. Their training entails a degree in law (or a non-law degree plus a one year's conversion course) followed by a one-year Bar Vocational Course regulated by the General Council of the Bar.

Following successful completion of their professional training, barristers undertake a period of training (termed 'pupillage') in the chambers of an established barrister or that of a relevant legal employer. They normally receive their work from solicitors rather than a direct approach from the general public and become involved in a case either when a solicitor seeks the opinion of a specialist or when a case goes to a higher court.

Solicitors and barristers are represented by different professional bodies. The Law Society of England and Wales represents solicitors in England and Wales. It was formed in 1825 (replacing the London Law Institutions which had been formed in 1823), although it did not officially adopt the title of 'Law Society' until 1903. Its charter was granted in 1843. The Solicitors' Regulation Authority (SRA) was to set up in 2007 to act as an independent regulatory authority of the Law Society for all solicitors in England and Wales and the Legal Complaints Service (LCS) is an independent complaints-handling body for the Law Society that investigates complaints made against solicitors.

The General Council of the Bar was established in 1894 to represent the interests of barristers in England and Wales. It is the governing body of the Bar and seeks to promote and improve its services and functions and represent its interests on all matters related to the profession. It is composed of around 100 barristers who are elected and represent the Inns of Court and interest groups. The regulation of barristers is the responsibility of the Bar Council's Bar Standards Board. This is an independent regulatory arm of the Bar Council that was established in 2006 and has a different membership to that of the Bar Council.

Senior members of the legal profession (around 10 per cent of the total number of barristers) may be appointed Queen's Counsel (QCs). This process is known as 'taking silk' and is awarded to those who have displayed excellence in advocacy in the higher courts. An independent selection panel advises the Lord Chancellor/Secretary of State for Justice regarding the selection of QCs who are formally appointed by Letters Patent issued by the monarch.

Historically, only barristers could be QCs, but since 1997 solicitors have also been appointed. This is, however, a very small number: in 1999 only 700 solicitors out of a total of 80,000 were eligible for consideration as QCs (Peach, 1999: 27), and in 2007 there were around 12 solicitor QCs. The QCs are viewed as the elite of the legal professions, and although the skills required for advocacy are not necessarily identical with those required of a judge, traditionally judges were selected from their ranks. Thus biases affecting the appointment of QCs have exerted a significant influence on the composition of the judiciary.

The place of QCs in the modern legal profession is, however, now being challenged. In 1998 a report published by the Adam Smith Institute urged that QCs should be abolished (Reeve, 1998). The primary reason for these calls is that the QC system inflates costs. Historically, a QC could not appear in court unless accompanied by a junior barrister and although this practice was theoretically abolished in 1977 it remained widely practised. Additionally, QCs command high fees when they appear in court, where their work is frequently financed out of public funds.

The two-tier nature of the legal profession drives up the cost of legal proceedings. Although there remain important distinctions between the work performed by the two professions (only solicitors, for example, are able to act as attorneys and conduct litigation on behalf of their clients), the rigid distinction between the work of solicitors and barristers was broken down in 1990 when the Courts and Legal Services Act enabled solicitors to appear as advocates in the higher courts. These – termed 'solicitor advocates' – numbered around 3,700 in 2007. Additionally, some barristers may now be contacted directly by members of the public without the need to consult a solicitor first.

An important issue relating to the legal profession concerns how complaints by members of the public are handled. Professions typically rely on self-regulation that was historically performed by either the Law Society (for solicitors) or the Bar Council (for barristers).

In 1996 the Law Society set up the Office for the Supervision of Solicitors (OSS) to handle complaints from the public. It was overseen by the legal services ombudsman (who also scrutinized the way in which the Bar handled complaints against barristers). Complainants who were dissatisfied with the way in which their complaints had been dealt with could refer the matter to the ombudsman for a ruling as to whether it had been handled satisfactorily.

Concerns relating to the number of complaints made by members of the public against solicitors (including a growth in claims for negligence) and the length of time taken to resolve them (so that in 1999 the OSS had a backlog of 17,000 cases) resulted in a perception that self-regulation was proving ineffective. This led the government to provide itself with reserve powers in the 1997 Access to Justice Act that would be invoked if self-regulation failed to improve. In 2004 the OSS was replaced by the Consumer Complaints Service. This was part of the Law Society, whose main role was to deal with complaints about poor service provided by solicitors.

Proposals to reform the way in which complaints about legal services were handled (Clementi, 2004; Department for Constitutional Affairs, 2005) paved the way for the 2007 Legal Services Act. This legislation created the Office of Legal Complaints (OLC) whose role was to administer an independent ombudsman system to deal with complaints made by members of the general public regarding legal services provided by both solicitors and barristers.

The OLC is a public body sponsored by the Ministry of Justice and is independent both of the government and the legal profession. It is intended that this new system which is overseen by the Legal Services Board (also created by the 2007 Act) will be operational by the end of 2010. Until then complaints against solicitors or barristers are dealt with by the relevant Approved Regulators who were designated by the 2007 Act (consisting of the Law Society, SRA and LCS for solicitors and the Bar Council and Bar Standards Board for barristers).

See also: Crown Prosecution Service, judges, criminal court system England and Wales

References and further reading

Clementi, Sir D. (2004) *Review of the Regulatory Framework for Legal Services in England and Wales: Final Report.* London: Legal Services Review Team.

Department for Constitutional Affairs (2005) *The Future of the Legal Services: Putting the Consumer First.* London: Department for Constitutional Affairs, Cm 6679.

Peach, Sir L. (1999) *An Independent Scrutiny of the Appointment Processes of Judges and Queen's Counsel in England and Wales.* London: Lord Chancellor's Department.

Reeve, P. (1998) *Silk Cut.* London: Adam Smith Institute.

Legal Services Board

See **legal profession England and Wales**

lex talionis

See **Punishment (aims of)**

M

magistrates

Magistrates are responsible for trying those accused of the less serious criminal cases and also for sentencing those found guilty of committing them.

Those who staff Magistrates' Courts are mainly laypersons serving in a part-time capacity and are referred to as Justices of the Peace. This is an ancient office that originated when King Edward III appointed persons in each county whose role was to maintain the peace and whose function subsequently expanded into more general forms of law enforcement. These officials adopted the title given to them in the 1361 legislation as 'Justices of the Peace' who later assumed the title of Magistrate in the sixteenth century. These developments were at the expense of the role performed by the sheriff whose power was viewed as a threat to the monarch and whose power entered into decline towards the end of the twelfth century.

Lay magistrates are aged 18–70 but cannot be appointed over the age of 65. They are unpaid and serve on a part-time basis that amounts to at least 26 half-days each year. They are not required to possess any legal knowledge or qualifications but are tested at interview on key qualities that include good character, social awareness, sound judgement and commitment and reliability. Once appointed they receive training which is supervised by the Judicial Studies Board.

When working in a court lay magistrates are advised by a Justices' Clerk who is legally trained. Each local justice area has at least one clerk who is assisted by deputy and assistant clerks. Clerks take a prominent part in the proceedings of Magistrates' Courts and can give advice proactively to the magistrates rather than having to wait for them to request it.

In 2003 there were around 30,000 of these officials who tried more than 95 per cent of all criminal cases (Department for Constitutional Affairs, 2003: 20) involving around 2 million defendants. In 2009 there were 356 Magistrates' Courts.

Local political nomination is an important source of recruitment for the lay magistracy. Responsibility for appointing magistrates was historically shared between the Lord Chancellor's Department and (in connection with the County Palatine of Lancaster) the Duchy of Lancaster, although the 2003 Courts Act terminated this arrangement. This legislation provided lay magistrates with jurisdiction covering England and Wales, and established one Commission of the Peace for England and Wales, divided into local justice areas. Appointments are made by the Secretary of State, although existing arrangements providing for local input into their appointment through advice to the minister given by the local Advisory Committees was retained. Around 1,500 appointments are made each year.

The main advantages with the lay magistracy is that cases can be heard speedily and at a far lesser cost than would be the case if all trials were heard in Crown Courts. Magistrates also tend to be more socially representative than judges thus enhancing the legitimacy of the legal process to the general public. However, there are also problems associated with the lay magistracy, in particular the proportion of middle-class appointees (especially from professional persons) and the high conviction rate in these courts. This might suggest a bias of lay magistrates towards the prosecution, although it may also be explained by the high proportion of guilty pleas entered by defendants who appear in these courts.

A small number of magistrates serve in a full-time capacity and have training either as barristers or solicitors. These officials originate from the 1792 Middlesex Justices Act and were formerly termed stipendiary magistrates. The 1999 Access to Justice Act re-titled them as 'District Judges (Magistrates' Courts)' and expanded their jurisdiction to enable them to sit in every Justice of the Peace Commission area in England and Wales. The volume of work they perform has significantly increased in recent years, mainly in the larger cities (Sanders, 2001). In 2008 there were 136 District Judges (Magistrates' Courts) and 167 Deputy District Judges (Magistrates' Courts).

See also: criminal court system England and Wales, out of court disposals

References and further reading

Department for Constitutional Affairs (2003) *Constitutional reform: A Supreme Court for the United Kingdom, A Consultation Paper Prepared by the Department for Constitutional Affairs.* London: Department for Constitutional Affairs, Consultation Paper CP 11/03, July.

Gillespie, A. (2007) *The English Legal System.* Oxford: Oxford University Press.

Sanders, A. (2001) *Community Justice: Modernising the Magistracy in England and Wale.* London: Central Books.

mandatory sentence

A mandatory sentence requires a sentencer (who is a judge or a magistrate) to deliver an obligatory penalty to a person who has been found guilty of committing a crime.

Mandatory sentences remove the discretion that sentencers possess regarding the penalty they should impose on a person who has been convicted of a criminal offence. They are not able to take the circumstances of the crime or the characteristics of the case or of the offender into account (Walsh, 2007: 64). Historically murder carried the mandatory sentence of execution which (following the enactment of the 1965 Murder (Abolition of Death Penalty) Act) became a mandatory sentence of life imprisonment.

Concerns regarding sentencers using their discretion to award lenient sentences (one response to which was the 1988 Criminal Justice Act which gave the Attorney General the right to appeal against sentences deemed to be excessively lenient) and the inconsistency between sentencers that resulted in similar crimes committed in comparable circumstances receiving different levels of sentence resulted in an additional range of mandatory sentences.

The 1997 Crime (Sentences) Act required offenders convicted for a second time of a violent or sex offence to receive an automatic life sentence and those convicted of a drug-trafficking offence with two or more previous convictions for similar offences to receive a mandatory sentence of seven years' imprisonment. Additionally a person convicted of domestic burglary with two or more convictions for similar offences had to receive a prison sentence of three years under the 'three strikes and you're out' provisions of the Act which derived from initiatives pioneered in Washington State and California in the early 1990s. Although sentencing discretion was not entirely eliminated, the flexibility possessed by sentencers was considerably restricted by this legislation.

In 1997 the in-coming Labour government staggered the introduction of the mandatory sentence provisions of this legislation with the provisions affecting domestic burglary coming into force in December 1999. The mandatory sentencing provisions contained in the 1997 Act were consolidated in the 2000 Powers of Criminal Courts (Sentencing) Act but that relating to a mandatory life sentence for a second serious offence was repealed by the 2003 Criminal Justice Act.

Post-1997 Labour governments added to the raft of mandatory sentences. The 1999 Youth Justice and Criminal Evidence Act introduced the mandatory penalty of a referral order and subsequent appearance before a Youth Offender Panel and the 2000 Criminal Justice and Court Service Act provided for the imposition of mandatory disqualification orders which prevented those who were convicted of an offence against children from working with them (whether they intended to do so or not) (Thomas, 2003: 62–4). Additionally, the 1998 Crime and Disorder Act and the 2000 Powers of the Criminal Courts (Sentencing) Act imposed requirements on sentencers to treat evidence of racial or religious hostility as aggravating factors when determining sentence.

See also: discretion, magistrates, judges, policy transfer, youth justice system

References and further reading

Henman, R. (1998) 'Making Sense of the Crime (Sentences) Act 1997', *Modern Law Review,* 61(2): 223–35.

Thomas, D. (2003) 'Judicial Discretion in Sentencing' in L.Gelsthorpe and N. Padfield, *Exercising Discretion: Decision-Making in the Criminal Justice System and Beyond.* Cullompton, Devon: Willan Publishing.

Walsh, J. (2007) *Three Strikes Law.* Westport, CT: Greenwood Press.

Megan's Law

Megan's Law refers to a legal requirement for law enforcement agencies to make information regarding sex offenders available to the general public.

This development occurred following the kidnap, rape and murder of 7-year-old Megan Kanka by a repeat sexual offender in the American State of New Jersey in 1994. This prompted states to enact legislation that typically entailed a registration process for sex offenders and a community notification procedure.

At federal (national) level the 1994 Sexual Offender (Jacob Wetterling) Act required states to register persons convicted of sexual offences against children. They were required to notify local law enforcement agencies of any change of address or employment following their release from a custodial sentence. The requirement to notify can be for a fixed period or be permanent.

In the United Kingdom the abduction and murder of Sarah Payne in 2000 by a person with a prior conviction for abduction and sexual assault of a child led to the *News of the World* newspaper spearheading a campaign for the introduction of a Sarah's Law in the United Kingdom (Carmichael, 2003: 15–16). This sought to give parents access to the Sex Offenders' Register that was launched in 1997 following the enactment of the 1997 Sex Offenders Act requiring sex offenders to register with the police. This would enable parents to be aware of the location details of convicted child sex offenders (or paedophiles) in their area.

A number of developments were pursued following this campaign that included a review of the Sex Offenders' Register. Changes were introduced in the 2000 Criminal Justice and Court Services Act which included raising the maximum penalty for failure to register and the introduction of a restraining order that allowed sentencers to set restrictions on a convicted sex offender's future behaviour (Matravers, 2003: 17). Additionally, the legislation amended the 1999 Protection of Children Act by introducing new arrangements designed to prevent unsuitable persons from working with children.

The 2003 Criminal Justice Act subsequently stiffened the penalties that could be used against sex offenders, including the indeterminate sentence for public protection and extended sentences in connection with violent or sexual offences committed by those aged below 18.

The 2003 Sexual Offences Act introduced new offences aimed at predatory sexual offenders that encompassed sexual grooming and amended the 1997 measure in connection with requiring sex offenders to register with the police. A national database, the Violent and Sex Offenders Register (ViSOR) was set up to record the details of all those jailed for more than 12 months for a violent crime and unconvicted persons felt to be at risk of offending of this nature.

Since 2010 parents have possessed the right to secure information on the presence of child sex offenders within communities. Additionally, the police or Multi-Agency Public Protection Arrangements (MAPPAs) (which were introduced in 2001) are responsible for informing individuals and the community on a case-by-case basis when they believe such an offender poses a risk to the general public.

See also: criminal record, Multi-Agency Public Protection Arrangements, self-policing society

References and further reading

Carmichael, K. (2003) *Sin and Forgiveness: New Responses in a Changing World*. Aldershot: Ashgate.

Fitch, K. (2006) *Megan's Law: Does it Protect Children?* London: NCPCC.

Matravers, A. (2003) *Sex Offenders in the Community: Managing the Risks*. Cullompton, Devon: Willan Publishing.

Military Assistance to the Civilian Authorities (MACA)

Military Assistance to the Civilian Authorities involves the use of soldiers in non-military operations.

During the 1970s the circumstances under which soldiers could be used in this capacity were rationalized under three headings: Military Aid to the Civilian Communities (MACC), Military Aid to other Government Departments (MAGD, formerly Military Aid to the Civilian Ministries, MACM) and Military Aid to the Civil Power (MACP).

MACC involves the deployment of soldiers to deal with 'an occasion when there is a danger to human life or a major breakdown of services vital to the welfare of the community' (Ministry of Defence, 1989: 3). This includes natural disasters such as flooding or major accidents.

MAGD entails the use of troops to assist functions performed by or associated with government departments, often by performing the work of those engaged in industrial disputes. Examples of this included the use of soldiers to fight fires during the 1977–78 national fire brigade strike and in subsequent local disputes of this nature such as that in Derbyshire in 1996 and Merseyside in 2001. MAGD may involve activities other than strike-breaking as was the case in the 2001 outbreak of foot and mouth disease when soldiers were used at the behest of the Ministry of Agriculture, Food and Fisheries to cull animals and dispose of their carcasses to stop the spread of this disease.

MACP concerns the use of troops in situations in which disorder was occurring on a scale that the civilian police were unable to contain and which posed a threat to the parliamentary system of government or where 'a minority, by violent means and armed force, was attempting to challenge the very authority of Government with a view to changing or overthrowing it' (Bramhall, 1980: 480–4). Troops were used in this capacity in Northern Ireland between 1969 and 2007 (under 'Operation Banner') and for briefer emergencies that included controlling security arrangements at Heathrow Airport during the Gulf War in the early 1990s. Specialist military units (such as the Special Air Services Regiment or bomb disposal teams) might also be used in individual operations related to hostage and hijack situations, surveillance and protection services.

Historically military aid for non-military circumstances was summoned by the 'civil authority' who was a magistrate. Subsequently other parties became involved in such a decision: for example the use of troops under MACP would involve relevant chief constables, the Home Secretary and the Secretary of State for Defence (Bramhall, 1980: 480–4).

In order to utilize troops effectively, joint operations with the police are sometimes conducted and advance planning to cater for civil emergencies occurs at national level through the Civil Contingencies Unit within the Cabinet Office. Sub-national machinery (such as Regional Emergency Committees that were established in 1979) may be involved in organizing the deployment of troops to specific incidents. The key legislation that caters for emergency planning arrangements for events that include terrorism is the 2004 Civil Contingencies Act.

See also: mutual aid

References and further reading

Bramhall, E. (1980) 'The Place of the British Army in Public Order', *Journal of the Royal Society of Arts,* June: 480–6.

Ministry of Defence (1989) *Military Aid to the Civilian Community.* London: HMSO, third edition.

Joyce, P. (2002) *The Politics of Protest: Extra-parliamentary Politics in Britain since 1970.* Basingstoke: Palgrave.

Peak, S. (1984) *Troops in Strikes: Military Intervention in Industrial Disputes.* London: Cobden Trust.

Ministry of Justice

See **political oversight of the criminal justice system**

miscarriage of justice

A miscarriage of justice arises when a person is found guilty by a court of a crime which he or she did not commit. This results in an innocent person being wrongly punished.

There are a number of reasons why a wrongful conviction may arise. A person may be unfairly convicted because the lawyers defending him or her failed to perform their job effectively (Justice, 1993). Improper pressure may be placed by the police on a suspect to confess to a crime that he or she did not commit or be exerted on witnesses to give false evidence. Alternatively, the police may fabricate (or 'plant') evidence on a suspect in order to ensure that a watertight case exists against a person or persons suspected by the police of having committed a crime. Reforms to reduce the likelihood of such actions have included the introduction of tape-recording interviews in police stations provided for in the 1984 Police and Criminal Evidence Act.

A miscarriage of justice may occur because the prosecution fail to disclose to the defence information uncovered during a police investigation. The failure to do this may severely prejudice the ability of defence lawyers to defend their client(s). Reforms to the procedure regarding the disclosure of evidence by the prosecution to the defence were made by the 1996 Criminal Procedure and Investigation Act (and the subsequent 2003 Criminal Justice Act).

Finally, the opinion expressed by expert witnesses has sometimes formed the basis of the prosecution's case and resulted in a wrongful conviction.

An allegation of a miscarriage of justice was traditionally handled by the Home Office (or in Northern Ireland by the Northern Ireland Office) that was able to refer cases back to the Court of Appeal if it felt an injustice may have been committed. However, the procedures adopted were slow, secretive and lacked independence, and decisions tended to support the status quo.

Suggestions were made that a body independent of the Home Secretary should be appointed to consider issues of this nature (Devlin, 1976) and the wrongful convictions of the 'Guildford Four' and the 'Birmingham Six' highlighted the need for stronger safeguards regarding miscarriages of justice. This led to the establishment of a new independent body, the Criminal Cases Review Commission (CCRC), which was proposed by the Royal Commission on Criminal Justice chaired by Lord Runciman (Runciman, 1993).

This body was established under the provisions of the 1995 Criminal Appeals Act and commenced work in April 1997. The remit of this body extended to Northern Ireland, and a similar body was established for Scotland under the provisions of the 1997 Crime and Punishment (Scotland) Act.

The CCRC may receive complaints directly from individuals or their representatives (such as solicitors) if they believe a person has either been wrongfully convicted of a criminal offence or has been wrongly sentenced. The ability of the Criminal Cases Review Commission to re-examine a case is governed by three conditions: it will normally only consider a case that has been through the appeals process (and the appeal failed or leave to appeal was refused), with regard to conviction there must be new evidence that was either not available or not disclosed at the original trial (or at any subsequent appeal) and concerning sentence there must be new information not raised during the original trial or at any subsequent appeal.

An initial assessment by CCRC staff will determine whether these conditions are met and whether the case is eligible for consideration by the CCRC. If it is, a CCRC caseworker and a Commission member will carry out a more detailed examination. At the end of this process a view is formulated as to whether the case should be referred back to the Court of Appeal. If the CCRC decides not to refer a case to the Court of Appeal, it may be re-approached if new evidence subsequently emerges.

Although the CCRC possesses a number of advantages over the previous system used to investigate allegations of a miscarriage of justice it has faced a number of difficulties at the outset. These have included the volume of work and the adequacy of its funding.

See also: expert witness, criminal court system England and Wales

References and further reading

Devlin, Lord (1976) *Report of the Departmental Committee on Evidence of Identification in Criminal Trials*. London: House of Commons, Session 1975–76, Paper 338.

Justice (1993) *Miscarriages of Justice: A Defendant's Eye View*. London: Justice.

Runciman, Lord (1993) Royal Commission on Criminal Justice Report. London: HMSO, Cm 2263.

moral panic

A moral panic is defined as a situation whereby 'a condition, episode, person or group of persons emerges to become defined as a threat to societal values and interests' (Cohen, 1980: 9). This becomes a pretext for state intervention directed at the identified problem which results in an enhanced degree of social control through the use of coercive methods.

The concept of a moral panic is derived from a number of criminological perspectives, in particular labelling and conflict theories, and seeks to explain how widespread popular endorsement for a law and order response to social problems that threaten the position of the ruling elite can be created. This perspective argues that the manufacturing of a moral panic involves a number of processes in which the media play a crucial role. A specific group of citizens (who are termed 'folk devils') are identified as the cause of a problem which is put forward as symptomatic of deep-rooted social malaise. This is accompanied by a campaign of denigration or vilification to establish a link in the public mind between the targeted group and deviant or criminal behaviour. This legitimizes the use of discriminatory practices against them.

Moral panics are said to occur in periods of rapid social change and are frequently identified with crises in capitalism. Problems such as recession, unemployment or the growth of monopoly capitalism lead many members of the general public to become disquieted concerning the direction society is taking, especially those whose interests or values seemed directly threatened by these changes. Those affected by feelings of social anxiety are especially receptive to the simplistic solutions provided by scapegoating a segment of the population and depicting them as the physical embodiment of all that is wrong with society. This results in a law and order response to problems whose roots are economic in nature.

The behaviour of young people (often, but not exclusively of working-class origin) is frequently the subject on which moral panics are based. Examples of moral panics included the clashes between 'mods' and 'rockers' at south coast holiday resorts in the 1960s (Cohen, 1980) and mugging in the 1970s where it was argued (by Hall *et al.*, 1978) that this term (which embraced a number of forms of street crime) was socially constructed by the media and utilized in a political way to divert attention from other problems of a structural nature that were then facing society.

Subsequent examples of moral panics included activities associated with the 'underclass' (particularly urban disorder and juvenile crime) in the 1980s and 1990s. A particularly significant event was the abduction and murder of James Bulger by two 10-year-old boys in 1993; it became the flashpoint 'which ignited a new moral panic and led to further demonization of young people and, increasingly in the 1990s, also of lone mothers' (Newburn, 1997: 648). In more recent years young men carrying knives has been the source of a moral panic.

Moral panics are thus viewed as being socially constructed – they are artificial and deliberately manufactured to maintain the existing power relationships within society by diverting attention away from the fundamental causes of social problems through focusing attention on the habits and behaviour of a marginalized minority.

However, arguments alleging that moral panics are based upon manufactured sentiments are not universally accepted. There is no evidence to sustain allegations of conspiracies to create moral panics (Williams, 2001: 452). Further, left realism asserts that the behaviour on which a moral panic was based constituted a genuine source of public concern and was not simply a product created by the media (Young, 1986).

See also: youth justice system

References and further reading

Cohen, S. (1980) *Folk Devils and Moral Panics.* Oxford: Martin Robertson, second edition, first published in 1972.

Hall, S., Critcher, C., Jefferson, T. and Roberts, B. (1978) *Policing the Crisis: Mugging, the State and Law and Order.* London: Macmillan.

Newburn, T. (1997) 'Youth, Crime and Justice' in M. Maguire, R. Morgan and R. Reiner, *The Oxford Handbook of Criminology.* Oxford: Oxford University Press, second edition.

Williams, K. (2001) *Textbook on Criminology.* Oxford: Oxford University Press, fourth edition.

Young, J. (1986) 'The Failure of Criminology: The Need for a Radical Realism' in R. Matthews and J. Young (eds) *Confronting Crime.* London: Sage.

Multi-Agency Public Protection Arrangements (MAPPAs)

Multi-Agency Public Protection Arrangements (MAPPAs) provide a mechanism whereby a number of agencies can cooperate to develop policies that seek to assess and manage the risk to the public posed by violent, dangerous or sex offenders when they are released from custody and placed back into the community.

The MAPPA process entails four stages: identifying the offender, sharing information between agencies, assessing the risk (using assessment tools such as OASyS) and managing that risk.

Following the 1997 Sex Offenders Act (which required convicted sex offenders to register with the police), Public Protection Panels were set up to facilitate information-sharing between relevant agencies in order to provide for the assessment and management of risk posed by these offenders.

The 2000 Criminal Justice and Court Services Act required the police and probation services (termed 'responsible authorities') to cooperate to make arrangements to assess and manage the risk posed by sex or violent offenders and others who presented a risk to the public when they were placed in the community. The 2003 Criminal Justice Act included the Prison Service as a responsible authority and placed a duty to cooperate on a range of other statutory and other social care agencies that included Youth Offending Teams (YOTs) and local social services, education authorities and housing authorities.

There are three categories of offenders who are subject to the MAPPA arrangements. Category 1 consists of registered sex offenders who have been convicted or cautioned since September 1997. The police have the responsibility to identify those in this category.

Category 2 consists of violent or other sex offenders who have received a custodial sentence of 12 months or more since April 2001, a hospital or guardianship order or who have been disqualified from working with children. Those in this category are subject to supervision by the National Probation Service and are thus identified by this agency.

Category 3 consists of other offenders deemed by the 'responsible authority' to pose a risk of serious harm to the general public. Those in this category are identified by the relevant responsible authority.

There are three levels of risk assessment: level 1 applies to offenders who present a low or medium risk and who can be managed by the agency that initially identified the offender; level 2 applies to offenders deemed to pose a higher level of risk which requires the involvement of more than one agency in devising risk management plans but who are not deemed to pose a risk appropriate to the next level, level 3, which applies to offenders who pose a high risk or whose management in the community requires resources from more than one of the partnership agencies.

Risk management for high-risk offenders is implemented and overseen by a Multi-Agency Public Protection Panel (MAPPC) which consists of senior managers from the participating agencies. The more routine cases are overseen by a lower-tier and more local committee known as a Multi-Agency Risk Assessment Conference (MARAC) (Tilley, 2005: 542). Since 2003, the overall responsibility for MAPPA work was given to strategic management boards (SMBs) established by the responsible authorities to review and monitor the effectiveness of MAPPAs.

In 2003/4 there were 39,429 offenders being managed by MAPPAs: 62 per cent were registered sex offenders (category 1), 32 per cent were in category 2 and 6 per cent in category 3 (Kemshall et al., 2005: 3). The initiatives that have been used to manage risk are wide-ranging and include tagging, supervised accommodation and accredited programmes.

See also: accredited programmes, assessment tool, joined-up government, Megan's Law, Probation Service, electronic monitoring ('tagging')

References and further reading

Kemshall, H., Mackenzie, G., Wood, J., Bailey, R. and Yates, J.

(2005) *Strengthening Multi-Agency Public Protection Arrangements*. London: Home Office, Home Office Development and Practice Report 45.

Tilley, N. (ed.) (2005) *Handbook of Crime Prevention and Community Safety*. Cullompton, Devon: Willan Publishing.

mutual aid

Mutual aid entails one chief constable calling on another for assistance. Requests of this nature are usually made in connection with public order events when a chief constable feels that his or her force cannot manage the situation without outside help.

Mutual aid was initially organized on an *ad hoc* basis until the 1890 Police Act formalized the practice, enabling police forces voluntarily to enter into standing arrangements to supply officers to each other in the event of major disorder. The arrangements governing mutual aid were not significantly altered until 1964, when section 14 (2) of the 1964 Police Act effectively made it obligatory for forces to come to the aid of another to provide an effective response to public disorder.

The decision to apply for mutual aid and from where to seek it was initially in the hands of a chief constable faced with disorder. However, following the success of the National Union of Miners in forcing the closure of Saltley Coke Depot during the 1972 miners' dispute (when the local City of Birmingham police force was overwhelmed by the number of pickets), these matters have been determined centrally.

In 1972 ACPO established a mechanism that was initially known as the National Reporting Centre (NRC) later termed the Mutual Aid Coordination Centre (or MACC). This body operated from New Scotland Yard, was operationally under the control of ACPO's president and was activated when an event that posed major implications for public order arose. Its role was to coordinate the deployment of police officers from across the country to the area affected by disorder. This arrangement was utilized in the 1984/5 miners' dispute (Bunyan, 1985: 298–9).

The coordination of policing public order events was further developed in connection with the 1999 millennium celebrations, the 2000 fuel protests and the responses to post-9/11 events in 2001. These witnessed the creation of a new body, the Police National Information and Coordination Centre (PNICC). This was initially formed on a temporary, *ad hoc,* basis but later became a permanent creation responsible for the coordination of mutual aid in connection with public disorder or other incidents such as a major disaster.

Although mutual aid may provide a safeguard against the total breakdown of law and order, its use raises a number of issues. The ability of a central body to organize the deployment of police officers from all 43 police forces to a specific venue indicates a departure from the traditional way in which policing is organized in England and Wales. As was discovered during the 1984/5 miners' dispute, local police authorities had no power to influence the loss of 'their' officers to other police forces under mutual aid arrangements.

Police officers drawn from outside forces have no need to cultivate good public relationships with the communities in which they are placed. This may encourage the use of aggressive and confrontational tactics which undermine the concept of policing by consent. It has been argued that the clash between the police and striking miners at Orgreave in June 1984 'represented the unveiling of colonial policing tactics in mainland Britain' (Northam, 1988: 59).

Mutual aid has also encouraged the standardization of police weaponry, tactics and training. This has arisen because the use of officers drawn from a number of different forces to police one specific event generates pressures for standardization of police practices. Developments to facilitate this include the *Public Order Manual of Tactical Operations and Related Matters* which was initially issued by ACPO in 1982 to provide guidance to forces regarding public order tactics. This was subsequently superseded in 2007 by the ACPO *Manual of Guidance on Keeping the Peace.*

See also: Military Assistance to the Civilian Authorities, paramilitary policing, police authority, policing by consent

References and further reading

Bunyan, T. (1985) 'From Saltley to Orgreave via Brixton', *Journal of Law and Society,* 12(3), Winter: 293–304.

Joyce, P. (2002) *The Politics of Protest: Extra-parliamentary Politics in Britain since 1970.* Basingstoke: Palgrave.

Northam, G. (1988) *Shooting in the Dark: Riot Police in Britain.* London: Faber and Faber.

N

Narrowing the Justice Gap

See **detection rates**

National Black Police Association

See **Police Staff Associations**

National Crime Reporting Standard

See **crime statistics**

National DNA Database (NDNAD)

The National DNA Database (NDNAD) stores information related to DNA samples which consist of biological material (such as blood or saliva) either taken by the police from individuals who are suspected of having committed a crime or which have been discovered at crime scenes. These samples are analysed to produce code numbers (called 'profiles') that are stored on the National DNA Database. NDNAD was set up in 1995 and the custodian of this database is the National Police Improvement Agency.

The 1994 Criminal Justice and Public Order Act amended the 1984 Police and Criminal Evidence Act to authorize the collection of DNA samples by the police service. Samples could be taken if a person was charged with, reported for summons or convicted for a recordable offence. Additionally, the samples and DNA profiles that were obtained could be retained and speculatively searched against other samples and profiles held on, or on behalf of, the police.

If a person was not prosecuted, or was acquitted by a court, the samples and profiles were to be destroyed. However, the 2001

Criminal Justice and Police Act removed the requirement to destroy samples following an acquittal or prosecution, although these retained samples could only be used for the purposes of preventing and detecting crime, investigating an offence or conducting a prosecution. The 2003 Criminal Justice Act further allowed the police to take DNA and fingerprints without consent from anyone who was arrested for a recordable offence and who was subsequently detained in a police station.

On 31 October 2007 there were 4,188,033 persons whose DNA profile was retained in the National DNA Database (which included the UK and other forces such as the Channel Islands). Of these, 4,165,300 consisted of samples provided after arrest and 22,700 were voluntary samples. For England alone, the figures were 3,916,500 samples provided following arrest and 21,600 provided voluntarily (Hillier, 2007).

DNA is a key weapon in the war against crimes that entail some form of physical contact between the criminal and his or her target. The capabilities of DNA as a method of detecting crime have been enhanced in the early years of the twenty-first century by the development by the Forensic Science Service of 'DNAboost' which could help to distinguish between samples taken from a surface that a number of people had touched or when only a small DNA sample had been collected.

The NDNAD plays an important role in contemporary crime-solving – 'a typical month has seen suspects identified for 15 murders, 31 rapes and 770 car crimes' (Flint, 2004: 1). A further benefit of the use of the database in police detection work is that it is an aid in solving old, serious crimes for which no person was apprehended at the time but for which DNA samples were retained and which are now capable of analysis. The process of reopening old cases of this nature and applying modern technology in an attempt to solve them is referred to as cold case review.

Additionally, cold case review could be used in an attempt to establish the innocence of a person who has been convicted of a crime that he or she claims they did not commit. Cold case review has not historically been used in this manner in the UK but could be developed as a further defence against miscarriages of justice.

However, although it is argued that DNA is more or less foolproof, it is not completely infallible and may still result in innocent people being convicted. Samples can be mixed up and, additionally, the decision as to whether a match has been discovered is made by human beings whose work can be subject to human error. Accusations of racial bias have been levelled at NDNAD, one MP alleging that there were disproportionate numbers of black people on the database – '27 per cent of the entire black population, 42 per cent of the male black population, 77 per cent of young black men, and 9 per cent of all Asians are on the database, compared with just 6 per cent of the white population' (Teather, 2008). The government, however, disputed accusations of this nature.

There are also important civil liberties considerations affecting the NDNAD which especially affected those whose DNA samples were retained on NDNAD although they had either not been charged with a crime or had been acquitted by a court. The government was very keen that these DNA samples should be retained. It was stated that around 8,500 profiles were linked with crime scene profiles involving 1,400 offences including 114 murders, 116 rapes and 68 sexual offences (Hillier, 2008). However, in late 2008 the European Court of Human Rights declared this practice to be unlawful and in 2009 the government announced that it would remove around 800,000 profiles on the database belonging to people who had no criminal convictions.

See also: miscarriage of justice

References and further reading

Flint, C. (2004) 'Parliamentary Under-Secretary of State's Foreword, in Home Office, *Police Science and Technology Strategy 2004–2009*. London: Home Office, Science Policy Unit.

Hillier, M. (2007) HC Debates, 10 December, Vol. 469, Col. 84W.

Hillier, M. (2008) HC Debates, 29 February, Vol. 472 Col. 1433.

Teather, S. (2008) HC Debates, 29 February, Vol. 472, Col. 1426.

National Offender Management Service (NOMS)

The National Offender Management Service (NOMS) provides a mechanism to coordinate the work of the probation and prisons service. It brings together the headquarters of these two services in order to provide a coherence of purpose, although they remain separate organizations. NOMS was set up in 2004 and assumed its present structure in 2008.

The level of cooperation between the probation and prison services had traditionally not been effective. It was alleged that information-sharing between the two services was often poor (a difficulty compounded by organizational boundaries that raised data protection issues), that programmes and interventions received in prison were not always followed up in the community and that no single organization was ultimately responsible for the offender which meant 'there is no clear ownership on the front line for reducing re-offending' (Carter, 2003: 35).

Accordingly, the creation of a new body – the National Offender Management Service (NOMS) – was called for which would focus on the management of offenders throughout the whole of their sentence (Carter, 2003: 5), an approach that was referred to as 'end-to-end offender management' (Home Office, 2004: 14). One aspect of this was that interventions commenced by an inmate whilst in prison would be continued when the offender was released into the community. A prime concern of NOMS was to reduce the rate of re-offending (Carter, 2003: 35).

NOMS is an executive agency of the Ministry of Justice and operates through nine regional offices in England and one office in Wales. Each English region is headed by a Regional Offender Manager (titled Director of Offender Management in Wales) whose role includes commissioning services that are delivered by a 'mixed economy' of public, private and third sector providers that are designed to punish and rehabilitate adult offenders both in custody and in the community. NOMS also is charged with developing a regional delivery plan to reduce re-offending and to coordinate regional and local partnerships.

One aspect of the coordination of the probation and prison services was intended to be a joint IT system, C-NOMIS, that would enable offenders to be tracked both in prison and in the community. However, following a series of technical problems and spiralling costs, it was decided in 2007 that this system (now called NOMIS) would be available only to the public sector prison service to replace its existing case management system LIDS. Crams – the existing case management system used in most probation areas – would be continued with. A more limited application, 'Data share' would enable core information relating to offenders to be shared by both agencies to aid offender management.

See also: desistance, prisons, Probation Service, recidivism, third sector

References and further reading

Carter, P. (2003) *Managing Offenders, Reducing Crime: A New Approach.* London: Home Office Strategy Unit.

Home Office (2004) *Reducing Crime – Changing Lives: The Government's Plans for Transforming the Management of Offenders.* London: Home Office.

National Offender Management Service (2006) *The NOMS Offender Management Model.* [Online] http://www.noms.justice.gov.uk/news-publications-events/publications/strategy/offender-management-model-1.1?view=Binary

National Police Improvement Agency (NPIA)

The National Police Improvement Agency (NPIA) is a central body within (and owned by) the police service that was set up to provide for the continuous reform of the operations of the service.

One difficulty with the policing reforms carried out by the 2001–5 Labour government was that a variety of bodies were given responsibility to oversee various aspects of policing, resulting in overlapping of responsibilities. To remedy this, the government proposed to establish a National Police Improvement Agency (NPIA). It was intended that it would focus on three key areas: the development of good policing practice, the implementation of the support function and operational policing support. It would also be responsible for driving the delivery of a small number of 'mission critical priorities' that would be established in the National Policing Plan (Home Office, 2004: 112).

The NPIA was formed in 2007 under the auspices of the Police and Justice Act 2006 and replaced a number of Home Office agencies that provided support for policing in England and Wales. These included the Police Information Technology Organization (PITO) and Centrex the Central Police Training and Development Authority.

The responsibilities carried out by the NPIA include the delivery of training, the development of doctrine and the improvement of the way that the service uses science and information technology. All the work that they undertake is now covered in the newly developed (2009) National Improvement Strategy for Policing (NISP) which outlines key strategic plans for the next ten years.

One of their newest roles has derived from the Policing Green Paper (Home Office, 2008) which proposed to reshape the police performance and inspection regime. A new Capability Support function has been formed to support those forces which have been subject to adverse inspection reporting by Her Majesty's Inspectorate of Constabulary (HMIC). The Scottish Police Services Authority (SPSA) provides a similar service but also has responsibility to oversee the Scottish Crime and Drugs Enforcement Agency.

See also: Police Service England and Wales

References and further reading

Home Office, (2004) *Building Communities, Beating Crime: A Better Police Service for the 21st Century*. London: Home Office, Cm 6360.

Home Office (2008) *From the Neighbourhood to the National: Policing our Communities Together*. London: Home Office, Cm 7448.

neighbourhood management

Neighbourhood management seeks to secure a partnership approach to tackle a wide range of local problems that traditionally would have been handled by single agencies working in isolation. The joined-up approach of neighbourhood management thus makes local services more responsive to local needs through making the workforce of a diverse range of agencies neighbourhood-focused.

Although currently in its infancy, developments compatible with neighbourhood management have been pursued, including the deployment of local government community safety coordinators alongside neighbourhood policing teams. In some areas neighbourhood policing teams have also been provided with analysts employed by local government to evaluate neighbourhood data that goes beyond crime-related information generated by the police.

In 2001 the Neighbourhood Renewal Unit established a Neighbourhood Management Pathfinder Programme. An evaluation of these projects revealed that effectiveness often derived from focusing on priority issues that included community safety, environment, housing and local health (Neighbourhood Renewal Unit, 2004: 5–6). Examples of the initiatives that were pursued by the Pathfinders included basing police officers within the neighbourhood area who were co-located with other services and the piloting of crime prevention initiatives such as property marking schemes and protocols to improve the detection of domestic violence (Neighbourhood Renewal Unit, 2004: 8).

Neighbourhood management is of particular importance to contemporary criminal justice policy. Sir Ronnie Flanagan's *Review of Policing* proposed that neighbourhood policing should be developed into a broader neighbourhood management structure in which local partners would deliver a wide range of issues affecting community safety and quality of life (Flanagan, 2008: 67). The government endorsed these recommendations and suggested that the neighbourhood structure should be composed of senior officers from the police service, local authority and other organizations, be headed by a neighbourhood manager or coordinator and underpinned by participatory budgeting. It was intended that this structure, a Community Safety Partnership, would be piloted in a few police force areas during 2008 and subsequently be rolled out nationally.

The future development of neighbourhood management entails innovations that might include joint-tasking, joint performance measures, pooling of budgets, joint training with teams operating from dedicated premises under the overall direction of a neighbourhood manager (Home Affairs Committee, 2008: para 250). To achieve this approach, however, there are potential impediments to progress that need to be addressed. These include ensuring that middle managers in participating agencies are not in a position to block progress to achieve aims agreed upon at neighbourhood level. Neighbourhood management also requires changes in the working habits of key personnel since staff employed by agencies such as local government often have a 9–5 working timetable and may thus not be available at times when their services are required to respond to neighbourhood problems.

See also: empowerment, joined-up government, neighbourhood policing

References and further reading

Flanagan, Sir R. (2008) *The Review of Policing Final Report*. London: Review of Policing.

Home Affairs Committee (2008) *Policing in the Twenty-first Century*. Session 2007–8, Seventh Report, House of Commons Paper 364.

Home Office (2008) *From the Neighbourhood to the National: Policing our Communities Together*. London: Home Office, Cm 7448.

Neighbourhood Renewal Unit (2004) *Neighbourhood Management Pathfinder Programme National Evaluation: Annual Review 2003/4 Key Findings*. Wetherby, West Yorkshire, Office of the Deputy Prime Minister.

neighbourhood policing

Neighbourhood policing is a modern method of delivering policing to local communities that has developed earlier initiatives in community policing.

A central aspect of Labour's Third Way agenda was to develop a sense of responsibility and citizenship by treating citizens as key stakeholders in the services they used (Giddens, 1998). This led to an important development affecting police methods that was referred to as neighbourhood policing (a term adopted in 2005). This went beyond placing enhanced numbers of uniformed personnel on the streets in localities and extended to creating structures and processes to promote police engagement with the public (Singer, 2004: 7) thereby entailing a collaborative approach to problem-solving. A key objective was to tackle the fear of crime.

The essence of this approach was the creation of neighbourhood policing teams composed of fully trained officers working alongside Police Community Support Officers (PCSOs), Special Constables and other personnel who adopted 'an intelligence-led, proactive, problem-solving approach to enable them to focus on and tackle specific local issues' (Home Office, 2004: 7). 'Neighbourhood' often equated with local government ward boundaries but this was not invariably the case.

According to the National Police Improvement Agency, the purpose of neighbourhood policing was to provide people who lived and worked in an area with

- access
- influence
- interventions and
- answers

concerning the policing of their community and the manner in which problems were addressed (NPIA, quoted in Casey, 2008: 23). It possesses the potential to be further developed in directions that include neighbourhood management.

The virtues of neighbourhood policing extended beyond local issues to embrace matters that included gathering intelligence relating to more serious forms of criminality including terrorism. The justification for this approach was that it is rare within a community for one individual to be in possession of a full range of information relating to criminal activity. Instead a range of individuals may possess snippets of information which a neighbourhood policing team could pull together and translate into a coherent picture (an issue discussed in Innes, 2006). It was in this sense that neighbourhood policing was described as 'a golden thread that runs through every aspect of policing. It is not something to be separated, that in some way is totally detached from our counter-terrorist thrust.' (Sir Ronnie Flanagan, quoted in Home Affairs Committee, 2008: para 25).

See also: Police Community Support Officer, Special Constabulary

References and further reading

Casey, L. (2008) *Engaging Communities in Fighting Crime – A Review by Louise Casey.* London: The Cabinet Office.

Giddens, A. (1998) *The Third Way.* Cambridge: Polity Press.

Home Affairs Committee (2008) *Policing in the Twenty-first Century.* Session 2007–8, Seventh

Report, House of Commons Paper 364.

Home Office,(2004) *Building Communities, Beating Crime: A Better Police Service for the 21st Century*. London: TSO, Cm 6360.

Innes, M. (2006) 'Policing Uncertainty: Countering Terror through Community Intelligence and Democratic Policing'. *The Annals of the American Academy of Political and Social Science,* 605: 222–41.

Singer, L. (2004) *Reassurance Policing: An Evaluation of the Local Management of Community Safety*. London: Home Office, Home Office Research Study 288.

net widening

See **out of court disposals**

new policing system (development in nineteenth century)

'New' policing replaced the 'old' system of policing in England and Wales in the early decades of the nineteenth century. Its key feature was the abandonment of the unpaid office of parish constable which was replaced by police officers who were paid a wage to enforce the law. Additionally, the organization of policing was related to the new urban centres of population where (outside of London) a considerable degree of local control was provided for. 'New' (or 'professional') systems of policing were also introduced in Ireland and Scotland.

The first measure to bring about a new system of policing was the 1829 Metropolitan Police Act which provided for a police force across London and the surrounding area (with the exception of the City of London which developed its own 'new' policing arrangements in the 1839 City of London Police Act). It was initially controlled by two commissioners (Charles Rowan and Richard Mayne) and was under the ultimate control of the Home Secretary. This situation whereby the Home Secretary was the police authority for the Metropolitan Police Force remained until the enactment of the 1999 Greater London Assembly Act which established an independent Metropolitan Police Authority (MPA) to oversee policing in London.

The 1829 measure was followed by the 1835 Municipal Corporations Act which established locally elected councils in urban England and Wales, one of whose responsibilities was policing which was controlled by a committee of the council termed the Watch Committee and paid for by rates levied on local property owners. The Watch Committee initially exerted a considerable degree of control over local policing arrangements.

New policing arrangements in rural England and Wales were initially provided for by the 1839 Rural Constabulary Act. This Act gave magistrates at Quarter Sessions the discretionary power to establish 'new' police forces throughout the county, paid for out of the rates and controlled by a chief constable whom the magistrates appointed. Although subject to considerable control by the magistrates, county forces established by this Act were subject to a greater degree of control by the Home Secretary than their urban counterparts.

This measure was not widely adopted for reasons that included the cost of the new policing arrangements and the perception that it would result in the loss of the rural elites' traditional control over their own affairs. The adoption of the measure was also influenced by political considerations, the Tories being against reform while the Whigs favoured it. Thus by the end of 1841 the measure had only been adopted in 22 English counties in whole or in part (Eastwood, 1994: 240). The 1842 Parish Constables Act (which aimed to shore up the old system of policing) was seen in many rural areas as an alternative to the implementation of the 1839 Act.

The compulsory introduction of new policing across England and Wales was ultimately provided for in the 1856 County and Borough Police Act which required 'new' police forces to be established in both towns and counties. A key reason for this insistence was the contemporary concern relating to the threat of vagrant crime associated with unemployed soldiers returning from the Crimean War. This justified the uniform provision of policing across England and Wales (Steedman, 1984: 26).

As an inducement to this compulsion, central government funding, initially equivalent to one-quarter of the costs of pay and clothing (increased to one-half in 1874), was given to forces certified as efficient by the newly created Inspectorate. Additionally, in most counties, the petty sessions divisions (rather than Quarter Sessions) exercised the main responsibilities for local policing arrangements, thereby retaining the geographic and administrative power of the local magistrates (Steedman, 1984: 47).

Further measures affecting the development of new policing in the nineteenth century were the 1882 Municipal Corporations Act and the 1888 Local Government Act.

The former measure sought to limit the existence of small police forces by providing that newly incorporated Boroughs could only have their own police forces if they had a population in excess of 20,000. The 1888 Local Government Act was primarily concerned with introducing elected local government in counties to replace the existing system of government by magistrates. This affected the mechanism of local control over policing which henceforth would be the responsibility of a standing joint committee consisting of 50 per cent elected councillors and 50 per cent magistrates.

See also: police authority, Police Service England and Wales, Police Service Northern Ireland, Police Service Scotland, policing by consent

References and further reading

Critchley, T. (1978) *A History of Police in England and Wales.* London: Constable.

Eastwood, D. (1994) *Governing Rural England.* Oxford: Oxford University Press.

Steedman, C. (1984) *Policing the Victorian Community: The Formation of English Provincial Forces, 1856 –80.* London: Routledge and Kegan Paul.

new public management

New public management sought to introduce the principles of efficiency and value for money into the operations of the public sector. It was developed during the 1980s with the introduction of the Conservative government's Financial Management Initiative and exerted considerable influence over the operations and governance of the criminal justice system.

New public management has been described as 'a way of reorganising public sector bodies to bring their management and reporting closer to a particular conception of business methods' (Dunleavy and Hood, 1994: 9) to redress perceived organizational inefficiencies and promote enhanced value for money.

New public management was associated with a number of reforms that were designed to subject public sector services to the discipline of market forces and was an important underpinning of criminal justice legislation that included the 1994 Police and Magistrates' Courts Act. These reforms included the use of management techniques traditionally associated with the private sector (such as performance targets measured by a wide range of performance indicators, business plans, and the costing and market testing of all activities) and the enhanced use of the private sector to fund and deliver services in whole or in part. The latter was achieved through measures that included privatization (in which functions performed by public sector bodies were 'hived off' to private sector service deliverers) and compulsory competitive tendering (whereby contracts to deliver public sector services were subject to a bidding procedure that might involve existing public sector service providers competing with rivals in the private sector). This process of 'load shedding' resulted in the fragmentation of government (Leishman, *et al.*, 1996: 11–12).

New public management was also associated with attempts to separate policy-making from service delivery with the latter performed by a number of executive agencies that operated at arm's length from their parent government department. The Prison Service, for example, became an executive agency in 1993. The intention of this was to enable agency heads the maximum freedom to deliver services as they saw fit, within the confines of strategic structures set by policy-makers such as organizational goals and cash-limited budgets.

New public management also sought to promote quality of service in order to ensure that public services were underpinned by an ethos of consumerism. Public satisfaction with the manner in which services were provided became a major test of organizational efficiency and gave rise to developments that included information in the form of league tables enabling members of the public to compare the delivery of services in their area with that of others.

Post-1997 Labour governments continued with many of the approaches associated with new public management, although there have been some important changes to the process. These include the replacement of compulsory competitive tendering with best value and the adoption of the principle of contestability in place of privatization which emphasizes the creation of a mixed economy of service delivery involving state, private and voluntary sectors.

Contestability has led to an enhanced role for the 'third sector' (consisting of non-governmental organizations that include voluntary organizations, charities, co-operatives and community groups) in delivering public services. This development is compatible with initiatives to promote community empowerment and has been spearheaded by the Office of the Third Sector (which is located in the Cabinet Office). A number of third sector organizations have secured funding through the Empowerment Fund of the Department of Communities and Local Government.

See also: Best Value, empowerment

References and further reading

Dunleavy, P. and Hood, C. (1994) 'From Old Public Administration to New Public Management', *Public Money and Management*, 14(3): 9–16.

Leishman, F., Cope, S. and Starie, P. (1996) 'Reinventing and Restructuring: Towards a "New Police Order"' in F. Leishman,

B. Loveday and S. Savage, *Core Issues in Policing.* Harlow: Longman.

non-custodial sentences

Non-custodial sentences are penalties imposed by the courts that are an alternative to imprisonment (or an equivalent regime for those aged below 21). These embrace sentences without supervision and those that contain it.

Non-custodial sentences that include an element of supervision are served in the community. These have a long history and include probation orders, community service orders, attendance centre orders, combination orders and curfew orders. The use of these penalties became associated with bifurcation which sought to tailor penalties according to the seriousness of the crime. The 1991 Criminal Justice Act labelled them 'community sentences' which were re-badged by the 2000 Criminal Justice and Court Services Act.

The 2003 Criminal Justice Act introduced a significant reform to supervised non-custodial sentences. The 2003 legislation made a clear distinction between dangerous and non-dangerous offenders and provided for a new sentence, that of a community order that enabled sentencers to draw from a list of 'requirements' to enable them to produce a sentence that was specifically tailored to each offender in order to accomplish the dual aims of punishment and rehabilitation. These requirements were:

- the compulsory unpaid work requirement (this is a reparative, payback element involving community service)
- the participation in a specified activity requirement
- the programme requirement (involvement in programmes that aim to change offending behaviour)
- the prohibited activity requirement
- the curfew requirement
- the exclusion from certain areas requirement
- the residence requirement
- the mental health treatment requirement (requires consent of the offender)
- the drug rehabilitation requirement (requires consent of the offender)
- the alcohol treatment requirement (requires consent of the offender)
- the supervision requirement
- the attendance centre requirement.

Sentencers were able to adopt a 'pick and mix' approach, selecting as many of these requirements as they felt to be appropriate to the offender in order to accomplish the dual aims of punishment and rehabilitation. In December 2008 the Ministry of Justice introduced Community Payback whereby the local community was able to have an input in determining the work performed by offenders.

The community order was designed to allay public concerns that community sentences were a soft option for those who committed crime. The order can also include electronic tagging to ensure that requirements are enforced (which is compulsory when a curfew requirement is imposed). This was designed to improve the administration of these penalties which was sometimes regarded an inefficient, allowing offenders to avoid the sanctions imposed on them.

It was initially intended that the community order would be available for all offenders aged 16 and above, but following the passage of the 2003 Act, the government suspended the implemention of the community order for offenders below the age of 18. Existing sentencing options remained in force for those aged 16 and 17 until the enactment of the 2008 Criminal Justice and Immigration Act that introduced a similar generic disposal for young offenders, the youth rehabilitation order.

With the exception of the curfew requirement (which is administered through electronic tagging), requirements imposed by the community order are implemented by the probation service and may not last for more than three years.

It has been argued that supervised non-custodial sentences possess the potential to be more effective than prisons in reducing re-offending (Home Affairs Committee, 1998) but in order to be credible with the public (who often regarded them as being 'soft' on crime) needed to be stringently enforced through the consistent use of breach procedures.

However, sentences of this nature have been criticized for the creation of the 'decarcerated criminal' (Cohen, 1985). It has been argued that community programmes 'far from reducing the restrictions on criminals who might otherwise have been sent to prison, create a new clientele of criminals who are controlled by other mechanisms. The boundaries between freedom and confinement become blurred. The "net" of social control is thus thrown ever wider into the community, its thinner mesh designed to entrap ever smaller "fish". Once caught in the net, the penetration of disciplinary intervention is ever deeper, reaching every aspect of the criminal's life' (Worrall, 1997: 25).

See also: bifurcation, desistance, electronic monitoring ('tagging'), Probation Service, recidivism, sentences of the criminal courts, youth justice system

References and further reading

Cohen, S. (1985) *Visions of Social Control*. Cambridge: Polity Press.

Home Affairs Committee (1998) *Alternatives to Prison Sentences,* Third Report, Session 1997/8, House of Commons Paper 486.

Worrall, A. (1997) *Punishment in the Community: The Future of Criminal Justice.* Harlow: Longman.

O

Offender Assessment System (OASys)

See **assessment tool**

Office of Legal Complaints

See **legal profession England and Wales**

old policing system

The term 'old' policing system refers to the style of policing that operated in England and Wales before the introduction of a 'new' or 'professional' system of policing in the early decades of the nineteenth century. Similar transitions from 'old' to 'new' systems of policing also occurred in Ireland and Scotland.

The origins of the English system of policing derive from the Anglo-Saxon period (400–1066) in which

the responsibility for preventing wrongdoings and initiating action against those who had broken the law was placed on the local community and victims of crime (Rawlings, 2008: 47). This system emphasized the mutual responsibility of all inhabitants for law enforcement in which all became responsible for each other's conduct.

The basis of this Anglo-Saxon system was that small groupings of people were organized into tythings which consisted of ten households, which were headed by a tythingman who was the forerunner of the office of constable which emerged during the reign of Edward III during the fourteenth century. Tythings were grouped into Hundreds, a sub-division of the county. The Hundred was headed by a Hundred-man who was responsible to the shire-reeve (or sheriff) who was in overall charge of the county.

The Norman Conquest (1066) developed this Anglo-Saxon system in a number of important ways. The system of Frankpledge built upon the existing principle that households grouped in tythings should exercise joint responsibility for each other's conduct by requiring all adult males to be members of a tything and to swear an oath to conduct themselves in a lawful manner. The 1166 Assize at Clarendon required the tything to denounce those of its members suspected of having committed a crime to the sheriff and the accusation was initially investigated by the tythingman and a jury of 12 members which took place at the tything Frankpledge hearings.

The 1285 Statute of Winchester further developed policing in England. It provided for the appointment of two high constables in each Hundred, below which there were the petty constables in each tything. It also introduced hue and cry whereby all able-bodied citizens were required to help arrest a criminal and required the Hundred to compensate the victim of a robbery when the hue and cry failed to apprehend an offender.

The 1285 Statute compelled all towns to establish a night watch to guard the entrances to the town and arrest suspicious strangers. The constable was responsible for supervising these arrangements which also included improved arrangements for day policing. This new system was referred to as 'watch and ward' – (watch by night and ward by day). The duty to participate in the watch was placed on all householders and its role was subsequently developed to that of keeping good order in the town at night.

By the eighteenth century a system of policing had evolved that was based on constables appointed in each locality (which was often the 'parish' although other jurisdictions such as 'township' were also used) whose role was supervised by magistrates. The constables were almost always male and generally unpaid although able to obtain income from fees derived from the administration of justice. They typically served in office for one year.

The system of unpaid parish constables supervised by magistrates characterized the old policing system. However, the twin forces of the agricultural and industrial revolutions and the consequent growth of towns made this system unsuitable for large areas of England and Wales. Key features of the old system of policing, such as raising the hue and cry, fell into disuse in this changed social setting.

Many contemporaries viewed crime as spiralling out of control and it has been observed that 'from the last quarter of the eighteenth century through to 1820 problems of crime and order maintenance

were regarded as particularly acute'
(Rawlings, 2002: 106).

The only solution to severe
outbreaks of disorder was to deploy
the military. However, the likely
response of the troops was to shoot
protesters which smacked of tyran-
nical government. These problems
were evidenced in the anti-Catholic
Gordon riots which lasted from 2–9
June 1780 and entailed the use of
cavalry and infantry. Almost 300
people died in this event and 200
were severely injured.

Problems of this nature paved the
way for police reform that commenced with the formation of the
Metropolitan Police in 1829 which
constituted the first professional (or
'new') police force in England and
Wales.

See also: jury system, new policing
system (development in nineteenth
century), Police Service England
and Wales, Police Service Northern
Ireland, Police Service Scotland,
policing by consent

References and further reading

Critchley, T. (1978) *A History of
Police in England and Wales.*
London: Constable.

Rawlings, P. (2002) *Policing: A
Short History.* Cullompton,
Devon: Willan Publishing.

Rawlings, P. (2008) 'Policing
Before the Police', in T.
Newburn (ed.) *Handbook of
Policing.* Cullompton, Devon:
Willan Publishing, second
edition.

out of court disposals

Out of court disposals are penalties
inflicted on those who have broken
the law without the offender being
taken to court for trial and sentencing.

The term 'summary justice' is
sometimes applied to sentences of
this nature which entails the speedy
application of legal procedures to
deal with minor infringements of
the law. Traditionally summary
justice was associated with Magistrates' Courts but in recent years
have become associated with what
is termed 'pre-court summary
justice' (Morgan, 2008: 8). This
entails sentencing powers being
exercised by the police and other
officials such as local authority
officers without referring the law-
breaker to court.

Although this approach has
especially been identified with New
Labour's approach to re-balance
the operations of the criminal
justice system in the interests of the
law-abiding majority (Morgan,
2008: 7), a wide range of responses
not involving the courts have
long been available for minor
offences. These include the system
of cautions and warnings for adults
and juvenile offenders and the
system of fixed penalty notices
(FPNs) by which a fine is handed

out either on the spot or subsequently when evidence gathered from devices such as speed cameras has been processed.

Fixed penalty notices were originally introduced in England and Wales during the 1950s to deal with minor parking offences and this approach was built upon by the 1988 Road Traffic Act which introduced fixed penalty notices for a range of minor traffic offences.

In recent years, fixed penalty notices have especially been used in connection with tackling various forms of anti-social behaviour.

The 2001 Criminal Justice and Police Act introduced Penalty Notices for Disorder (PNDs). These entail on-the-spot fines of £50 or £80 being handed out (usually by police officers) to anyone over the age of 16 who has committed various forms of anti-social behaviour or minor criminal actions such as theft to the value of £200 or criminal damage to the level of £500. PNDs can be challenged (in which case the offender may be taken to court or the PND may be dropped) but if the offender fails to pay the fine, it is raised and becomes enforced by the courts.

On 16 July 2009, revised operational guidance to police forces relating to PNDs was issued by the Justice Department in response to concerns that PNDs were being used inappropriately in connection with crimes that should have been referred to the courts. In connection with retail theft, the use of PNDs henceforth would be restricted to first-time offenders who were not substance misusers where the value of the goods was below £100 or where the damage caused was below £300. The definition of retail theft was also tightened to ensure that the PNDs would be used only for cases of shoplifting where the recovered goods could normally be offered for re-sale.

There are a number of advantages derived from PNDs which include reducing the bureaucratic burden placed on police officers and in enhancing the degree of public confidence in the criminal justice system derived from a speedy and visible response to low-level crimes and disorder. It also removes crime of this nature from the courts thus enabling them to concentrate on more serious forms of criminal behaviour.

However, this approach has been criticized for 'net widening' (Cohen, 1985) whereby minor offenders (especially younger people) become criminalized for actions that would previously not have merited any intervention from criminal justice practitioners, thereby running the risk that increased levels of criminalization will enhance the degree of social exclusion and anti-social behaviour. Other objections relate to the extent to which those who take decisions to dispense this form of summary justice are adequately accountable for their actions. A further problem, which is common to all forms of out of court disposals, is that penalties not transacted in open court deny transparency to those who are victims of crime.

The 2003 Criminal Justice Act introduced a further out of court disposal, known as the conditional caution. This was available on the recommendation of the CPS if the offender was 18 or over and admitted an offence for which there was sufficient evidence on which a charge could be based.

As amended by the 2006 Police and Justice Act, a conditional caution could (like a simple caution) be given by a police officer but had conditions attached to it that were designed to provide for rehabilitation and thereby prevent the risk of re-offending and/or provide for reparation directly or indirectly by the offender. The former may entail participation in interventions designed to address the root cause of offending behaviour (such as drug or alcohol misuse programmes) and the latter may entail financial compensation to the victim or unpaid work within the community.

If an offender fails to comply with the conditions attached to a conditional caution, the 2003 Act provides for criminal proceedings to be instituted and the caution cancelled. A conditional caution a does not constitute a criminal conviction but it may be considered if the offender appears in court charged with a subsequent offence.

See also: cautioning (formal), Crown Prosecution Service, magistrates, re-balancing the criminal justice system

References and further reading

Cohen, S. (1985) *Visions of Social Control.* Cambridge: Policy.

Morgan, R. (2008) *Summary Justice Fast – but Fair?* London: Centre for Crime and Justice Studies.

P

PACE Codes of Practice

The 1984 Police and Criminal Evidence Act (PACE) provided for Codes of Practice to be issued in connection with the exercise of a number of police powers in relation to those suspected of having committed a crime.

The 1984 legislation gave the police a number of key powers, which included the ability to:

- stop and search a person or a vehicle in a public place;
- enter private property, search the premises and seize material found there (with or without a warrant);
- arrest;
- take fingerprints and other non-intimate samples for the purposes of identification;
- detain a person in custody and to interview that person.

The usage and conditions under which powers granted by the Act can be exercised and what the police can and cannot do when implementing them is regulated by provisions contained in the Act itself and in detailed Codes of Practice. Codes of Practice are re-issued periodically. There are currently eight Codes of Practice issued under the authority of PACE, the most recent of which were issued in February 2008.

PACE Codes of Practice are separate from the parent 1984 legislation. They constitute a form of delegated legislation which is issued by ministers following a statutory process of consultation and require the approval of both Houses of Parliament. The current procedure governing this was amended in the 2003 Criminal Justice Act making for a more limited consultation process outside of Parliament (Gibson and Watkins, 2004: 26).

Although the Codes impose obligations on the police service, breach of them does not automatically lead to criminal or disciplinary proceedings although it may form the basis of a disciplinary hearing. Additionally, the Codes are accompanied by 'Notes for Guidance'. These amplify the content of the Codes but their legal status is less clear (Harlow and Rawlings, 1997: 157–8) and there have been occasions when they have not been strictly complied with.

See also: delegated legislation, institutional racism, Police Service England and Wales

References and further reading

Gibson, B. and Watkins, M. (2004) *Criminal Justice Act 2003: A Guide to the New Procedures and Sentencing.* Winchester: Waterside Press.

Harlow, C. and Rawlings, R. (1997) *Law and Administration.* Cambridge: Cambridge University Press.

panopticon

The panopticon was a blueprint for the design of prisons drawn up by Jeremy Bentham.

The idea was first put forward in a series of letters that he wrote from Crecheff (Kirchev) in White Russia (1787) and developed in postscripts written in 1790 and 1791. This material was subsequently published in a collected edition of his writings (Bowring, 1843).

His aim was to provide the architectural design for prison that would bring about the transformation of the behaviour of offenders. Central to his idea was the imposition of discipline through surveillance enabling an observer to monitor prisoners both collectively and individually without them being aware when they were being watched. To achieve this objective, Bentham proposed that prisons should be designed with a central tower which housed the unseen observers from which rows of single cells arranged in tiers and separate blocks would radiate. These cells would be isolated from each other.

This 'invisible omniscience' secured the constant conformity of inmates since they were unable to discern when their actions were not being observed. It induced in inmates 'a state of conscious and permanent visibility that assures the automatic functioning of power'. Surveillance was thus 'permanent in its effects, even if it is discontinuous in its action' (Foucault, 1977).

The 1794 Penitentiary Act provided for the construction of a penitentiary at Millbank. The project was abandoned in 1803 although Millbank was eventually completed (without Bentham's involvement) in 1821. Pentonville Prison (opened in 1842) was also influenced by this concept. A number of prisons constructed outside the United Kingdom also incorporated his ideas.

Michel Foucault was heavily influenced by Bentham's ideas, especially in connection with the way in which power and knowledge were intertwined: he argued that the disciplinary surveillance of the prison created knowledge of the convict's body thus creating a new kind of power (Foucault, 1977: 27). However, even with developments associated with surveillance technology such as CCTV, it is impossible to constantly monitor the actions of all prisoners at all times and knowledge of this situation by inmates may undermine the power that the authorities sought to exert over them.

See also: prisons, punishment (aims of), surveillance

References and further reading

Bentham, J. (1798) *Panopticon or The Inspection House: Containing the Idea of a New Principle of Construction Applicable to any sort of Establishment in which Persons of any Description are to be Kept under Inspection.* http://cartome.org/panopticon2.htm [online reference].

Bowring, D. (1843) *The Works of Jeremy Bentham.* Edinburgh: William Tait.

Foucault, M. (1977) *Discipline and Punish: The Birth of the Prison.* London: Allen Lane.

Semples, J. (1993) *Bentham's Prison: A Study of the Panopticon Penitentiary.* Oxford: Clarendon.

Wilson, D. (2002) 'Millbank, the Panopticon and their Victorian Audience'. *Howard Journal of Criminal Justice*, 41: 364–81.

paramilitary policing

The term 'paramilitary policing' refers to changes affecting the tactics, weaponry and equipment used by the police at public order events and the way in which the deployment of police resources was prepared for in advance of a specific event and controlled on the day of it. These changes were incrementally introduced during the 1980s, often as reactive responses to events such as the 1981 inner-city disorders and the 1984/5 miners' dispute.

Paramilitary policing has been described as 'the application of (quasi) military training, equipment and organization to questions of policing (whether under central control or not)' (Jefferson, 1990: 16). It has often been equated with aggressive policing in which those on the receiving end are viewed as the enemy and subjected to a violent police response. The presence of police officers at a specific incident who are dressed and equipped as if they were 'looking for trouble' has the potential to exacerbate violence (Jefferson, 1987: 51–3) and may provoke or legitimize the use of violence by a crowd.

This aspect of paramilitary policing is argued to have set it apart from the traditional ways in which the police responded to protest whereby the time-honoured notion of minimum force that underpinned policing since the early years of the nineteenth century (Brewer *et al.,*1996: 22) gave way to a style of policing that favoured the use of coercion in order to quell manifestations of dissent and was akin to methods associated with colonial policing tactics (Northam, 1989: 59).

However, arguments that equate paramilitary policing with an aggressive police response at public order events presents an incomplete account of the range of developments with which paramilitary policing was associated.

Particular attention has been drawn (P. Waddington 1987 and 1993) to the importance of command and control systems to paramilitary policing that enabled 'a more disciplined approach to disorderly and violent situations than is possible by traditional methods (Waddington, 1993: 353). These enhanced the degree of control that senior officers were able to exert over officers deployed in public order situations and served to suppress the discretion of individual

officers and undermine the influence that subcultural values might otherwise exert over their actions (Waddington, 1993: 357). Other developments associated with paramilitary policing included intelligence gathering and planning and the use of tension indicators (Waddington, 1987) which sought to avoid confrontation rather than to provoke it.

Additionally, the opinion that paramilitary policing characterized a more aggressive form of policing that set aside the time-honoured principle of minimum force has been challenged by arguments that suggest that changes to police methods introduced in the latter decades of the twentieth century were prompted in response to the violence to which police officers were often subjected. These changes did not undermine the concept of minimum force but the baseline was altered so that what level of force constituted 'minimum' was pushed upwards in response to the violence associated with protest (Reiner, 1998: 46).

Recent events involving the policing of protestors at the G20 summit in London on 1 April 2009 (which resulted in the death of one man and major criticism of the police tactic of containment, sometimes called 'kettling'), has reignited the debate around the paramilitary approach to policing of disorder. The resulting report by HMIC suggested that the tactics deployed were inappropriate and there was a need to strengthen and sustain the traditional British model of policing at these events (HMIC, 2009:7).

See also: mutual aid, policing by consent

References and further reading

Brewer, J., Guelke, A., Hume, I., Moxon-Browne, E. and Wilford, R. (1996) *The Police, Public Order and the State.* Basingstoke: Palgrave Macmillan, second edition.

Her Majesty's Inspectorate of Constabulary (HMIC) (2009) *Adapting to Protest.* London. Central Office of Information.

Jefferson. T. (1987) 'Beyond Paramilitarism', *British Journal of Criminology*, 27: 47–53.

Jefferson, T. (1990) *The Case Against Paramilitary Policing.* Buckingham: Open University Press.

Northam, G. (1989) *Shooting in the Dark: Riot Police in Britain.* London: Faber and Faber.

Reiner, R. (1998) 'Policing Protest and Disorder in Britain' in D. della Porta and H. Reiter (eds) *The Control of Mass Demonstrations in Western Democracies.* Minnesota: University of Minnesota Press.

Waddington, P. (1987) 'Towards Paramilitarism? Dilemma in the Policing of Public Disorder', *British Journal of Criminology,* 27: 37–46.

Waddington, P. (1993) 'The Case Against Paramilitary Policing Considered', *British Journal of Criminology,* 33(3): 353–73.

Parole Board for England and Wales

The Parole Board is an agency whose role is to consider applications by prisoners for their release from custody.

The 1967 Criminal Justice Act introduced a procedure whereby prisoners in England and Wales could be released before they had served the full sentence ordered by a court. This system of discretionary early release was named 'parole' and on the advice of the Parole Board the person was released into the community under licence, supervised by a probation officer.

The eligibility criteria for release were initially determined by this legislation – it was 'granted to "good" prisoners and required a prisoner to acknowledge their guilt' (Easton and Piper, 2007: 167). The criteria were amended by subsequent measures, most notably the 1991 Criminal Justice Act. Initially the Board made recommendations to the Secretary of State but the minister's power to intervene was limited by the 1998 Human Rights Act.

The 2003 Criminal Justice Act established new arrangements for the automatic release of many prisoners, limiting the role of the Parole Board to determine the release of two categories of prisoners. The first category was those serving indeterminate life sentences (whether these were mandatory, discretionary or automatic and also those serving the newly created Indeterminate Sentence for Public Protection). In all of these cases, the trial judge stipulates a minimum period of time (termed a 'tariff') that the prisoner must serve in custody and it is for the Parole Board to assess whether, having completed this term, it is safe for the inmate to be released into the community. If this course of action is adopted, life licence conditions are set as requirements to which the released prisoner must adhere.

The second category of prisoner that is relevant to the work of the Parole Board is those serving determinate sentences. These include discretionary conditional release prisoners serving determinate sentences of over four years for offences committed before 4 April 2005 and those given extended sentences for public protection for offences committed after 4 April 2005. The Parole Board assesses whether, having completed the minimum time the prisoner is required to spend in custody, it is safe to release him or her into the community. If the inmate is released, parole licence conditions are set as requirements to which the released prisoner must comply.

The role performed by the Parole Board has changed since its creation in 1968 from that of an advisory body to that of a decision-making agency. The decision to release a prisoner is based on an assessment by the Board of the risk this action would pose to the general public – 'at the heart of the matter is the process of risk assessment and public confidence that this process is there primarily to protect the public from the dangerous offender' (Nichol, 2006).

See also: human rights, prisons, sentencing tariff

References and further reading

Nichol, Sir D. (2006) Speech to the Centre for Crime and Criminal Justice, London (www.crimeand justice.org.uk/opus230/ retrieved 1 September 2008).

Padfield, N. (ed.) (2007) *Who to Release? Parole, Fairness and Criminal Justice.* Cullompton, Devon: Willan Publishing.

Easton, S. and Piper, C. (2007) *Sentencing and Punishment: The Quest for Justice.* Oxford: Oxford University Press.

Penalty Notices for Disorder (PNDs)

See **out of court disposals**

penology

See **punishment (aims of)**

plea bargaining

Plea bargaining refers to an arrangement between prosecution and defence lawyers and a judge or magistrate that secures a reduced sentence for a defendant who agrees to plead guilty.

As practised in the United Kingdom, plea bargaining entails one or other of two courses of action. An arrangement may be struck between the CPS, defence lawyer and magistrates or trial judge whereby a defendant agrees to plead guilty to a crime with which he or she has been charged and secures a reduced sentence for this cooperation. A variation of this is for a defendant charged with several crimes to plead guilty to some if the others are disregarded.

Plea bargaining may also involve a defendant agreeing to plead guilty to a lesser charge than the one with which he or she was originally charged in order to secure a less severe sentence. This is known as 'charge reduction' or 'downgrading'.

Although plea bargaining is an accepted aspect of the American criminal justice system, in the UK it traditionally existed on an informal basis. In 1970 Lord Chief Justice Parker put forward the 'Turner Rules' governing plea bargaining which insisted that the defendant should be free to make up his or her mind regarding how to plead and insisting that judges in open court should not give any indication of the variation in sentence that would derive from pleas of guilty or not guilty. However, it remained possible for barristers to seek this information from the judge privately, in chambers.

A more formalized system of plea bargaining was provided for in the 2003 Criminal Justice Act. This related to cases that were triable either way (in a Magistrates' or a Crown Court) and enabled magistrates to give an advanced indication as to whether the sentence they would deliver in response to a plea of guilty by the defendant at that stage would be custodial or non-custodial.

A formalized system of plea bargaining in Crown Courts was developed by the Court of Appeal in the Goodyear case which established a framework that enabled a judge, when requested by the defence, to give an indication in open court as to the maximum sentence for a guilty plea when this was immediately entered.

One problem with the procedures that were set out in the Goodyear case concerned the stage at which plea bargaining could be entered into. Complex cases often required agreements between suspects or defendants and prosecutors to be arranged before a case was taken to court in order to secure evidence on which a prosecution could be based.

Accordingly, the 2005 Serious Organized Crime and Police Act placed on a statutory basis the award of reduced sentences when defendants aided a prosecution. Subsequently, in 2009 the Attorney General issued guidelines whereby formal agreements could be entered into between the CPS and defence lawyers in connection with fraud cases which would include the length of sentence.

Plea bargaining may speed up court procedures especially in complex cases where proceedings may be lengthy and costly and perhaps where there is concern about the way in which a judge or jury will view the evidence that has been amassed during the investigation. Plea bargaining also avoids victims having to give evidence in court which may be a daunting and traumatic process for them especially in cases of sexual assault.

However, there are problems with plea bargaining. Serious crimes may not receive the penalty that they deserve (in which case victims will feel cheated of justice) especially if they believe that a downgrading agreement has been driven by financial considerations in order to move a case from a Crown Court to a Magistrates' Court.

It might also be argued that increasing the pressure on defendants to plead guilty undermines the presumption of innocence (Justice, 1993) and may result in miscarriages of justice whereby innocent people feel constrained to plead guilty to avoid a harsher sentence if they fear that their plea of not guilty will be rejected by the court (Justice, 2004: 8–9).

Plea bargaining is closely related to a formalized system of sentence discount for a timely plea of guilty by a defendant. This procedure was provided for in the 1994 Criminal Justice and Public Order Act (subsequently replaced by the 2000 Powers of the Criminal Courts (Sentencing) Act).

It was subsequently suggested that judicial sentencing guidelines should be introduced to provide for 'a system of sentencing discounts graduated so that the earlier the tender of plea of guilty the higher the discount for it' (Auld, 2001: 443). The government endorsed this reform and the Sentencing Guidelines Council that was created by the 2003 Criminal Justice Act is responsible for issuing sentencing guidelines regarding discounts for guilty pleas.

See also: Crown Prosecution Service, judges, jury system, criminal court system England and Wales, magistrates, miscarriage of justice, Sentencing Guidelines Council

References and further reading

Auld, Rt. Hon, Lord Justice (2001) *Review of the Criminal Courts of England and Wales.* London: TSO.

Justice (1993) *Negotiated Justice – A Closer Look at the Implications of Plea Bargains.* London: Justice.

Justice (2004) *Response to White Paper One Step Ahead – A 21st Century Strategy to Defeat Organised Crime.* London: Justice.

R *v* Turner (FR) [1970] 2 QB 321.

R *v* Goodyear [2005] EWCA Crim 888.

Slapper, G. and Kelly, D. (2006) *The English Legal System.* London: Routledge, sixth edition.

police authority

A police authority is a body that provides for the involvement of local people in the conduct of policing in England and Wales. It exercises responsibility alongside the Home Secretary and chief constables in the tripartite division of responsibility for police affairs.

Police authorities were created by the 1964 Police Act to assume the responsibilities that were formerly carried out by watch committees in urban areas and standing joint committees in rural areas. Although attached to the structure of local government (at county level), police authorities did not derive their powers by delegation from the local council (which had been the position previously) but directly from the Act itself. They became free-standing bodies under the provisions of the 1994 Police and Magistrates' Courts Act.

The composition of police authorities has been affected by subsequent legislation. They were initially composed of two-thirds councillors and one-third magistrates but the 1994 Police and Magistrates' Courts Act augmented their membership with a number of independent members so that the average police authority consisted of 17 members – 9 councillors (chosen by local authorities in the police authority area drawn from the political parties in proportion to their share of the vote), 3 magistrates (selected by Magistrates' Courts Selection Panels) and 5 persons appointed by members of the police authority from a short list submitted to them by the Home Secretary (which was derived from names initially submitted by a local selection panel).

The 2006 Police and Justice Act removed magistrates as a separate category of member, although the 2008 Police Authority Regulations stipulated that a police authority should contain at least one magistrate as an independent member. The 2008 Regulations required most police authorities to consist of 17 members (9 councillors and 8 independent members), with five consisting of 19 members (10 councillors and 9 independents).

The role of police authorities has also changed since 1964. Its initial role was to secure the maintenance of an 'adequate and efficient' police force for its area. This entailed a number of specific functions which have been augmented by the 1994 Police and Magistrates' Courts Act and the 1996 Police Act (which made police authorities responsible for the 'maintenance of an efficient and effective police force for its area') and the 2006 Police and Justice Act (which extended the role of a police authority beyond that of 'securing the maintenance of an efficient and effective force' to that of additionally requiring the police authority to hold the chief constable to account for the exercise of his or her functions and those of the officers and staff under their control). The key functions carried out by police authorities to discharge these responsibilities include publishing an annual local policing plan and a three-year strategy plan and setting the budget.

Different governance arrangements applied to the Metropolitan Police where the Home Secretary exercised the role of the police authority since the force's creation in 1829. This situation persisted until the enactment of the 1999 Greater London Assembly Act which established the Greater London Assembly and an independent Metropolitan Police Authority (MPA) to oversee policing in London. This now consists of 23 people – 12 members of the Greater London Assembly and 11 independent members. One of these is appointed by the Home Secretary and 10 are chosen through an open recruitment campaign.

See also: magistrates, political oversight of the criminal justice system, tripartite system of police governance

References and further reading

Jones, T. (2003) 'The Governance and Accountability of Policing' in T. Newburn (ed.) *Handbook of Policing*. Cullompton, Devon: Willan Publishing.

Joyce, P. (2001) 'The Governance of the Police in England and Wales, 1964–98', *Police Practice and Research,* 2(4): 315–44.

Loveday, B., McClory, J. and Lockhart, G. (2007) *Fitting the Bill: Local Policing for the Twenty-first Century*. London: Policy Exchange.

Police Community Support Officer (PCSO)

Police Community Support Officers (PCSOs) are an important aspect of neighbourhood policing, one aim of which is to provide a visible uniformed presence within communities in order to allay the fear of crime. In 2009 there were 16,000 PCSOs in England and Wales.

PCSOs were created by the 2002 Police Reform Act. They are funded by a combination of central government and local authority grants and are employed by both police forces and local councils. Their primary function is to provide a high-profile patrolling to local communities addressing local concerns and providing reassurance. They represent a significant element of the current move to modernize the police service which has been motivated by a recognition that police officers are a highly trained but an expensive resource that should be channelled into specific areas of work requiring the application of police powers.

PCSOs have fewer powers than police officers. Initially PCSOs had various powers designated to them at the discretion of individual chief constables. This created a wide variation in what PCSOs could and could not do, leading to uncertainty amongst the public and adding to the media's negative stereotype. In order to address this, in December 2007 all PCSOs across England and Wales were provided with a common set of 20 standard (or core) powers that were drawn up by the Home Secretary but which allowed chief constables flexibility on other powers.

In total 53 powers can be designated to which some local authority bylaws can also be added (NPIA, 2008: 11). These additional powers range from the confiscation of alcohol and tobacco from minors to the ability to detain a person for a specific period of time. Some chief constables have given all of these powers to PCSOs whilst others have only given some. The power of detention has only been provided to PCSOs in 50 per cent of forces (Home Office, 2007).

Reviews of PCSOs have suggested that if forces try to use them in a back office role for minor administrative support, with a view to freeing up officers, it is likely that their visibility and impact on reassurance would decline (HMIC, 2004: 144). An evaluation of the deployment, use and effectiveness of PCSOs has highlighted concerns of role drift and variation, with some engaged in roles seen as outside of their core role of high-profile patrol in neighbourhoods by performing roles that include roads policing and offender management (NPIA, 2008: 34–5). These are likely to place them in confrontational situations which might undermine the relationships they have developed with local communities.

In 2004 the government gave a commitment to increase the number of PCSOs and Neighbourhood Wardens in England and Wales to 25,000 by 2008 (Home Office, 2004). However, this was later rescinded and a concern now exists around their long-term future due to a lack of clarity over government funding beyond 2010 and the challenging economic outlook for the public sector (Flanagan, 2008).

See also: neighbourhood policing, reassurance policing

References and further reading

Flanagan, Sir R. (2008) *The Review of Policing Final Report.* London: Review of Policing.

Her Majesty's Inspectorate of Constabulary (HMIC) (2004) *Modernising the Police Service. A Thematic Inspection of Workforce Modernisation.* London: Home Office.

Home Office (2004) *Building Communities, Beating Crime: A Better Police Service for the 21st Century.* London: Home Office, Cm 6360.

Home Office (2007) PCSO Powers [Online] http://police.homeoffice. gov.uk/publications/community-policing/PCSOs_Audit_Table_ May_2007_1.pdf?view=Binary

National Police Improvement Agency (NPIA) (2008) *Neighbourhood Policing Programme: PCSO Review.* London: NPIA.

Police Federation of England and Wales

See **Police Staff Associations**

police property

The term 'police property' describes the relationship between the police and those at the bottom end of the social ladder.

A key role performed by the police in the nineteenth century was to regulate the behaviour of the lower social orders and to impose on them the moral habits and standards of behaviour of 'respectable' members of society. It was in this sense that they have been described as 'domestic missionaries' (Storch, 1976). The elites who controlled policing were willing to give the police a relatively free hand to discharge this function (acting aggressively within the law or perhaps outside of it) and this situation gave rise to the concept of 'police property' (Lee, 1981). This term is applied to social groups which possess little or no rights in society and thus are not in a position to formally object to their treatment by the police. Vigorous action undertaken by the police towards them also serves to secure consent towards the police from those occupying positions higher up the social ladder.

The definition of which groups constitute police property is not stable and changes over time. It may embrace any grouping whose habits or behaviour are deemed to be unacceptable by those wielding power in society or which are deemed to pose a threat to their social position. In nineteenth-century Liverpool 'participants in the street economy' (Brogden, 1982: 232) were accorded this status which was later imposed on minority ethnic communities in the twentieth century.

Although groups which are treated aggressively by the police lack formal means (or lack the access to these means) to redress their treatment, they may articulate their grievances through alternative methods. In Liverpool, for example, a link has been drawn between the outbreaks of disorder directed at the police by those who were regarded as police property in the nineteenth century and the riots that occurred in Toxteth in 1981 (Brogden, 1982). Outbreaks of disorder may give rise to pressures on the police from political or economic elites to alter their behaviour towards targeted social groups since continued mistreatment can lead to disorder on a scale that poses a threat to the existing social order.

See also: policing by consent

References and further reading

Brogden, M. (1982) *The Police: Autonomy and Consent.* London: Academic Press.

Lee, J. (1981) 'Some Structural Aspects of Police Deviance in Relation to Minority Groups' in C. Shearing (ed.) *Organisational Police Deviance.* Toronto: Butter-worths.

Storch, R. (1976) 'The Policeman as Domestic Missionary', *Journal of Social History*, IX(4), Summer: 481–509.

Police Service England and Wales

The Police Service in England and Wales consists of a number of separate police forces which perform a wide range of functions that seek to provide a safe and secure environment for its citizens.

The role of the police (as stated in 1829 by Metropolitan Police Commissioner Sir Richard Mayne in his instructions to the newly formed Metropolitan Police) was to prevent crime, protect life and property and preserve public tranquillity (Mayne, cited in Villiers, 2009: 17). To these functions others might be added – enforcing the law, bringing offenders to justice (which until the creation of the Crown Prosecution Service included the prosecution of offenders) and 'befriending the public'. The latter responsibility entails performing activities which have little to do with law enforcement but which entail answering requests by the public for assistance, whatever the nature of the problem. This is referred to as the 'service function' of policing and it performed an important role in securing widespread popular consent for policing in its formative years in the nineteenth century. In more recent years there have been attempts to scale down activities of this nature on the grounds that they distracted from the 'real' (or core) tasks of policing.

England and Wales has no unified police service; instead there are 43 separate police forces each with its own police authority. Each is headed by a chief constable (the term 'Commissioner' being used in London for the Metropolitan Police Service). Each force is divided into a number of territorial areas. These were formerly referred to as divisions although the term basic command unit (BCU) is now commonly used by many forces. Divisions/BCUs are usually under the control of a chief superintendent although the Metropolitan Police Service utilizes the term commander for an officer performing this function.

Police work is carried out by a variety of personnel. In 2009 there were approximately 140,000 police officers in England and Wales. In addition to police officers, police work is performed by a number of other officials, most importantly the Special Constabulary and Police Community Support Officers (PCSOs).

The police service also includes police support staff. In 2009 here were 76,000 persons employed in this capacity in England and Wales.

The costs of policing are paid for by central government grants (primarily in the form of a police general grant which is supplemented by a number of specific grants) and from money obtained from Council Tax levied by the local authority.

The government revenue spending for police authorities is set for a three-year period within the context of the Comprehensive Spending Review through which the Treasury assesses government priorities and allocates money to public services over a three-year period. The total provision for police revenue grants in 2009/10 was £9,428 billion.

The distribution of the police general grant to individual police authorities is determined by a complex calculation based on a number of components. The most important of these is the needs-based formula. The main determinant in the formula is the projected resident population but cost adjustments are built in for the socio-economic and demographic factors that may impact on crime levels.

The contribution made by local government finance towards policing varies considerably across England and Wales but it is a growing source of funding (Home Affairs Committee, 2007: para. 41). The amount of police spending financed through the council tax precept has doubled in real terms between 2001 and 2006/7.

See also: Basic Command Units, Crown Prosecution Service, old policing system, new policing system, new public management, police authority, Special Constabulary, tripartite system of police governance

References and further reading

Home Affairs Committee (2007) *Police Funding.* Fourth Report of Session 2006–7. London: TSO, House of Commons Paper 553.

Rowe, M. (2008) *Introduction to Policing.* London: Sage.

Villiers, P. (2009) *Police and Policing: An Introduction.* Sheffield: Waterside.

Police Service Northern Ireland

The Police Service in Northern Ireland consists of one police force (the Police Service of Northern Ireland (PSNI)) which performs a wide range of functions that seek to provide a safe and secure environment for its citizens.

Until the partition of Ireland in 1922 which created the state of Northern Ireland and the Irish Republic, Ireland was part of the United Kingdom. The police system developed differently from that of England and Wales. Whereas policing in England and Wales is founded on the Common Law tradition, policing in Ireland was based on the Roman Law tradition.

Its prime role was to ensure the continuance of the rule of the British government in a country where this was widely contested. This gave policing in Ireland a political orientation above a concern to deal with 'ordinary' crime and lawlessness.

The 'old' system of policing in Ireland was performed by High Constables (appointed by County Grand Juries) and Petty Constables (appointed by Court Leets or Sheriffs Tourns, operating at parish level). By the eighteenth century this system was ineffective.

Initial reform sought to shore up the old system. In 1787 outside of Dublin the Lord Lieutenant was authorized to appoint chief constables for each baronial district. (A baronial district, or barony, was derived from Tudor administration in Ireland and was the unit of administration below the County.) County Grand Juries would appoint sub-constables to these districts. This measure was augmented by a further piece of legislation in 1792. But neither provided for a system of policing that operated throughout Ireland (in particular because County Grand Juries became increasingly reluctant to appoint constables) and much reliance was placed on the military to counter disturbances that occurred in the late eighteenth and early decades of the nineteenth centuries.

A further measure to shore up the old system was the creation of the

Peace Preservation Force (usually referred to as Peelers) in 1814. The Lord Lieutenant was able to declare a county (or a barony or a half barony) to be in a state of disturbance. A police force consisting of a chief constable and up to 50 constables would then garrison the area until the disturbance had passed. Initially local ratepayers footed the bill for this force, but in 1817 an amendment to the legislation permitted central government to contribute up to two-thirds of the cost. By 1822 the force numbered around 2,300 and operated in about half of Ireland's counties.

The legislation of 1787 and 1792 was replaced by the 1822 Irish Constabulary Act which created a new system of policing for Ireland. The initial intention of the government was to place this new police force under central control but compromises were made whereby the barony remained the basic unit of police organization. The Lord Lieutenant appointed a chief constable to each barony and in turn he appointed a number of constables. The chief constable was required to submit a report to the Lord Lieutenant every three months. Baronies were grouped into four provincial areas, and in each the Lord Lieutenant appointed an Inspector General (sometimes referred to as a General Superintendent) whose role included drawing up general regulations for the police in their area.

The style of policing provided by the Irish Constabulary was paramilitary, constables were armed and housed in barracks and police stations throughout Ireland. The great bulk of constables were from Catholic backgrounds, but the officers tended to be Protestant.

Further reform was provided by the 1836 Irish Constabulary Act. The main effect of this measure was to centralize control over policing. The four provincial areas headed by an Inspector General were replaced by one Inspector General and two Deputies who exercised control throughout Ireland (with the exception of Dublin). After 1846 the government provided fully for the funding of the Irish Constabulary.

Much of the work of the new force was directed at disturbances that were a frequent feature of Irish political life. The role of the Irish Constabulary in dealing with Fenian violence was recognized by the Queen who renamed the force the Royal Irish Constabulary (RIC) in 1867. The force was abolished following partition in 1922. However, the RIC was the model for the policing arrangements conducted in Northern Ireland by the newly formed Royal Ulster Constabulary (RUC).

Policing in Dublin differed from the system throughout the remainder of Ireland. Dublin was the first area in the United Kingdom to be provided with a 'new' policing system. The 1786 Dublin Police Act established the Dublin Metropolitan Police District headed by a High Constable. The Police District was divided into four districts, each headed by a chief constable. A salaried magistrate was appointed to each of these districts, appointed by the Lord Lieutenant. The police force was armed, officers were paid and were mainly Protestant. The 1808 Dublin Metropolitan Police Act extended the jurisdiction of the force which now operated over six districts and the 1836 Dublin Police Act removed the last vestiges of local control over the force which was placed in the hands of the Chief Secretary for Ireland, with day-to-day control being placed in the hands of two magistrates appointed by the Lord Lieutenant.

The force was abolished as a separate organization in 1925 when it became part of the Irish Republic's police force, the *Garda Siochana*.

Following partition in 1922, Northern Ireland became self-governing in connection with its domestic affairs. The RUC was controlled by the Northern Ireland Minister for Home Affairs. It operated across the six counties that comprised Northern Ireland and was a paramilitary force. It was mainly Protestant in composition and was augmented by the Ulster Special Constabulary (usually referred to as the B-Specials).

The sectarian orientation of the RUC and B-Specials was especially obvious when the demand for civil rights for Catholics emerged during the 1960s. By the late 1960s the level of sectarian violence spiralled out of control. The RUC could not cope and in 1969 the British government ordered troops onto the streets of Belfast. However, the use of troops in a policing role could not be a permanent one and in the mid-1970s the policy of 'police primacy' was adopted (Kennedy-Pipe, 1997: 103–4).

This entailed reforming the RUC in a number of important ways. It was enlarged and re-equipped to enable it to counter terrorist violence and attempts were made to make the force less sectarian and more professional; a key feature of this reform was the establishment of the Northern Ireland Police Authority in 1970.

Under the control of Kenneth Newman and John Hermon during the mid-1970s until the end of the 1980s, attempts were made to develop community policing, enrol more Catholics to the force and to pursue policies that included banning Protestants from parading in predominantly Catholic areas.

However, these reforms failed to make the RUC a police force that was acceptable to both sides of the sectarian divide in Northern Ireland. Its role in countering terrorism entailed the use of tactics that included interrogation, the supergrass policy and the alleged 'shoot to kill' policy in the early 1980s. The RUC was viewed as operating in a sectarian manner which meant that it had little legitimacy in nationalist (that is, Catholic) communities.

During the 1990s, attempts were made to find a political solution to the political violence in Northern Ireland. These culminated in the signing of the 1998 Good Friday Peace Agreement. This created a new structure of devolved government for Northern Ireland consisting of the Northern Ireland Assembly and an executive headed by a first minister and composed of representatives of Northern Ireland's main political parties who entered into a power-sharing arrangement.

One aspect of the Belfast (or 'Good Friday') Agreement was the establishment of a commission to examine the future policing arrangements in Northern Ireland. This took the form of an enquiry (Independent Commission on Policing in Northern Ireland, 1999) that was chaired by Chris Patten. This recommended the creation of a Police Service for Northern Ireland, overseen by a Northern Ireland Policing Board to monitor the efficiency and effectiveness of the force, acting as the equivalent of a police authority that exists in England, Wales and Scotland. This Board and the new police force was created by the 2000 Police (Northern Ireland) Act.

The Board is composed of 19 political and independent members.

Sinn Fein, however, initially refused to join the Northern Ireland Policing Board, although the SDLP did so. One of its main objections was that insufficient power over policing had been devolved locally. However in February 2007 Sinn Fein agreed to join the Northern Ireland Policing Board and participate in the District Policing Partnerships. This decision paved the way for the ultimate devolution of police and criminal justice functions to the Northern Ireland Assembly in 2010.

This new police force took over from the RUC on 4 November 2001. Its features included recruiting new members on the basis of 50 per cent Catholics and 50 per cent non-Catholics from April 2002 until a target figure of 30 per cent Catholic membership (as recommended by Patten) had been attained. By early 2008 this target was relatively close to being reached. The force numbers around 7,500 officers and almost 4,000 civilian staff. Its budget in 2008/9 was almost £1.2 billion which the Policing Board negotiates with the Northern Ireland Office.

In addition to neighbourhood policing which has been rolled out across Northern Ireland's eight policing districts, local involvement in police affairs is secured through District Policing Partnerships. There are 29 of these across Northern

Ireland which serve as a mechanism to link the district council, councillors and representatives of the local community and enable local people to influence the way in which their community is policed.

See also: informants (grasses/ supergrasses), neighbourhood policing, new policing system, old policing system, Police Service England and Wales, Police Service Scotland

References and further reading

Independent Commission on Policing in Northern Ireland (1999) *A New Beginning: Policing in Northern Ireland. The Report of the Independent Commission on Policing in Northern Ireland.* London: TSO.

Kennedy-Pipe, C. (1997) *The Origins of the Present Troubles in Northern Ireland.* London: Longman.

Ryder, C. (2000) *The RUC 1922 – 2000: A Force Under Fire.* London: Arrow Books, second edition.

Police Service Scotland

The Police Service in Scotland consists of a number of separate police forces which perform a wide range of functions that seek to provide a safe and secure environment for its citizens.

Scottish policing initially rested on the voluntary principle, the first constables being appointed in 1617. In the cities, the constables were augmented by watchmen to guard the area at night. By the eighteenth century, constables appointed by the justices performed a range of functions in connection with the maintenance of order and were empowered to summon public aid in order to quell disturbances. Although they were often paid, their tenure in office was of a limited duration.

A professional police force was briefly established in Glasgow in 1779 but collapsed because there was no provision for it to be supported by the levying of a local rate (Donnelly and Scott, 2005: 45–6).

The 1800 Glasgow Police Act provided for a professional police force for that city whose underlying ethos was crime prevention. It was financed by a rate levied on houses and businesses by the City Council and was under the control of the Lord Provost, three baillies (magistrates) and nine commissioners who were elected each year from the traders and merchants of the city (Donnelly and Scott, 2005: 47).

Separate Acts of Parliament subsequently established similar policing arrangements for a number of other cities and burghs. A general power to establish professional police forces in the burghs was provided by the 1833 Burghs and

Police (Scotland) Act which also enabled burghs to adopt powers relating to cleansing, lighting and paving. The Policing of Towns (Scotland) Act 1850 and the General Police and Improvement (Scotland) Act 1862 extended these powers to other urban areas which resulted in the creation of around 100 burgh police forces.

The 1857 Police (Scotland) Act imposed a compulsory requirement on the Commissioners of Supply in each county (who performed most of the local government functions in these areas until their replacement by county councils by the 1890 Local Government (Scotland) Act) to establish police forces in the counties and also permitted existing burgh forces to be amalgamated with the county force if the magistrates and town council of the burgh and the commissioners of supply in the county were agreed on this course of action.

These forces were administered by a police committee that consisted of a maximum number of 15 commissioners and the Lord Lieutenant and Sheriff of the county. The commissioners of supply were responsible for levying a 'police assessment' to finance the force and a key role of the police committee was to appoint a chief constable who was responsible for the day-to-day activities of the force, and for appointing and dismissing constables.

The 1967 Police (Scotland) Act permitted police forces to amalgamate and this process of consolidation reduced the number of forces from 49 in 1945 to 22 in 1968 (Gordon, 1980: 30). The 1973 Local Government (Scotland) Act further reduced the number of forces to eight – six covered areas controlled by one regional authority and two covered more than one regional authority. These forces are maintained either by a police authority or a joint police board. The universal introduction of a unitary system of local government for Scotland that was created by the 1994 Local Government etc. (Scotland) Act did not affect the structure of policing.

Since 1999, policing has been a devolved responsibility to the Scottish government that comes under the overall jurisdiction of the Cabinet Secretary for Justice. In June 2009 there were in excess of 17,000 police officers in Scotland and around 6,500 civilian employees. There are no PCSOs in Scotland, but the delivery of local policing involves the use of community wardens who are funded by local government. The overall cost of policing is above £1 billion a year (HMIC Scotland, 2009: para. 1.7).

See also: Police Service England and Wales, Police Service Northern Ireland

References and further reading

Donnelly, D. and Scott, K. (eds) (2005) *Policing Scotland.* Cullompton, Devon: Willan Publishing.

HMIC Scotland (2009) *Independent Review of Policing: A Report for the Cabinet Secretary for Justice.* Edinburgh: HMIC Scotland.

Gordon, P. (1980) *Policing Scotland.* Glasgow: Scottish Council of Civil Liberties.

Police Staff Associations

The Police Staff Associations consist of a number of organizations that represent various groupings within the police service. These were traditionally based around rank structure (consisting of the Association of Chief Police Officers (ACPO), the Police Federation, and the Police Superintendent's Association) but in recent years have been joined by a number of single-issue organizations that represent interests shared by a number of officers regardless of rank.

The origins of the Association of Chief Police Officers (ACPO) date from the formation of the County Chief Constables' Club in 1858 and the Chief Constables' Association of England and Wales in 1896 (which represented the chief officers of urban forces). These two bodies amalgamated in 1948 to form ACPO and the Royal Ulster Constabulary was incorporated in 1970. The organization consists of the most senior ranks of the police service (assistant chief constable and above) which numbered 280 in 2009. ACPO is funded by a Home Office grant, contributions from the 44 police authorities, membership subscriptions and from the proceeds of its annual exhibition. The senior ranks of the Scottish Police Service are represented by the Association of Chief Police Officers in Scotland (ACPOS).

During the nineteenth century the chief constables' organizations did little more than facilitate social contact between its members. However, the role of ACPO in the twentieth century became broader, seeking to promote the effectiveness, efficiency and professional interests of the police service in addition to safeguarding the individual and collective interests of its members. In 1996 these two functions were separated, with the newly formed Chief Police Officers' Staff Association becoming responsible for negotiating with the Police Negotiation Board on issues related to its members' salaries and conditions of service. This meant that henceforth ACPO could concentrate on the development of police policy both in the sense of influencing the activities pursued by individual forces (a role that had formerly been hindered by the doctrine of constabulary independence) and seeking to influence the content of centrally directed police policy (a function that was aided by its position as an 'insider' group within the Whitehall corridors of power).

Since the 1990s, ACPO committees have become extremely influential in formulating decisions regarding policing strategy and advising the government on the future direction of police policy (Bassett et al., 2009: 12). Its role in connection with both policy and performance evaluation have resulted in ACPO being a key centralizing influence on the police service (Jones, 2003: 615) and acting as its corporate voice.

The concerns of rank-and-file police officers are voiced by a different organization, the Police Federation for England and Wales. This body emerged as the consequence of the police strikes of 1918 and 1919 that were organized by the National Union of Police and Prison Officers. The resultant 1919 Police Act forbade police officers to join trade unions but set up the Police Federation as a statutory advisory body to represent the views of police officers (now up to the rank of chief inspector) on all matters related to their welfare and efficiency. Its work included negotiating on pay and conditions of service and it is consulted on the formulation of police regulations. The Police Federation of Northern Ireland and the Scottish Police

Federation perform similar functions elsewhere in the UK.

Like ACPO, the Police Federation has evolved from a staff association into an organization that seeks to exert influence on police and criminal justice policy. Unlike ACPO, it mainly performs this role from outside the corridors of power, a role that was developed after 1955 when it was granted the ability to levy a subscription from its members in order to conduct campaigning.

Initial Federation campaigns were concerned with issues such as police pay and support for the death penalty, but a watershed in its political role occurred during the 1970s when factors that included the increase of crime and the negative views held by some left-wing politicians towards the police prompted the Federation to more vigorously seek to influence public opinion. These campaigns witnessed the use of lobbying techniques allied with methods such as press advertising to appeal directly to the public over the heads of senior police officers and the government (McLaughlin and Murji, 1998). An example of this was the Federation's 1975 law and order campaign (McLaughlin and Murji, 1998) which sought to mobilize the silent majority in favour of tougher law and order policies. Campaigning also takes the form of rallies and demonstrations, such as the procession of police officers through central London in 2008 to voice opposition to the Home Secretary's decision not to backdate a pay award.

A third staff association that seeks to influence the policing agenda is the Police Superintendents' Association (PSA) of England and Wales. This was set up in 1920 to represent Superintendents and Chief Superintendents. It currently performs two key roles: to provide advice and support to its members and to contribute and influence police policy and practice at a national level. Initially the PSA was seen as little more than a senior officers' dining club but it subsequently pursued a more significant (if intermittent) role on policing and criminal justice policy (Savage *et al.*, 2000).

The PSA is the main mouthpiece for BCU commanders and its influence over police policy may increase should the position occupied by these officers in delivering the local police agenda increase in future years. The Association of Scottish Police Superintendents and the Police Superintendents' Association of Northern Ireland perform similar functions elsewhere in the UK.

In addition to the three staff associations organized around the rank structure of the police service, there are a number of single organizations. An objective shared by many of them (termed Police Diversity Staff Support Associa-

tions (DSSAs)) is to promote the principle of diversity within the service. Some of these benefit from government financial funding, others do not.

In 1994 a Black Police Association was launched within the Metropolitan Police and it became a national organization, the National Black Police Association, in 1998. The role of this body was initially concerned with the operations of the internal aspects of the police service (especially in connection with racial discrimination and the high wastage rate of minority ethnic officers) but its activities have subsequently extended into campaigning outside of the service to voice the concerns of the Black community and ensure that all persons receive fair treatment from the police service.

The National Association of Muslim Police was launched in July 2007 as a national representative body of Muslim Police Officers and Police Staff within the United Kingdom. Its specific aims are to promote recruitment, retention and progression of Muslim Police Officers and Staff within the service and to support the welfare and religious needs of its members. Its role also extends beyond the service to promote an understanding of Islam within the police service and the wider community, thereby contributing to community cohesion.

The British Association for Women in Policing was set up in

1987 to promote awareness of issues that specifically affected women in the police service and to contribute to debates on issues of concern to all officers by providing the female perspective. It performs these functions by organizing events and meetings and through liaison with the Home Office.

See also: Basic Command Units, Police Service England and Wales

References and further reading

Bassett, D., Haldenby, A., Thraves, L. and Truss, E. (2009) *A New Force.* London: Reform.

Jones, T. (2003) 'The Governance and Accountability of Policing' in T. Newburn (ed.) *Handbook of Policing.* Cullompton, Devon: Willan Publishing.

McLaughlin, E. and Murji, K. (1998) 'Resistance Through Representation: "Storylines", Advertising and Police Federation Campaigns', *Policing and Society,* 8: 367–99.

Savage, S., Charman, S. and Cope, S. (2000) *Policing and the Power of Persuasion.* London: Blackstone Press.

Police Superintendents' Association of England and Wales

See **Police Staff Associations**

policing by consent (development in nineteenth century)

Policing by consent is a style of policing which seeks to secure the active support of members of the general public. This objective distinguishes it from policing by coercion in which the police are viewed as servants of the government who do not require to cultivate good relationships with those they police.

The new system of policing did not have the immediate support of the general public and there was opposition towards it drawn from all social classes. It was thus necessary for the new system of policing to sell itself to the general public. The principle of policing by consent emphasized the importance of the police service operating with the support of the public. The objective underpinned a number of developments affecting the delivery of policing in its formative years in the nineteenth century.

Outside of London policing was organized locally and controlled by local people who were initially drawn from the property-owning classes. Watch committees in the towns and magistrates in rural areas exercised considerable authority over policing in its formative years in order to dispel the impression that the new system would be the agent of the government, to the detriment of the rights of the people.

One of the main objectives of policing was to prevent crime and this task was performed by police officers patrolling small geographic areas on foot (termed the 'home beat' method of policing) based on the belief that their physical presence would deter the commission of crime. They were not encouraged to pursue a more active role within the community to avoid unnecessary intrusions into people's lives which might undermine support for the reformed system of policing. The emphasis that was placed on preventive policing was at the expense of detective work which although not a neglected function of policing was given a relatively low profile in early nineteenth-century police forces.

The principle of policing by consent was furthered by the requirement that the performance of professional police officers in England and Wales should be subject to the rule of law. Police officers were required to use formalized procedures against those who had broken the law and apply it without fear or favour. Additionally, at the outset of professional policing, officers were given no special powers with which to discharge their duties since this was thought to be inconsistent with the citizens' exercise of civil and political liberties. Accordingly, the police were initially able to exercise only common law powers.

Minimum force was an important aspect underpinning policing by consent. This especially affected the weaponry with which they were provided. Police officers were not routinely armed and merely carried a truncheon for their personal protection. The absence of weaponry which could be used in an offensive posture was designed to ensure that when the police were required to intervene to uphold law and order they would initially rely on 'persuasion, advice and warning' (Reith, 1956: 287) and only if this failed would they use the minimum degree of physical force that was required to achieve their objective.

The recruitment policies adopted by new police forces also sought to advance the goal of policing by consent. Initially police forces recruited their personnel from the working class (save for the most senior ranks of the service who were frequently ex-army officers). This policy was partly pursued for economic reasons (since working-class recruits could be paid less than members of higher social groups) but was also a means through which members of the working class could be incorporated into the machinery of the newly emerging capitalist state. The tendency for officers below the rank of chief constable to be selected from serving policemen offered the possibility of police work as an avenue of social mobility for working-class people. Additionally, police officers drawn from the lower end of the social scale might find it easier to relate to fellow members of the working class with whom they came into contact and to discharge their duties without displaying a sense of class hatred towards them.

Working-class recruitment also ensured that police officers would act deferentially to those who were their social superiors and act in accordance with their instructions which especially sought to regulate vagrants and disorderly behaviour caused by prostitution and drunkenness which offended the propertied classes. This was an important factor in securing the consent of 'respectable' people to the new system of policing.

Policing by consent also furthered the 'service role' of policing. The role to protect life and property was of most benefit to the wealthy who owned property. Thus in order to 'sell' policing to a wider audience (and in particular to the working classes), the police function extended beyond law enforcement. This resulted in the police performing a wide range of activities (many of which were not crime-related) in an attempt to befriend the community and to dispel the image that police work was exclusively concerned with the exercise of coercive authority against the lower social orders.

The extent to which policing by consent was achieved by the end of the nineteenth century is the subject of academic debate. The view of orthodox police historians was that initial opposition to the police culminated in the 1830s and that their success in combating crime and disorder enabled them to overcome any serious resistance to their presence on the streets and secure the cooperation (hence the consent) of most sections of society (Critchley, 1978: 55–6).

However, this view has been challenged by revisionist historians who emphasized that the motive for the introduction of a new policing system in the nineteenth century was 'the maintenance of order required by the capitalist class' which meant that the attention of the police was directed at all actions that threatened to undermine it – 'crime, riot, political dissidence and public morality' (Reiner, 1985: 25).

Revisionist accounts thus reject the orthodox position that hostility towards the new police was a relatively short-lived phenomenon and instead conclude that consent was determined by a person's position on the social ladder. The level of consent was greatest from the property-owning middle classes (including those who comprised the petty bourgeoisie such as shopkeepers) who stood to gain most from police activities. However, working-class hostility was more enduring, characterized for those at the lower end of the social ladder by 'passive acquiescence', broken by frequent outbreaks of conflict throughout the nineteenth century (Brogden, 1982: 202–28).

See also: Bourbon system of policing, new policing system (development in nineteenth century), Police Service England and Wales

References and further reading

Brogden, M. (1982) *The Police: Autonomy and Consent.* London: Academic Press.

Critchley, T. (1978) *A History of Police in England and Wales.* London: Constable.

Reiner, R. (1985) *The Politics of the Police.* Brighton: Wheatsheaf Books.

Reith, C. (1956) *A New Study of Police History.* London: Oliver and Boyd.

Storch, R. (1976) 'The Policeman as Domestic Missionary', *Journal of Social History*, IX(4), Summer: 481–509.

Policing Performance Assessment Framework

See **Best Value**

policy transfer

Policy transfer is a process 'in which knowledge about policies, administrative arrangements, institutions and ideas in one political setting (past or present) is used in the development of policies, administrative arrangements, institutions and ideas in another political setting' (Dolowitz and Marsh, 2000: 5). In connection with criminal justice policy, policy transfer refers to the deliberate adoption by one country of policies and practices that have been pioneered in another.

Many contemporary policies and practices in the UK relating to crime control and criminal justice policy derive from initiatives that were developed in the United States. These include the extension of mandatory sentences in the 1997 Crime (Sentences) Act which embraced the 'three strikes and you're out' approach to domestic burglars that originated from an initiative pioneered in the State of Washington in 1993, 'load shedding' that enabled some prisons in England and Wales to be managed by private sector companies rather than HM Prison Service, the adoption of situational approaches to crime prevention and the adoption of problem-oriented and zero tolerance policing methods in England and Wales.

Approaches to policy transfer distinguish between policy transfer and policy convergence (Newburn and Jones, 2006). The former refers to similarities in the approaches adopted by two countries that derive from a deliberate emulation by one of the practices developed in another. This situation may arise from a range of factors that include international networking arrangements achieved through mechanisms such as think-tanks. However, similarities in the approaches of two countries may derive from factors other than deliberate copying of one from the other and convergence may derive from factors such as shared cultural or political conditions.

Additionally, the crime control policies adopted by individual countries may converge for reasons derived from globalization that has resulted in the emergence of criminal enterprise operating across national boundaries. These necessitate the emergence of regional and global responses to crime through agencies that include Europol.

See also: crime prevention, Europol, new public management, prisons

References and further reading

Dolowitz, D. and Marsh, D. (2000) 'Learning from Abroad: The Role of Policy Transfer in Contemporary Policy-Making. *Governance*, 13(1): 5–24.
Newburn, T. and Jones, T. (2006) *Policy Transfer and Criminal Justice. Exploring U.S. Influence over British Crime Control Policy.* Buckinghamshire: Open University Press.

political oversight of the criminal justice system

Political oversight refers to the control that is exerted over the separate agencies that comprise the criminal justice system and the accountability of these agencies to the executive and legislative branches of government.

The activities of the criminal justice system are superintended by the executive and legislative branches of government. The executive branch of government is responsible for setting the priorities and objectives of individual criminal justice agencies and for financing the tasks they each perform. The legislative branch of government monitors the activities performed by the criminal justice agencies and may hold these agencies and their political leaders accountable for perceived failings or omissions.

Central government control over the criminal justice system is exercised through three departments: the Attorney General's Office, the Home Office and the Ministry of Justice.

The Attorney General's Office houses the Attorney General and the Solicitor General. These, together with the Advocate General for Scotland, comprise the Law Officers of the Crown.

The law officers perform three major functions. They act as legal advisers to the government with responsibility for all Crown litigation both domestic and international, including issues arising from EU and international law that may affect the UK. Second, they exercise overall responsibility for the work of the Treasury Solicitor's Department, the Crown Prosecution Service, the Serious Fraud Office, the Revenue and Customs Prosecution Office and Her Majesty's Crown Prosecution Service Inspectorate. They exercise a statutory responsibility to superintend the operations of the Director of Public Prosecutions (and the Director of Public Prosecutions for Northern Ireland), the Director of the Serious Fraud Office and the Director of the Revenue and Customs Prosecution Office.

Finally, the law officers also act as independent guardians of the public interest. This entails functions that include appealing against unduly lenient sentences, referring cases to the Court of Appeal on a point of law and bringing proceedings under the Contempt of Court Act. Additionally, other functions may be allocated to the Attorney General, one of which has been to act as Ministerial Champion for the Narrowing the Justice Gap initiative which seeks to bring more offenders to justice.

The remaining responsibilities for the criminal justice system are exercised by the Home Office (sometimes referred to as the Home Department) and the Ministry of Justice. The former is headed by the Home Secretary and the latter by the Secretary of State for Justice who also occupies the position of Lord Chancellor (although the Minister is not required to sit in the House of Lords).

The work of the Home Office was revamped in 2007 and it now exercises responsibility for policing, anti-social behaviour, drugs policy, crime prevention, immigration and passports, asylum and identity, security and counter terrorism. The contemporary significance of terrorism means that homeland security is an important aspect of the work of the Home Office and in 2007 an Office for Security and Counter Terrorism was set up within this department to take responsibility for implementing the long-term strategy to counter international terrorism (CONTEST). Additionally, a new research, information and communications unit was set up in the department to focus on ideas and values.

The Ministry of Justice was created in May 2007. It replaced the Department for Constitutional Affairs (which had itself replaced the Lord Chancellor's Department in 2003) and has responsibility for policy affecting the criminal, civil, family and administrative justice system (including sentencing policy).

Much of the operational work of the Home Office and Ministry of Justice is conducted by executive agencies. These were developed as a consequence of the Ibbs Report (Ibbs, 1988) and sought to separate policy planning and service delivery. Executive agencies are characterized by possessing a high degree of operational autonomy whilst working within guidelines, financial constraints and performance targets imposed by central government departments to which they are ultimately accountable.

The Home Office has three executive agencies: the UK Border Agency, the Identity and Passport Service and the Criminal Records Bureau.

The UK Border Agency is responsible for securing the UK borders and controlling migration in the United Kingdom. It manages border control for the United Kingdom by enforcing immigration and customs regulations. It also considers applications for permission to enter or stay in the United Kingdom and handles requests for citizenship and asylum. A major development affecting the work of this agency is the e-borders project which aims to utilize electronic technology to collect and analyse information on everyone who travels to and from the UK. This will be used in conjunction with other technology to identify travellers, especially biometrics.

The Identity and Passport Service is responsible for issuing UK passports and identity cards and for registering births, marriages and deaths in England and Wales. The role of the Criminal Records Bureau is to operate a system to enable the background of those seeking to work with children or vulnerable adults to be checked in order to ensure the suitability of those recruited into positions of trust.

The Ministry of Justice houses two key executive agencies: the National Offender Management Service (NOMS) and Her Majesty's Courts Service (HMCS).

The National Offender Management Service (NOMS) was created in 2004 and brings together the headquarters of the Probation Service and HM Prison Service (both of which were historically located within the Home Office) to enable more effective delivery of services and in particular to provide for end-to-end offender management. Prison and probation services ensure the sentences of the courts are properly carried out and work with offenders to tackle the causes of their offending behaviour.

Her Majesty's Courts Service is responsible for providing administration of the criminal, civil and family courts in England and Wales. A key purpose of HMCS is to ensure speedy access to justice for all who are parties to civil disputes or criminal proceedings. The administration of tribunals across the UK is provided for by a different body, the Tribunals Service whose key purpose is to provide administrative support for those who hear cases and determine appeals.

The Ministry of Justice also houses the Office for Criminal Justice Reform. This provides support to secure the joined-up delivery of criminal justice policy and reports to the Home Office, Ministry of Justice and the Attorney General's Office. The OCJR is responsible for progressing improvements to the criminal justice system put forward by the National Criminal Justice Board which is made up of ministers, heads of criminal justice services and senior civil servants. Forty-two Local Criminal Justice Boards coordinate activity and share responsibility for delivering criminal justice in their areas.

Parliamentary scrutiny of the criminal justice system is secured through the work of two Select Committees of the House of Commons: the Home Affairs Committee and the Justice Committee. Additionally, the Joint Committee on Human Rights, composed of members of both Houses of Parliament, investigates matters that frequently have a bearing on the operations of key criminal justice agencies. These committees hear evidence and publish reports which are frequently the subject of parliamentary debates. The House of Lords European Union Select Committee has also initiated enquiries into issues affecting policing and security throughout the EU.

See also: accountability, criminal record, Crown Prosecution Service, joined-up government, National Offender Management Service, prisons

References and further reading

Attorney General's Office – http://www.attorneygeneral.gov.uk/

European Union Select Committee – http://www.parliament.uk/parlia mentary_committees/lords_eu_ select_committee.cfm

Home Affairs Committee – http://www.parliament.uk/parlia mentary_committees/home_ affairs_committee.cfm

Home Office – http://www. homeoffice.gov.uk/

Ibbs, Sir R. (1988) *Improving Management in Government: The Next Steps.* London: HMSO.

Joint Committee on Human Rights – http://www.parliament.uk/ parliamentary_committees/joint_ committee_on_human_rights. cfm

Justice Committee – http://www. parliament.uk/parliamentary_ committees/justice.cfm

Ministry of Justice – http://www. justice.gov.uk/

pre-sentence report

See **sentences of the criminal courts**

prisons

A prison houses offenders who have been given a custodial sentence by the courts as the result of having committed a crime that requires their removal from the community.

Prisons initially existed as institutions to house those awaiting sentence or the implementation of it (either execution or transportation) or to hold debtors and those guilty of relatively minor crimes. Under the influence of late eighteenth- and early nineteenth-century evangelical reformers (such as Elizabeth Fry and John Howard) and utilitarian thinkers (such as Jeremy Bentham) prisons assumed a new purpose as institutions which could alter the attitudes and behaviour of criminals. The 1779 Penitentiary Act indicated this change in their purpose.

Towards the end of the nineteenth century a new approach, that of rehabilitation, emerged as a key function of prisons. The difference between reform and rehabilitation was that the latter promoted a more positive role for the state to bring about changes to those offenders who were receptive to changing their ways. The Gladstone Report of 1895 was a key development in promoting the role of prisons as rehabilitative institutions (see Hudson, 1987: 3–11). It was based on the belief that prisoners were sent to these institutions *as* punish-ment rather than *for* punishment and sought to turn convicted offenders out of prison better men and women, both physically and morally, than when they came in (Gladstone, 1895). The report's key provisions were incorporated into the 1898 Prisons Act.

The emphasis placed on prisons as mechanisms to secure the rehabilitation of prisoners was underpinned by positivist assumptions that it was legitimate to focus remedial attention on the individual with a view to treating the causes of their offending behaviour. This approach gave rise to the 'treatment model' that was the main aim of prisons for much of the twentieth century.

The individualist philosophy which 1979–97 Conservative governments promoted had implications for the attitude adopted towards those who broke the law. The emphasis placed by the treatment model on rehabilitation gave way to an approach that sought to imbue punishment with a retributivist objective (which was termed the justice model). This approach was reinforced by a political goal to 'get tough with criminals' which placed prisons at the forefront of Conservative penal policy. It was argued that 'prison works' (Howard, 1993) in particular by the incapacitation of offenders who could not commit crime whilst they were locked up. This caused prison numbers to increase and had a direct impact on the prisoners' environment since it resulted in overcrowding.

Policy changes also affected conditions within prisons. The regime associated with the treatment model was replaced by a harsher, 'decent but austere' environment that could be presented as additional proof that those who committed crime were being appropriately punished for their wrongdoings. A number of high-profile escapes in the early 1990s resulted in renewed emphasis being placed on security. This approach was directed by the Learmont Report (1995) which viewed custody as the primary purpose of prisons and put forward 127 recommendations to achieve this (Home Office, 1995:139–42).

However, the emphasis placed on tough regimes was balanced by reforms seeking to make the prison regime fairer to its inmates. A major riot and siege in Strangeways Prison, Manchester, in 1990, resulted in a report by Lord Woolf in which he argued there was the need for a balance to be struck within prisons between security, control and justice (Home Office, 1991: 17). The government endorsed some of these recommendations including those related to contracts for prisoners, accredited standards and the establishment of a prison ombudsman.

Post-1997 Labour governments continued with many aspects of their predecessor's policies and prison numbers continued to rise – totalling 83,000 in 2009. There have, however, been certain differences. Jack Straw (Labour's Home Secretary between 1997 and 2002) was especially concerned to ensure that prison regimes were constructive. This approach emphasized the importance of purposeful activities.

The prison service is administered by the Ministry of Justice. Most prisons are in the public sector but there are a small number of privately managed prisons. In 2008 there were 126 public sector prisons in England and Wales and 11 private sector prisons. All prisons are managed by a service level agreement between the relevant Director of Offender Management and the prison.

On entry into a prison, prisoners are given a security category (A, B, C or D). Categories A, B and C are housed in closed prisons and category D are placed in open prisons. A similar categorization applies to female prisoners. The interests of prisoners are safeguarded by independent monitoring boards (one for each prison) and the Prison and Probation Ombudsman. The Prison Inspectorate has also traditionally exerted influence over the manner in which establishments treat prisoners.

It costs around £24,000 per person per year to keep an inmate in prison and the total cost of the prison service is around £2.0 billion per year. The extent of recidivism questions whether prisons provide value for money and is one rationale for the use of non-custodial alternatives delivered in the community.

See also: cognitive behavioural pro- grammes, National Offender Man- agement Service, non-custodial sentences, panopticon, punishment (aims of), purposeful activities, recidivism

References and further reading

Home Office, (1991) *Prison Disturbances 1990: Report of an Inquiry by the Rt Hon Lord Justice Woolf (part I and II) and His Honour Judge Stephen Tumin (part I)*. London: HMSO, Cm 1456, the Woolf Report.

Home Office (1995) *Review of Prison Service Security in England and Wales and the Escape from Parkhurst Prison on Tuesday 3rd January 1995*. London: HMSO, Cm 3020, the Learmont Report.

Gladstone, H. (1895) *Report from the Departmental Committee on Prisons*. London: HMSO, Sessional Paper 1895, c. 7702.

Howard, M. (1993) Speech to the Conservative Party Conference, Blackpool, 6 October.

Hudson, B. (1987) *Justice Through Punishment: A Critique of the 'Justice' Model of Correction*. Basingstoke: Macmillan.

Ramsbotham, D. (2005) *Prisongate – The Shocking State of Britain's Prisons and the Need for Visionary Change*. London: Free Press.

Probation Service

The Probation Service was estab- lished to advise, assist and befriend those who had been sentenced by the courts in order to change their behaviour and avoid short terms of imprisonment.

The origins of the present probation service date from the 1907 Probation of Offenders Act. This placed probation work on a statutory footing by introducing probation orders and authorizing courts to appoint and pay probation officers. Probation was available to all courts and applied to most offences provided that the offender agreed to the process and also consented to abide by standard conditions that included maintaining regular contact with the probation officer. In 1925 the appointment of at least one proba- tion officer to each court became a mandatory requirement.

The work performed by the probation service has experienced numerous changes in the latter half of the twentieth century. Work carried out in prisons assumed considerable importance after 1966 and the introduction of parole in 1968 extended the work of proba- tion officers to the supervision of offenders following their release from prison. New court sentences such as community service orders introduced by the 1972 Criminal Justice Act added to the work of probation officers who were responsible for supervising these and other non-custodial sentences that were subsequently introduced.

Towards the end of the 1990s the service's focus on supervising individual offenders to secure their rehabilitation was supplanted by a new emphasis on offender management whose key aim was to protect the public from the risks posed by offending behaviour. This has been described as a transition from 'old' to 'new' penology (Feeley and Simon, 1992).

Offenders were evaluated by a standardized risk assessment tool termed OASys (Offender Assessment System) and on the basis of this would be directed by probation officers to accredited cognitive and behavioural programmes. This assessment also helped to determine the level of resources (the 'tiering framework') that was required for the case management of individual offenders (Burnett et al., 2007: 222).

Accredited programmes derived from the Home Office's Effective Practice Initiative (1998) which sought to promote the use of evidence-based practice into the work of the probation service. They were accompanied by targets and performance indicators covering issues such as attendance rates and completion. Although these developments tended to marginalize the traditional form of one-to-one counselling, this remained as an element of case management in which some of the skills became re-badged as specific approaches such as 'motivational interviewing' and 'mentoring' (Burnett et al., 2007: 218).

Initially, the probation service had a local orientation. It was administered through 54 areas, each governed by a Probation Committee composed of magistrates, judges, local authority representatives and local persons. The Probation Committee's role was to manage the service provided in their area. However, the role of the Home Office increased after 1936 through the establishment of a Central Advisory Committee that provided for services that included inspection and training. Subsequent changes derived from the new public management agenda served to enhance the degree of centralized control, an important development being the publication of National Standards for the Probation Service in 1992.

The structure of the service was significantly affected by the 2000 Criminal Justice and Court Services Act. This legislation established a unified National Probation Service for England and Wales, which was set up on April 2001. Its operations were conducted through 42 areas which coincided with those used by the police service, CPS and the courts. These areas are grouped into ten regions across England and Wales. The service was also affected by the formation of the National Offender Management Service (NOMS) following the 2003 Carter Review.

Further changes affecting the structure of the service were made by the 2007 Offender Management Act which provided for the creation of Probation Trusts to buy services related to probation supervision, tackling offending behaviour and providing for other forms of specialist support. This has resulted in the service in England and Wales being currently administered by 6 probation trusts and 36 Local Probation Boards.

See also: accredited programmes, assessment tool, cognitive behavioural programmes, National Offender Management Service, new public management, noncustodial sentences, sentences of the criminal courts

References and further reading

Burnett, R., Baker, K. and Roberts, C. (2007) 'Assessment, Supervision and Intervention: Fundamental Practice in Probation' in L. Gelsthorpe and R. Morgan (eds) *Handbook of Probation.* Cullompton, Devon: Willan Publishing.

Feeley, M. and Simon, J. (1992) 'The New Penology: Notes on the Emerging Strategy of Correctionalism and its Implications', *Criminology*, 30(4): 449–74.

Raynor, P. and Vanstone, M. (2002) *Understanding Community Penalties: Probation, Policy and Social Change.* Buckingham: Open University Press.

punishment (aims of)

Those whom a court finds guilty of having committed a crime will have a penalty inflicted upon them in the name of the state. The scientific study of punishment is known as penology; it is concerned with the motives and methods used to punish offenders and prevent crime. An important aspect of penology concerns the theories and purposes of punishment.

There are various purposes that might be served by inflicting a penalty on a wrongdoer. These include reductivism, retributivism, denunciation and the reintegration of offenders into society.

Reductivism views punishment as a means to prevent crime from taking place in the future. This approach is associated with a range of strategies that include deterrence, incapacitation or programmes that seek to secure the rehabilitation of offenders.

Deterrence may be individual or general. Individual deterrence seeks to influence the future behaviour of a convicted offender whereas general deterrence seeks to influence the future actions of the public at large. Individual deterrence may be delivered through means that include harsh custodial regimes (imposing conditions to which offenders will not wish to return) and general deterrence is often associated with severe penalties that are designed to dissuade criminal actions.

Deterrence views offenders as rational beings who calculate the costs and benefits of their behaviour, and punishment is designed to ensure that the potential costs outweigh any advantages that might be derived from committing a crime. A major problem with this approach is that it ignores the possibility that crime may be a spontaneous act, propelled by factors that override logical considerations. General deterrence also assumes that the behaviour of all members of the general public can be influenced by similar constraints and that it is possible to precisely identify what level of punishment will prevent a criminal act from being committed.

Incapacitation inflicts a penalty on an offender in order to protect society from his or her future actions. This will typically entail removing convicted offenders from society (a goal that was historically implemented through transporta-tion but which is now associated with imprisonment).

Incapacitation may also involve various forms of pre-emptive action, targeting persons deemed to be potential offenders, even if criminal behaviour has not occurred when the intervention takes place. This latter approach has been associated with attempts to identify factors that predispose individuals to commit crime and then to implement remedial action.

Punishment may also be a mechanism to bring about the reform and rehabilitation of those who have committed crime. This approach seeks to change the personal values and habits of criminals so that their future behaviour conforms to mainstream social standards.

Penal reformers in the late eighteenth and early nineteenth centuries (whether driven by evangelical or utilitarian impulses) viewed prisons as arenas in which bad people could be transformed into good and useful members of society.

Contemporary prisons augment the punitive aspects of imprisonment with other initiatives including cognitive behavioural progammes and purposeful activities that are designed to bring about the reform and rehabilitation of offenders, but there are several factors affecting the prison environment that serve to undermine this ideal. Reform and rehabilitation may also be delivered through a range of community-based penalties.

A particular problem with reductivist strategies is whether the future behaviour of offenders can be altered through punishment, whatever form it takes. While punishment may temporarily suppress anti-social behaviour, once the punishment is removed the previous behaviour may return (Huesmann and Podolski, 2003: 77). Accordingly, it is also necessary to identify and address the factors which underpin that behaviour in order to prevent future offending: 'people must "internalise" mechanisms that regulate behaviour so that in the absence of the threat of punishment, they will choose not to act aggressively – not because of the threat of punishment, but because they agree with the behaviour which has been taught' (Huesmann and Podolski, 2003: 78). The problems inherent in seeking to change behaviour through punishment have led many who advocate restorative justice to disassociate this response to crime with punishment.

The various strategies associated with reductivism focus their concern on future behaviour. An alternative approach is retributivism. This is backward-looking, in which punishment is justified in relation to offending behaviour which has already taken place.

Many societies have based their response to crime on the principle of retributivism. The *lex talionis* was referred to in the Bible whereby the response to crime was of an equivalent nature to the crime itself ('an eye for an eye and a tooth for a tooth'). Other retributive penal systems were based upon a proportionate response to crime, in which the punishment reflected the seriousness of the crime (as this was perceived by either society or the victim).

Retributivism insists 'that punishment is justified solely by the offender's dessert and blameworthiness in committing the offence' (Lacey, 2003: 176) – criminals are punished because they deserve it. This approach to punishment is akin to vengeance since pain is inflicted on transgressors for pain's sake rather than from a desire to bring about their rehabilitation (Lacey, 2003: 176): it enables society to 'get its own back' on those who commit criminal acts. A difficulty with this approach is that the deliberate infliction of violence by the state may legitimize the use of violence by its citizens.

The association of retribution with vengeance made this response to crime an unpopular one for much of the twentieth century in Western societies but it was resurrected (termed 'new' retributivism) because problems were perceived in the sentencing policies associated with the reductivist goal of rehabilitation that were fashionable in a number of post-war Western societies. New retributivism focused on the offence an offender had committed, asserted that the response to crime should be proportionate to the seriousness of the offence and viewed punishment as the main aim of the penal system. Depriving an individual of his or her liberty through imprisonment is a key aspect of contemporary retributivist approaches to crime in England and Wales.

A third aim of punishment is denunciation. This is closely associated with retributivism as it focuses on a past criminal act. The punishment meted out to an offender reflects the seriousness with which the community views the offence and provides it with a mechanism thorough which it can express its sentiments thereby reinforcing the official disapproval of the act that has been committed with the community's social censure. This implies that punishment is justified not because it influences the behaviour of others not to commit similar acts but simply because it expresses society's abhorrence of crime.

However, public sentiments regarding how a particular crime should be dealt with may be out of line with the views of officials, in particular with politicians (who make the law) and sentencers (who implement it). The ability of the public to air their concerns (for example on what they regard as an over-lenient sentence to a specific crime) may encourage public debate that helps to set the boundaries of society – 'we collectively define what sort of people we are by denouncing the type of people we are not' (Davies, 1993: 15).

A fourth aim of punishment is that of enabling the offender to make good the harm that he or she has done by some form of reparation, either to the victim or to the community in general. This aim is associated with a further objective of punishment, that of securing the reintegration of offenders into society. Restorative justice is an important mechanism through which this aim may be accomplished.

See also: cognitive behavioural programmes, non-custodial sentences, panopticon, prisons, purposeful activities, restorative justice

References and further reading

Cavadino, M. and Dignan, J. (2007) *The Penal System: An Introduction.* London: Sage, fourth edition.

Davies, M. (1993) *Punishing Criminals: Developing Community-based Intermediate Sanctions.* Westport, CT: Greenwood.

Hudson, B. (2003) *Understanding Justice.* Buckingham: Open University Press, second edition.

Huesmann, L. and Podolski, C. (2003) 'Punishment: A Psychological Perspective' in S. McConville (ed.) *The Use of Punishment.* Cullompton, Devon: Willan Publishing.

Lacey, N. (2003) 'Penal Theory and Penal Practice: A Communitarian Approach', in S. McConville (ed.) *The Use of Punishment.* Cullompton, Devon: Willan Publishing.

Tonry, M. 2004: *Punishment and Politics: Evidence and Emulation in the Making of English Crime Control Policy.* Cullompton, Devon: Willan Publishing.

purposeful activities

The term 'purposeful activity' describes a wide range of pursuits that are available to prisoners when not confined to their cells. These activities include prison work, education and training courses, physical education, cognitive behavioural programmes, anti-bullying initiatives, family visits, and performing work in prison gardens and workshops (Home Affairs Committee, 2005).

Purposeful activities are designed to provide prisoners with constructive use of their time whilst in prison. They are integral to the maintenance of order within these institutions and an essential aid to the rehabilitation of inmates when released. They are not, however, always delivered effectively.

The rehabilitation of most prisoners is heavily dependent on the acquisition of skills that will boost employment prospects upon release. However, prisons have not consistently offered medium- and long-term offenders meaningful educational or training opportunities. Education was traditionally viewed as a privilege rather than a right whose provision varied from one prison to another. The nature of the subjects taught were not necessarily appropriate to prisoners, many of whom lacked basic literacy and numeracy skills. This issue was addressed by the 1997 Labour government that concentrated prison education resources on basic skills. In 2002/3 over 41,000 basic skills qualifications were gained by prisoners (Home Office, 2004: 4).

Work conducted within prisons was traditionally associated with menial tasks that seemed more concerned with aiding the passage of time than with providing work-relevant skills. It was argued that 'production and manufacture in prison is likely to be inefficient and in many respects is "primitive" and "pre-capitalist"' (Matthews, 1995: 44). However, changes to this situation have been introduced and prisoners became able to earn above the average 'prison wage' by performing work for outside companies. This was aided by the 1996 Prisoners' Earnings Act that provided for the payment of realistic wages.

Recent developments to aid prisoners to find work upon release have included the provision of facilities (both within prisons and the community) to obtain key work and training skills qualifications, and the Custody to Work initiative that was launched in 2000. This was spearheaded by the Custody to Work Unit whose prime responsibility was to deliver the objective of the resettlement of prisoners in the community using the mechanism of resettlement partnerships. By 2002/3 30 per cent of prisoners were released with a job or training place to go to (Home Office, 2004: 5).

Continued problems in the provision of purposeful activities were highlighted by a study in 2005 which stated that

> disturbingly high proportions of prisoners are engaged in little or no purposeful activity. Very few prisons provide for adequate amounts of purposeful activity across all, or most, of the main categories of such activities. The reasons for this include overcrowding and disruptions to education, vocational and treatment programmes caused by prisoner transfer, reducing prison staffing and generally poor admin-

istration. The consequences for prisoners are too many hours 'banged up' in their cells, with an adverse impact on their mental and physical health, and missed opportunities for rehabilitation.

> (Home Affairs Committee, 2005)

See also: cognitive behavioural programmes, prisons, recidivism

References and further reading

Home Affairs Committee (2005) *Rehabilitation of Prisoners.* First Report, Session 2004/5, House of Commons Paper 193.

Home Office (2004) *Reducing Crime – Changing Lives: The Government's Plans for Transforming the Management of Offenders.* London: Home Office.

Matthews, R. (1995) *Doing Time: An Introduction to the Sociology of Imprisonment.* Basingstoke: Macmillan.

Ramsbotham, D. (2005) *Prisongate – The Shocking State of Britain's Prisons and the Need for Visionary Change.* London: Free Press.

Q

Queen's Counsel

See **legal profession England and Wales**

Queen's evidence

See **informants (grasses/super-grasses)**

R

reassurance policing

Reassurance policing was coined in the United States (Bahn, 1974) 'and has become a catch-all category encompassing a variety of ideas including public engagement by the police as well as public satisfaction with and confidence in policing' (Singer, 2004: 1).

The reassurance agenda was promoted after an assessment conducted by HMIC (2001) and was followed by a number of initiatives that included the safer neighbourhoods programme. The National Reassurance Policing Programme was initiated between 2003 and 2005 and entailed the adoption of neighbourhood policing in a small number of trial sites in eight police forces. This was designed to allay fears through an increased visibility of a uniformed presence in communities. It also emphasized the importance of involvement with the public in selecting problems and designing remedies for them.

The National Reassurance Policing Programme additionally devoted particular attention to tackling what were termed 'signal crimes and disorders'. These were events and incidents (that included anti-social behaviour) that had 'a disproportionate impact upon levels of fear in a community, because they are interpreted as warning signals about the distribution of risks and threats' (Ditton and Innes, 2005: 608). They thus exerted an adverse impact on people's sense of security and caused them to alter their beliefs or behaviour. Success in tackling such issues would thus have a disproportionate impact on neighbourhoods, especially in alleviating their fear of crime, and would serve to strengthen community cohesion.

See also: neighbourhood policing, Police Community Support Officers, Police Service England and Wales, policy transfer

References and further reading

Bahn, C. (1974) 'The Reassurance Factor in Police Patrol', *Criminology*, 12(3): 338–45.

Ditton, J. and Innes, M. (2005) 'The Role of Perception Intervention in the Management of Crime Fear' in N. Tilley (ed.) *Handbook of Crime Prevention and Community Safety.* Cullompton, Devon: Willan Publishing.

Her Majesty's Inspectorate of Constabulary (HMIC) (2001) *Open All Hours – A Thematic Inspection Report on the Role of Police Visibility and Accessibility in Public Reassurance.* London: Her Majesty's Inspectorate of Constabulary.

Singer, L. (2004) *Reassurance Policing: An Evaluation of the Local Management of Community Safety.* London: Home Office Research, Development and Statistics Directorate, Research Study 288.

re-balancing the criminal justice system

The objective of re-balancing the criminal justice system indicates a desire to make the system provide an improved level of service to victims of crime and offer enhanced protection to the general public at the expense of the perceived bias that it has traditionally displayed towards offenders.

A number of developments have been put forward since 1945 to improve the position of victims and witnesses of crime. These include the introduction of the Criminal Injuries Compensation Scheme in 1964, the publication of the Victims' Charter in 1990, the launching of the Crown Court Witness Service (initially as a pilot scheme in 1990 and later extended to all Crown Courts), the initiation of the Victim Personal Statement Scheme in 2001 and the extended use of compensation orders imposed upon convicted offenders by the criminal courts, ordering them to pay compensation to their victims for personal injury, loss or damage arising from the offence. The 2000 Criminal Justice and Court Services Act imposed a statutory duty on the Probation Service to keep victims informed about the custodial process for offenders who received a custodial sentence of 12 months or more for a sexual or violent crime.

However, none of these developments were totally successful in making a significant improvement to the way in which the criminal justice system catered for victims of crime and in recent years the objective of 're-balancing' the criminal justice system in favour of the victim and society at large has assumed an important aspect of contemporary criminal justice policy.

A number of new measures have been pursued to 'ensure that victims and witnesses are at the heart of the system' (Home Office, Lord Chancellor's Department and Crown Prosecution Service, 2002: 38). An independent commissioner for victims and witnesses was proposed in the 2004 Domestic Violence, Crime and Victims Act and a Code of Practice for the Victims of Crime was put forward in 2005 to set out what protection, practical support and information victims had a right to expect from criminal justice agencies.

The principle of joined-up government also sought to improve the level of service to victims and witnesses. All criminal justice agencies were required to work towards achieving a joint Public Service Agreement target to meet the needs of victims and witnesses (Home Office, Lord Chancellor's Department and Crown Prosecution Service, 2002: 48–9). In 2003 the Criminal Case Management Programme was launched to ensure that the police, CPS and courts co-operated more effectively with each other and with other key stake-holders in the prosecution process. Witness Care Units, operated jointly by the police and CPS to provide information, advice and support to both victims and witnesses, were introduced by local criminal justice

boards for all cases where someone was charged with an offence. Enhanced Police–CPS cooperation was secured through the establishment of Criminal Justice Units.

The objective of closing the gap between what the public expected of a criminal justice system and what they saw it delivering remained at the forefront of government criminal justice policy following the 2005 general election. It was forcibly articulated by the then Prime Minister, Tony Blair, in a speech at Bristol on 23 June 2006, and was expressed in the argument that 'the needs of victims must be at the heart of what the criminal justice system does' (Home Office, 2006: 4).

A number of proposals to achieve this were put forward which included the introduction of a victim's voice in the most serious cases that came before the Parole Board, increasing the amount of compensation paid by offenders to victims and to clarify that all relevant criminal justice agencies had a duty to protect the public. Changes in sentencing procedures were also put forward. The establishment of an integrated national enforcement service was proposed. It was also recommended that the Criminal Justice Exchange should be further developed to enable information on offenders to be shared across the criminal justice system (Home Office, 2006). In 2009 the Ministry of Justice announced plans to set up a National Victims Service to provide for one-to-one care for victims of crime.

Although proposals and the sentiments that underpinned them to re-balance the criminal justice system sought to improve the position of victims of crime, they went beyond this and had a broader objective that sought to re-establish overall public confidence in the operations of the criminal justice system.

In addition to affording enhanced protections to victims of crime and to society as a whole, re-balancing the criminal justice system has entailed initiatives directed at defendants in criminal cases. The 2003 Criminal Justice Act abolished common law rules governing the admissibility of evidence relating to a defendant's bad character in criminal proceedings and made changes to the admissibility of hearsay evidence in such cases. This legislation also enabled juries to be dispensed with in cases where there was a danger of jury tampering. A number of new proposals affecting defendants and sentencing policy were included in the 2008 Criminal Justice and Immigration Act. This measure provided for tougher measures to combat crime, the end of automatic sentencing discounts and the removal of the use of procedural irregularities to quash the sentences of those who were plainly guilty of the offence for which they were convicted.

However, attempts to re-balance the criminal justice process by reducing the rights of defendants expose the tensions between the due process and crime control models of the criminal justice process (Packer, 1964). Developments that seek to facilitate convictions in order to appease public concerns regarding inadequate responses to crime encounter arguments that seek to assert the rights of the individual against mistakes that might result in a wrongful conviction. This perspective defines victims as those who are deprived of their civil liberties and wrongly convicted of crimes.

See also: attrition, detection rates, joined-up government, jury system, out of court disposals, victimology

References and further reading

Bottoms, A. and Roberts, J. (2010) *Victims in Contemporary Criminal Justice: A Need for Rebalancing?* Cullompton, Devon: Willan Publishing.

Home Office, Lord Chancellor's Office and the Crown Prosecution Service (2002) *Justice For All.* London: TSO, Cm 5563.

Home Office (2006) *Rebalancing the Criminal Justice System in Favour of the Law-abiding Majority: Cutting Crime, Reducing Re-offending and Protecting the Public.* London: Home Office.

Packer, H. (1964) 'Two Models of the Criminal Process', *University of Pennsylvania Law Review*, 13: 25–43.

recidivism

Recidivism refers to the repetition of criminal behaviour by a person who has previously been convicted and punished for committing a crime.

In 2007 the number of adults aged 18 and above who were released from custody or who commenced a court order under the supervision of the probation service for the first quarter of 2007 and who subsequently re-offended within one year (measured by a court conviction) constituted 39 per cent of the cohort of around 50,000 (Ministry of Justice, 2009: 9). However, statistics also suggest that this proportion increases with time – the re-offending rates of adults aged 18 and over released from prison in the first quarter of 2005 stood at 49.1 per cent within one year but rose to 62 per cent within two years (Hanson, 2009).

Recidivism may measure the deterrent effect of punishment and can also be used as an indicator of the success (or otherwise) of initiatives such as cognitive behavioural programmes, although their usefulness in doing this is influenced by the accuracy of official crime statistics which may underestimate the extent to which former offenders re-offend (Falshaw *et al.*, 2003).

Additionally, repeat offenders constitute a large proportion of the criminal population and effective action to combat recidivism would result in a significant fall in crime which would have economic benefits. The cost of recorded crime committed by ex-offenders was estimated to be at least £11 billion a year (Social Exclusion Unit, 2002). Accordingly, the need to tackle recidivism occupied high prominence on the government's agenda in the early years of the twenty-first century.

Offenders have a background of social exclusion and in particular lack basic literacy, numeracy and writing skills (Social Exclusion Unit, 2002). This formed the background to a recommendation that a cross-government approach was needed to tackle re-offending that would involve providing help for prisoners in areas that included health, housing, education and vocational training delivered in the context of a National Rehabilitation Strategy.

A number of initiatives were pursued in order to advance objectives of this nature through which the government intended to reduce the rate of adult and juvenile re-offending by 10 per cent between 2005 and 2011.

These included the establishment of the National Offender Management Service in 2004 to provide for the end-to-end management of offenders both in prison and in the community and the resettlement agenda which entails the prison service pursuing actions in areas that include education, training, housing and work (often in partnership with other bodies) to provide for the effective resettlement of offenders into communities upon release. Other approaches identified in research into desistance have suggested the need to focus on offenders' self-motivation and mental processes and have emphasized the importance of mentoring to prevent re-offending.

See also: cognitive behavioural programmes, crime statistics, desistance, prisons, National Offender Management Service

References and further reading

Falshaw, L., Friendship, C. and Bates, A. (2003) *Sexual Offenders – Measuring Reconviction, Reoffending and Recidivism.* London: Home Office Research, Development and Statistics Directorate, Findings 183.
Hanson, D. (2009) HC Debates 3 March, Vol. 488, Col. 1509W.
Ministry of Justice (2009) *Reoffending of Adults: Results from the 2007 Cohort England and Wales.* London: Ministry of Justice Statistics Bulletin.

Social Exclusion Unit (2002) *Reducing Reoffending by Ex-Prisoners.* London: Social Exclusion Unit.

reductivism

See **punishment (aims of)**

regulatory supervision

Regulatory supervision refers to measures that are designed to exercise control over the actions of commercial organizations, the breach of which is not regarded as a criminal offence although it may result in a penalty being imposed on them.

Regulatory supervision may entail self-regulation by the organizations concerned (an approach that may be voluntary or enforced) or it may involve regulation by external bodies. The philosophy of these two approaches is different – external regulation is frequently associated with punitive aims, whereas self-regulation is primarily motivated to deter (Slapper and Tombs, 1999: 184). Some regulatory mechanisms (such as the Financial Services Authority) contain elements of self- and external regulation.

Self-regulation possesses a number of advantages. 'Insiders' may possess a better grasp of corporate practices than those not intimately involved with a commercial undertaking and are thus best placed to spot wrongdoings. They may also be better placed to conduct more frequent and detailed investigations than external regulators (Braithwaite and Fisse, 1987: 222–4).

External (or statutory) controls over the actions of commercial concerns may seek to protect consumers or workers employed in the industry. Examples of this form of regulatory supervision include the 1974 Health and Safety at Work Act, the 1994 General Product Safety Regulations, the 1988 Merchant Shipping Act, the 1989 Air Navigation Order, the 1990 Environmental Protection Act and the 1991 Water Resources Act (Bergman, 2000: 55). These are enforced by a wide range of bodies, examples of which include the Health and Safety Executive, the Environment Agency, the Office of Fair Trading, and local authority Trading Standards Departments and Environmental Health Departments.

There are, however, several weaknesses associated with external control over corporate activities. Regulatory bodies are often reluctant to prosecute and may prefer to secure compliance with laws and regulations through ways other than prosecution, which is frequently used only as a last resort when other courses of action have failed (Croall, 2001: 104–5). Additionally, the penalties that are associated with breaches of regulatory measures are often insufficient although the 2003 Water Act established the Water Services Regulatory Authority that is empowered to fine water or sewerage companies up to 10 per cent of their turnover if they fail to meet their standards of performance.

The effectiveness of any form of supervisory regulation is dependent on the extent to which the machinery that implements it adopts a proactive as opposed to a reactive stance regarding intervention. It was observed that the Financial Services Authority had 'failed dreadfully in its supervision of the banking sector' as was exhibited in its handling of the Northern Rock crisis which resulted in the introduction of the Supervisory Enhancement Programme designed to increase the intensity of supervision over the financial services sector (Treasury Committee, 2009: para. 22).

See also: administrative law

References and further reading

Bergman, D. (2000) *The Case for Corporate Responsibility: Corporate Violence and the Criminal Justice System.* London: Disaster Action.

Braithwaite, J. and Fisse, B. (1987) 'Self Regulation and the Control of Corporate Crime', in C. Shearing and P. Stenning (eds) *Private Policing.* Beverley Hills: Sage.

Croall, H. (2001) *Understanding White Collar Crime*. Buckingham: Open University Press.

Slapper, G. and Tombs, S. (1999) *Corporate Crime*. Harlow: Longman.

Treasury Committee (2009) *Banking Crisis: Regulation and Supervision*. Fourteenth Report of Session 2008–9, House of Commons Paper 767. London: TSO.

rehabilitation

See **prisons**

remand in custody

See **bail**

reprimands (juvenile justice)

See **cautioning (formal)**

resettlement

See **recidivism**

restorative justice

Restorative justice is a community-based response to crime. It is based upon the view that crime is an action that causes harm and hurt to those who are victims of it and seeks to enable the person who has broken the law to repair the damage that has been caused to the direct victim and/or to society at large by his or her criminal behaviour. By doing so, the criminal is more readily reintegrated into society.

Restorative justice has been defined as consisting of 'values, aims and processes that have as their common factor attempts to repair the harm caused by criminal behaviour' (Young and Hoyle, 2003: 200). It consists of an approach which seeks to replace the values of vindictiveness and vengeance which frequently underpin criminal justice interventions with those of healing and conciliation (Braithwaite and Strang, 2001: 1–2).

Restorative justice entails some form of forum in which the criminal and victim are brought face to face so that the victim can explain the harm that the criminal act has caused him or her and the person who has committed the wrongdoing can both apologize, explain the actions that caused the criminal act to take place and agree to take steps to make amends for the harm that has been caused.

These meetings take several forms and frequently adopt some form of conferencing format at which the victim and wrongdoer are joined by other family and community members and criminal justice practitioners. In this sense, the principle of restorative dialogue is at the heart of conferencing (Roberts, 2004: 245), 'that brings people together . . . to gain understanding and repair the harm caused by a crime or conflict' (Roberts, 2004: 251).

A key advantage of restorative justice is that crime is no longer viewed as an impersonal act which has breached an abstract legal code but is seen as an act that has caused genuine harm to a real person. It enables the victim and wrongdoer who are often marginalized by court procedures (becoming 'idle by-standers in what, after all, is *their* conflict' (Barton, 2003: 26–7)) to speak for themselves and each give their account of the incident. The main intention of this process is that offenders can be more readily reintegrated into society than would be the case if they merely received punishment for their actions which, in the case of a custodial sentence, may result in long-term or permanent exclusion from society.

There are, however, problems with this approach. Those who support a retributive response to crime criticize restorative justice for being too soft an option whereby a person who says 'sorry' (whether they mean it or not) may escape the more severe sentence that their actions merited. Also victims may not wish to face those who have harmed them. There is also the danger that wrongdoers who are subjected to conferencing procedures may resent the process and refuse to cooperate with it.

One way in which restorative justice functions is to make the wrongdoer feel ashamed of their actions and thus emotionally susceptible to making amends for them. This has been termed 'reintegrative shaming' (Braithwaite, 1989). However, if the law-breaker does not genuinely feel that his or her actions were wrong, the process will not produce positive outcomes.

See also: criminal court system England and Wales, punishment (aims of)

References and further reading

Barton, C. (2003) *Restorative Justice: The Empowerment Model.* Sydney: Hawkins Press.

Braithwaite, J. (1989) *Crime, Shame and Reintegration.* Cambridge: Cambridge University Press.

Braithwaite, J. and Strang, H. (2001) 'Introduction: Restorative Justice and Civil Society', in H. Strang and J. Braithwaite (eds) *Restorative Justice and Civil Society.* Cambridge: Cambridge University Press.

Johnstone, G. and Van Ness, D. (2006) (eds) *Handbook of Restorative Justice.* Cullompton, Devon: Willan Publishing.

Roberts, A. (2004) 'Is Restorative Justice Tied to Specific Models of Practice?' in H. Zehr and B. Toews, *Critical Issues in Restorative Justice.* New York: Criminal Justice Press.

Young, R. and Hoyle, C. (2003) 'Restorative Justice and Punishment' in S. McConville (ed.) *The*

Use of Punishment. Cullompton, Devon: Willan Publishing.

retributivism

See **punishment (aims of)**

right to silence

The right to silence denoted that a person who had been arrested was not required to answer any subsequent questions put to him or her by a police officer.

The right to silence provided a defence against self-incrimination and placed the burden of proving a person's guilt firmly on the shoulders of the prosecution. It was formalized in Judges' Rules in 1912 and was endorsed by Article 6 of the European Convention on Human Rights and Fundamental Freedoms which guaranteed the right of an accused person to a 'fair and public hearing'.

However, criminal justice practitioners were concerned that this right was abused by criminals and their legal advisers, sometimes resulting in courts acquitting guilty persons. This led to certain qualifications being imposed on it.

The 1994 Criminal Justice and Public Order Act enabled the courts to draw inferences from a suspect's refusal to answer questions under four circumstances: when a defendant used a defence in court that they had failed to mention previously when questioned or charged by the police, when a defendant aged 14 or over refused to give evidence at a trial, when a suspect was issued with a 'special warning' under the Act which allowed inferences to be drawn from a suspect's failure to answer police questions in connection with incriminating circumstances (specifically if a suspect failed to account for incriminating objects, marks or substances) and when a person failed to account for their presence at a particular place (Bucke and Brown, 1997: 34 and 37).

Although relatively little use had been made by suspects of the right to silence, the impact of this reform was to reduce its overall use. However, factors that included the seriousness of the offence and racial and gender differences exerted an influence on suspects' use of silence – African-Caribbeans were found to be more likely to exercise this right than other racial groups and men were more likely to exercise it than women (Bucke and Brown, 1997: 35–6).

Changes to the right of silence brought about by the 1994 legislation were reflected in the caution that an arrested person receives by a police officer before being questioned. This was amended to state: 'you do not have to say anything but it may harm your defence if you do not mention now anything you later rely on in court. Anything you do say will be given in evidence'.

The right to silence has been limited in other ways. The 1987 Criminal Justice Act required a person to answer questions, provide information or produce documents for the purposes of an investigation being conducted by the Serious Fraud Office. Similar powers were given to the Serious Organized Crime Agency by the 2005 Serious Organized Crime and Police Act. The 2000 Regulation of Investigatory Powers Act also eroded the right to silence by making it a criminal offence not to disclose when requested the key to unlock encrypted information. Limitations to the right of silence imposed by requirements of this nature might, however, conflict with Article 6 of the European Convention on Human Rights (Newburn *et al.*, 2007: 593).

See also: human rights, Judges' Rules, Serious Organized Crime Agency

References and further reading

Bucke, T. and Brown, D. (1997) *In Police Custody: Police Powers and Suspects' Rights under the Revised PACE Codes of Practice*. London: Home Office, Research and Statistics Directorate, Home Office Research Study 174.

Newburn, T., Wiliamson, T. and Wright, A. (eds) (2007) *Handbook of Criminal Investigation*. Cullompton, Devon: Willan Publishing.

Owen, T. *et al.* (2005) *Blackstone's Guide to the Serious Organised Crime and Police Act 2005*. Oxford: Oxford University Press.

royal prerogative of mercy

The royal prerogative of mercy is a procedure whereby judicial decisions related to the conviction or sentencing of a person can be overturned or modified by a government minister acting in the name of the Sovereign.

The royal prerogative of mercy derives from powers that were initially exercised by the Sovereign without having to secure the agreement of Parliament. The Sovereign's power to mitigate the sentence of judges through his prerogative of mercy 'was the chief and ancient emblem of his majesty as the Almighty's representative on earth' (Gatrell, 1994: 201).

The prerogative of mercy was initially exercised by the monarch personally but by the eighteenth century it was common for judges to apply it if they believed there were mitigating circumstances that made the death penalty inappropriate to a case they had tried. In such cases, their decision was theoretically subject to review by the monarch. This prerogative power is now exercised by a

Minister of the Crown thus providing an element of Parliamentary accountability to the procedure.

Initially the royal prerogative of mercy was applied to commuting the death penalty but latterly became exercised in connection to a wider range of actions concerning the penalty or sentence imposed on a convicted person. It now embraces a free (sometimes called 'Royal') pardon, a conditional pardon or the remission or part remission of a sentence imposed by the courts and is exercised on the recommendation of the Justice Secretary (formerly by the Home Secretary). In the latter circumstance a person may be released from a sentence without a pardon. The effect of this is that the state fails to acknowledge that the person was innocent of the crime for which he or she was convicted but accepts that the evidence on which the conviction was based was unsafe.

The exercise of the royal prerogative is a technical breach of the rule of law, but may under certain circumstances be subject to judicial review. In 1985 (in connection with the banning of trade unions from GCHQ) the House of Lords ruled that although some areas of the prerogative power were ill-suited to such a process, it was appropriate to subject other aspects of its use to the process of judicial review. This includes the exercise of the prerogative of mercy which was affirmed in the Bentley case in 1993.

The royal prerogative of mercy can be exercised in any country where the UK monarch is Head of State. In these cases it is exercised on behalf of the Sovereign by the Governor General.

See also: judicial review, rule of law

References and further reading

Council of the Civil Service *v.* Minister for the Civil Service [1985] AC 374.

Gatrell, V. (1994) *The Hanging Tree; Execution and the English People 1770–1868.* Oxford: Oxford University Press.

R. *v.* Secretary of State for the Home Department, ex parte Bentley [1993] 4All ER 433.

Select Committee on Public Administration (2004) *Ministerial Powers and the Prerogative,* Session 2003–4, 4th report, HC 642.

rule of law

The rule of law is a key constitutional principle that was popularized by A. V. Dicey (1982 [1885]). This principle asserted the supremacy of the law in a liberal democratic state as an instrument that governs both the actions of individual citizens in their relationships with each other and also controls the actions of the state in its dealings with citizens. Later definitions suggested that it imposes a requirement on all citizens to obey the law. This limits the ability of individuals to act in any way they choose thus upholding social order in the interests of all.

The rule of law insists that citizens can only be punished by the state using formalized procedures when they have broken the law and also that all citizens will be treated in the same way by the courts when they commit wrongdoings. Nobody is 'above the law' and the punishments given out for similar crimes should be the same, regardless of who has committed them. This implies that the law is applied dispassionately and should not be subject to the biases and prejudices of those who enforce it. Additionally, all citizens should be aware of the contents of the law. The rule of law, therefore, provides a powerful safeguard to citizens against arbitrary actions by the state and its officials and is best guaranteed by a judiciary which is independent of the other branches of government.

The rule of law may be grounded in common law (which is the situation in the UK) or be incorporated into a codified constitution (as is the case in America where the requirement of 'due process of law' provided for in the 5th and 14th amendments protects citizens against arbitrary actions or the use of wide discretionary authority by the government) (Vago, 1991: 40).

However, most liberal democratic states deviate on occasions from the strict application of the rule of law. Factors that include financial means, class, race or gender may play an influential part in determining whether a citizen who breaks the law is proceeded against by the state and may also have a major bearing on the outcome of any trial. The use of discretion by state officials may undermine the predictable outcome of law-breaking. Additionally, governments may depart from strict adherence to the rule of law in times of national emergency, for example by introducing exceptional procedures to combat terrorism that in the UK have included internment (2001 Anti-terrorism, Crime and Security Act) and control orders (2005 Prevention of Terrorism Act).

See also: discretion, internment, criminal court system England and Wales, criminal court system Scotland, royal prerogative of mercy

References and further reading

Dicey, A. V. (1982) *Law of the Constitution.* Indianapolis, IN: Liberty Fund Inc., originally published in 1885.

United Nations (1999) *Human Rights and the Rule of Law.* New York: United Nations.

Vago, S. (1991) *Law and Society.* Englewood Cliffs, NJ: Prentice Hall.

rules of evidence

Rules of evidence determine what evidence is admissible and can be presented before a court of law for the consideration of those who act as triers of fact (which in a criminal trial before a Crown Court in England and Wales is the jury).

Rules of evidence play an important part in criminal trials conducted under the principles of adversarial justice. In Crown Court trials in England and Wales, these rules require that only evidence that is relevant to the case can be brought forward. They authorize the calling of witnesses or the production of documents and other materials that relate to the case and regulate the way in which witnesses are questioned (for example they cannot be required to incriminate themselves). These rules also re-quire witnesses to give evidence of facts they have observed and not inferences they have drawn from these facts and also render inadmissible most forms of hearsay evidence (which was historically defined as 'rumour' and 'gossip').

It is usually the case that a verdict should be based on the evidence given in court rather than what a defendant has done on previous occasions (Hostettler, 2009: 238). However, rules of evidence permit exceptions to this. The 2003 Criminal Justice Act re-wrote rules concerning the production of evidence relating to an accused person's bad character. The prose-cution may also be able to put forward similar fact evidence whereby witnesses testify in order to establish a pattern or method affecting the accused person's behaviour in the past that is relevant to the case before the court.

In the case of evidence that is disputed (for example a confession that the defence argues was made without a caution having been administered), the trial judge will send the jury away and conduct a 'trial within a trial' where the defence and prosecution put forward evidence to support their arguments regarding admissibility. This procedure is known as *voir dire* and if the judge declares the evidence to be inadmissible, the jury will be unaware of its contents.

Some rules of evidence were formulated during the Middle Ages, but many of the modern rules of evidence that apply to criminal court proceedings date to decisions made by common law judges in the seventeenth and eighteenth cen-turies (Thomas, 1999: 154–5). Rules of evidence have also been developed by more recent statutes that include the 1984 Police and Criminal Evidence Act, the 1994 Criminal Justice and Public Order Act and the 2003 Criminal Justice Act.

See also: adversarial justice, criminal court system England and Wales, judges, jury system

References and further reading

Hostettler, J. (2009) *A History of Criminal Justice in England and Wales*. Hook, Hampshire: Waterside Press.

Thomas, R. (1999) *Espionage and Secrecy: The Official Secret Acts 1919–1989 of the United Kingdom*. London: Routledge.

S

Sarah's Law

See **Megan's Law**

Schengen Information System (SIS)

See **Schengen initiatives**

Schengen initiatives

The term 'Schengen initiatives' covers a range of developments that have been pursued within the European Union to enhance the cooperation of criminal justice agencies of member states and secure the coordination of their criminal justice policies.

The Schengen Agreement (1985) and Convention (1990) sought to further the objective of a single market by facilitating the freedom of movement of people, goods and transport. This objective gave rise to several new arrangements affecting criminal justice policy which included cooperation over drugs-related crime (especially to curb drug smuggling), enhanced assistance between police forces and legal authorities across national frontiers, the development of standardized policies in connection with illegal immigration and visas and the introduction of simpler extradition rules between member countries.

The Schengen Information System (SIS) is of particular importance for securing closer working relationships between the criminal justice agencies of EU member states. The SIS is an EU-wide database for the collection and exchange of information relating to immigration, policing and criminal law. It was formally established by the 1990 Schengen Convention and became operational in 1995.

Its development stemmed from the relaxation of border controls provided for in the 1985 Schengen

Agreement since pooled information was required to enable law enforcement and immigration control officers (working at borders or elsewhere within their respective countries) to carry out identification procedures in connection with what are referred to 'alerts'.

Alerts include persons wanted in a Schengen state, a list of non-EU citizens ('aliens') who should be denied entry, missing persons, persons wanted as witnesses or for the purposes of prosecution or the enforcement of sentences, persons or vehicles to be placed under surveillance and objects sought for the purposes of seizure for use in criminal proceedings (Schengen Convention 1990, cited in House of Lords European Union Committee, 2007: para. 12).

The information stored on the SIS is relatively basic (including details such as names and aliases, sex and physical characteristics, date and place of birth, nationality and whether the person is violent). Member states hold supplementary information on persons who are the subject of its alerts in a separate database known as Supplementary Information Request at the National Entry (SIRENE) to which all member states may request access. Each member state has a SIRENE bureau which acts as a link between member states' police forces and the SIS.

Limitations of the SIS (arising from the accession of new EU

member states) and the desirability of including biometric data (such as photographs, fingerprints, DNA profiles and retina scans) resulted in the development of a second generation SIS (called SIS II). Biometric identifiers will be stored on the second generation of the Schengen Information System SIS II. The new system will also provide for links between the different alerts stored on the system. It is intended that SIS II will become fully operational before the end of 2011.

A key aspect of the Schengen Agreement was the abolition of internal frontier controls within member states. The United Kingdom was, however, sceptical of this development, believing that open EU frontiers could be exploited by criminals, terrorists and illegal refugees and that in particular the UK would become exposed to 'uncontrollable immigration' (Davies, 2003: 207). Accordingly, the UK maintained its border controls with other member states and this course of action was affirmed at the Amsterdam summit in 1997 in connection with the subsequent Treaty of Amsterdam which integrated the Schengen Convention and measures that built upon it (collectively known as the Schengen *acquis*) into the EU framework and came into force in 1999.

However, in 2000 the UK was granted approval to participate in areas of the Schengen *acquis* relating to criminal law and policing and in some aspects of the Schengen Information System (SIS). Participation in the SIS was due to have commenced in January 2005 but did not take place because of technical difficulties.

The UK intends to join SIS II but since it is not a full participant it will not have access to the immigration data stored on SIS II. It will, however, have access to other data concerned with policing and criminal cooperation (House of Lords European Union Committee, 2007: para. 21).

When the UK joins SIS II, checks made through the Police National Computer will automatically trigger a check on the SIS. If a match is made, the officer making the enquiry will be referred to SIRENE UK (housed by SOCA) which will then act as a link between the UK and the SIS (House of Lords European Union Committee, 2007: para. 55).

See also: Europol, Serious Organized Crime Agency

References and further reading

Davies, G. (2003) *EU Internal Market Law*. London: Cavendish.
House of Lords European Union Committee (2007) *Schengen Information System, II (SIS II)* Session 2006–7, 9th Report.
London: TSO, House of Lords Paper 49.
The 1990 Convention Applying the Schengen Agreement [Online] Statewatch, http://www.state watch.org/news/2006/oct/Sch ImpCon.htm

Security Service (MI5)

The Security Service (MI5) was established in 1909 to foil the spying activities of foreign governments within Britain and it subsequently developed into an agency whose role was to counter subversion within the United Kingdom by monitoring political ideas and opinions that it deemed to pose some form of threat to the political, social or economic status quo in the UK or to the well-being of its citizens. MI5 is controlled by a Director General appointed by the Prime Minister and is operationally accountable to the Home Secretary.

MI5 is primarily an intelligence-gathering body which is passed over to other organizations to which it might be relevant. Historically it has collected information on subversive organizations and individuals through a number of methods that included mail interception, the interception ('tapping') of telephone calls and other forms of electronic communication, placing bugs in a target's home or premises or planting informants or agents in organizations.

Occasionally the role of MI5 has extended beyond intelligence gathering to embrace the use of 'dirty tricks' designed to sabotage or destabilize an organization that had been targeted as subversive. This accusation was made in connection with the alleged involvement of this agency in the 1984/5 miners' dispute (Milne, 1994) and implies the redrawing of the boundaries of the liberal democratic tradition 'by declaring to be illegitimate political and industrial activities which had been thought to have distinguished a liberal democracy from an authoritarian or fascist society' (State Research, 1979).

A key problem concerns the control of MI5 where a fine balance has to be drawn between the requirements of the agency to exercise a degree of operational independence against the need to ensure that it functions in accordance with the principles of liberal democratic political systems. Insufficient external control may lead to self-tasking which in extreme situations may result in members of democratically elected governments being targets of MI5 (Wright, 1987).

Criticisms that the agency was subject to insufficient external control led to a number of reforms in the 1980s and 1990s, in particular the 1989 Security Service Act which placed MI5 on a statutory basis and defined its sphere of operations. It also authorized the issuance of 'property warrants' to enable the agency to 'bug and burgle' in order to gather intelligence. A Security Services Tribunal was established to consider complaints by members of the public and the operations of the legislation in connection with property warrants was overseen by a Security Services Commissioner. The 1994 Intelligence Services Act subsequently created the Intelligence and Security Committee composed of MPs and peers to scrutinize the expenditure and administration of MI5.

Further external controls over the activities of MI5 were developed by the 2000 Regulation of Investigatory Powers Act. This developed existing safeguards related to *intrusive surveillance* (covering surveillance conducted in a private location that included a person's home or property such as a car where a presumption of privacy would normally apply) requiring warrants issued by a Secretary of State.

The 2000 Act also authorized covert intelligence gathering (or *directed surveillance*) including the use of informants. This typically takes place in a public place to obtain private information about a person and is authorized by police officers whose actions are subject to a Code of Practice. The safeguards established by the 2000 Act included a tribunal to hear complaints from members of the public.

The role of MI5 was latterly extended beyond political policing to embrace more routine criminal activities. In 1992 it was given the lead role in countering terrorism on mainland Britain. The 1996 Security Services Act further extended the role of MI5 into 'serious crime' which was defined as an offence that carried a sentence of three or more years on first conviction or any offence involving conduct by a large number of persons in pursuit of a common purpose.

See also: informants, surveillance

References and further reading

Milne, S. (1994) *The Enemy Within.* London: Pan Books.

State Research (1979) 'Introduction' in E.P. Thompson, *The Secret State.* London: Independent Research Publications, State Research Pamphlet No. 1.

Wright, P. (1987) *Spycatcher: The Candid Autobiography of a Senior Intelligence Officer.* New York: Heinemann.

self-policing society

A self-policing society is one in which some of the tasks of law enforcement are undertaken by local communities without recourse to the law enforcement agencies.

In order to accomplish a self-policing society, it is necessary to create structures from which a sense of community spirit can be generated. These may embrace a variety of neighbourhood forums that deal with a range of ongoing local affairs or are set up to deal with specific issues which, regardless of their original role, may be developed as mechanisms to provide a sense of community solidarity to combat crime and disorder.

The incorporation of 'the intermediate institutions which lie between the state and the individual' (Leadbeater, 1996: 34) constitute an example of what has been referred to as the 'responsibilization strategy' (Garland, 1996: 445) whereby the responsibility to maintain law and order is devolved from the central state and can be used as a means to empower localities to remedy some of their own problems, especially in connection with low-level disorder and crime.

There are, however, problems posed by this approach which include the possibility of displacing crime to other neighbourhoods which lack mechanisms to promote community solidarity and the extent to which initiatives of this nature may be used against marginalized and unpopular groups within a community which at its worst may transform community self-policing into vigilante justice.

Vigilante justice describes a situation in which an individual or group inflict punishment on a law-breaker (or assumed law-breaker) either because the state is powerless to act or because the penalties available to the state to deal with the problem are viewed as insufficient. Individuals or groups thus take the law into their own hands and dispense a penalty which they view to be appropriate to the crime that has been committed and/or seeks to drive the offending party out of the community. This raises the spectre of lynch mobs in the nineteenth-century American Wild West whereby mob rule is used to enforce the sentiments of the unenlightened and the intolerant.

An example of this occurred in the United Kingdom in 2000 in connection with a national newspaper campaign to 'name and shame' child sex offenders in an attempt to secure the enactment of a 'Sarah's Law'. A number of paedophiles were subjected to physical attack alongside other people (in one case a paediatrician) who were mistakenly identified as child sex offenders.

See also: empowerment, Megan's Law

References and further reading

Garland, D. (1996) 'The Limits of the Sovereign State', *British Journal of Criminology*, 36(4): 445–71.

Leadbeater, C. (1996) *The Self-Policing Society*. London: DEMOS.

self-report studies

Self-report studies constitute a method of compiling information on crime by asking individuals to record criminal activities that they have committed.

Self-report studies typically consist of a series of questions addressed to selected groups asking them about their personal involvement in criminal or other forms of rule-breaking behaviour.

Such studies have elicited important information connected with youth culture that suggests certain activities such as shoplifting or drug taking are relatively widespread (Mott and Mirrlees-Black, 1993). They have also provided information on victimless crimes and offences conducted within the privacy of a home, such as child abuse.

A recent study using self-report methods was the Offending, Crime and Justice Survey introduced in 2003. It was based upon interviews with around 12,000 people aged 10–65 in England and Wales. Its findings suggested that there were around 3.8 million active offenders (defined as persons who had committed at least one offence in the previous year). Those defined as 'serious or prolific offenders' (those who had committed six or more offences in the previous year) were said to comprise about 2 per cent of the population but accounted for around 82 per cent of all crime (Budd and Sharp, 2005).

There are several weaknesses associated with self-report studies. They are not addressed at a representative sample of the population, and they rely on the honesty of persons responding to the survey who may choose to exaggerate or downplay their involvement in such activities. They may also secure information on trivial offences that constitute minor infractions of the law not regarded as crimes by those who perpetrate them – such as using a work telephone to make a private call.

See also: crime statistics, field research, victimization surveys

References and further reading

Budd, T. and Sharp, C. (2005) *Offending in England and Wales: First Results from the 2003 Crime and Justice Survey.* London: Home Office, Home Office Research, Development and Statistics Directorate, Findings 244.

Mott, J. and Mirrlees-Black, C. (1993) *Self-Reported Drug Misuse in England and Wales: Main Findings from the 1992 British Crime Survey.* London: HMSO, Home Office Research and Statistics Department, Research Findings Number 7.

sentencers

See **bifurcation**, also **judges, magistrates**

sentences of the criminal courts

Sentences of the criminal courts refer to the decisions taken by sentencers (who are judges or magistrates) in connection with applying sanctions to persons who have been found guilty of committing a crime. The material in this section applies to adult offenders (those aged 21 and above).

The sentences available to the courts are set out in legislation. Major enactments include the 2000 Powers of the Criminal Courts (Sentencing) Act, much of which was repealed and replaced by provisions contained in the 2003 Criminal Justice Act. The 2003 legislation also set out the aims of sentencing. These were to provide for the punishment of offenders, to secure the reduction of crime, to bring about the reform and rehabilitation of offenders, to protect the public and for offenders to make reparation to those affected by their crimes.

One course of action available to a sentencer is to give the offender an absolute discharge. This means that the court believes that he or she is morally innocent of the offence with which they have been charged but is technically guilty of it. In this case the defendant is subject to no penalty save the stain on his or her character arising from the court not acquitting him or her and the criminal record that results from this (which lasts for a period of six months).

Alternatively, a person found guilty of an offence may be given a conditional discharge. In this case the person is freed by the courts but should she or he commit a further offence within a period that is stipulated by the sentencer (ranging from six months to three years), the offence for which the conditional discharge was given will be taken into account alongside the new offence and is likely to result in a more severe penalty being given than the new offence would normally warrant. A conditional discharge is not a conviction but does enter onto the offender's criminal record.

In cases where a court considers that a custodial sentence of below 12 months is appropriate, it may decide to give the offender one last chance and impose a suspended sentence order (SSO, also referred to as Custody Minus) and impose requirements derived from a community order (see below) on the offender. This procedure is governed by the 2003 Criminal Justice Act. The SSO has two components: the operational period (the time for which the original custodial sentence is suspended) and the supervision period (the time in which the requirements are to be undertaken). Both components may last for a period of between six months and two years (although the supervision period cannot be lengthier than the operational period). In the case of a breach the court may impose harsher requirements, lengthen the supervision period or imprison the offender (the latter no longer being an automatic response to a breach). This sentence was viewed as an offender's last opportunity to avoid a term of imprisonment.

A court may alternatively impose a deferred sentence on an offender. Under these circumstances the court decides not to impose any sentence at the time of the hearing but instead sets a period of time (up to six months) during which the offender is required to be of good behaviour. The 2003 Criminal Justice Act made changes to the operations of this sentence whereby the offender is required to undertake any requirements imposed by the court, compliance with which is monitored by the Probation Service. If the offender fails to comply he or she will be brought back to court and receive a sentence for the original offence. If the offender complies with these conditions a deferred sentence does not count as a conviction. Should the offender commit a further offence during the period of deferment, he or she will be punished for both the previous and the new crime.

A person found guilty of an offence that entails the use of threat of low-level violence could historically be bound over to be of good behaviour or to keep the peace. This penalty was available to magistrates in England and Wales and dated from the 1361 Justice of the Peace Act. A person who refused to be bound over could alternatively be given a prison sentence. He or she was subject to conditions stipulated by the magistrate and was required to pay a surety which would be forfeited if he or she failed to comply with these conditions. A binding over order is classed as a civil matter and thus does not appear on a person's criminal record.

The procedure of binding over was affected by the European Court of Human Rights in 2000 in connection with Article 10 (1). Following this ruling the Home Office recommended that courts should specify what conduct or activity the defendant should refrain from as opposed to imposing a general requirement on them to be of good behaviour or to keep the peace.

Fines constitute a further aspect of the powers available to criminal courts to deal with those found guilty. In this case the offender suffers a financial penalty as the punishment for his or her crime.

They may be applied to a wide range of offences. In the Magistrates' Courts offences that may be punished with a fine are graded from level 1 to 5. Level 1 offences are subject to a maximum fine of £200 and level 5 to a maximum of £5,000. There is no limit placed on a fine that the Crown Court can impose.

The major problem with fines was the failure to pay them and by 2002/3 the payment rate for these and similar impositions fell to 55 per cent (Home Office, 2004: 4). This prompted the Department of Constitutional Affairs to introduce reforms that included targeted interventions to improve performance in the worst court areas and new measures in the 2003 Courts Act that included automatic deductions from earnings or benefits from defaulters. Subsequently the collection of fines reached over 73 per cent in the first half of 2003, and it was anticipated that the creation of the Unified Courts Agency would make further improvements in this area of activity by providing for a national focus on, and management of, fine enforcement (Home Office, 2004: 4).

On-the-spot fines in the form of fixed penalty notices may also be handed out for certain low-level offences without the need for a court appearance. The fine does not count as a conviction and does not result in the offender having a criminal record.

A community sentence is a further form of punishment available to sentencers. The 2003 Criminal Justice Act placed a range of such penalties (termed 'requirements') under the umbrella of a community order. The community order replaced all existing community sentences for offences committed after April 2005. It allows magistrates and judges to dispense a tailor-made sentence for each offender taking into account the nature of their offences and their circumstances. The Act also required sentencers not to give a custodial sentence unless the offence was so serious that neither a fine nor community penalty could be justified.

A similar penalty – Youth Rehabilitation Orders (YROs) – were provided for children and young persons in the 2008 Criminal Justice and Immigration Act. The YRO contains 18 requirements and can be enforced by an electronic monitoring requirement. It came into force in October 2009. Referral orders and reparation orders for young offenders remain as separate orders.

Those who commit the more serious crimes are given a custodial sentence. In this case they are removed from the community. Adults are placed in prison and young offenders in accommodation that includes Young Offender Institutions (for those aged 18–20) and Secure Training Centres for younger offenders.

If an offender has committed more than one imprisonable offence, a judge has the discretion to impose a concurrent or a consecutive sentence. If a concurrent sentence is imposed, the offender serves all sentences at the same time, the time spent in prison being determined by the crime which attracted the longest sentence. If a consecutive sentence is imposed, the terms of imprisonment for each offence are added up and the offender serves the total length of time awarded for all of the offences.

The 2003 Criminal Justice Act also provided for new sentences. Under the 2003 Criminal Justice Act, all offenders whose prison sentence is less than 12 months were to become subject to a period of licence on release which was administered by the Probation Service. This was known as a Custody Plus order. The 2003 legislation also provided for an Intermittent Custody order whereby a sentence of between 26 and 51 weeks could be served intermittently either at weekends or weekdays. Between periods of custody the offender was on licence which could include similar requirements to those of a Community Order. The aim of intermittent custody was that the offender could maintain family and community ties and remain in employment at the same time as serving the sentence. However, Custody Plus has never been introduced and Intermittent Custody was abandoned in 2006.

When determining what sentence to impose, a court may require a pre-sentence report (PSR) (formerly termed a Social Enquiry Report) to be prepared by the Probation Service unless it is believes that this course of action is unnecessary. This arises when the offence is very minor or if the court is minded to impose a community penalty with a single requirement or where the sentence will not involve the Probation Service (Gelsthorpe and Morgan, 2007: 190).

Following the 2003 Criminal Justice Act, reports can take the form of an oral briefing to the court, a 'fast delivery' report (which is completed either on the day of the hearing or within five days of it) or a 'standard delivery' report which provides a detailed assessment (usually based on OASys). It is used for the more serious offences and should be completed within 15 days of the hearing.

A PSR is required if the court needs advice as to the nature of the sentence that it should impose. If it has made up its mind already (typically when it believes a community penalty is the appropriate course of action) it may ask a probation officer for a Specific Sentence Report (SSR) rather than a PSR. If a SSR is asked for, a probation officer would normally see the offender immediately and report back to the court.

See also: assessment tool, criminal record, electronic monitoring, judges, magistrates, non-custodial sentences, out of court disposals, prisons, Probation Service, punishment (aims of), youth justice system

References and further reading

Ashworth, A. and Player, E. (2005) 'Criminal Justice Act 2003: The Sentencing Provisions', *Modern Law Review,* 68(5): 822–38.

Hashman and Harrup *v.* United Kingdom (2000) 30 EHRR 241, [2000].

Home Office (2004) *Reducing Crime – Changing Lives: The Government's Plans for Transforming the Management of Offenders.* London: Home Office.

Gelsthorpe, L. and Morgan, R. (2007) *Handbook of Probation.* Cullompton, Devon: Willan Publishing.

Lacey, N., Wells, C. and Quick, O. (2004) *Reconstructing Criminal Law: Texts and Materials.* Cambridge: Cambridge University Press, third edition.

Sentencing Advisory Panel (SAP)

See **Sentencing Guidelines Council**

Sentencing Guidelines Council (SGC)

The Sentencing Guidelines Council (SGC) for England and Wales is a body whose role is to promote consistency in sentencing so that similar crimes receive comparable sentences regardless of where they were committed and who carried them out.

The SGC was developed in the context of seeking to place limits on judicial discretion in sentencing. The senior judiciary had historically performed this role. The introduction in 1908 of the Court of Criminal Appeal (renamed the Court of Appeal in 1966) enabled defendants to appeal against their sentences. The decisions reached by this Court when adjudicating on sentencing appeals tended to influence the actions subsequently taken by judges in similar cases, and the role of the Court of Appeal was extended during the 1970s by its issuance of 'guidelines judgement' that provided judges with generalized guidance as to how certain types of crime should be dealt with.

A key difficulty with this situation was that the coverage of the Court of Appeal was not comprehensive, being directed at the more serious offences that were heard in Crown Courts. Accordingly, the appeal court had not formulated guidelines for a large number of offences and the sentencing policies of Magistrates' Courts and non-custodial sentences tended to be ignored by this process of peer review.

The 1998 Crime and Disorder Act sought to enhance the role of the Court of Appeal in sentencing matters by setting up the Sentencing Advisory Panel. Its role was to stimulate the development of sentencing guidelines by this Court by suggesting areas where these needed to be drawn up. Its role was advisory only, but the Court of Appeal was required to consult it when preparing guidelines (Thomas, 2003: 70).

Further reform to sentencing policy was provided by the 2003 Criminal Justice Act. This legislation established the Sentencing Guidelines Council (SGC). The existing Sentencing Advisory Panel provided advice to the new body and its remit was extended to enable it to comment on any issue affecting sentencing rather than being confined to the consideration of specific offences.

The rationale for the SGC was 'to develop a coherent approach to sentencing across the board' (Home Office, 2004: 10) by providing sentencers with 'comprehensive, clear and practical guidance' to cover all offences which would enable judges and magistrates to know what was needed in terms of punishment and, aided by advice provided by offender managers, what was most likely to work with individuals in reducing their chances of re-offending (Home Office, 2004: 10).

One difficulty with this approach was that the circumstances related to criminal behaviour assumed lesser importance and might account for developments such as the increased incarceration of women (Hudson, 2003: 181–2). Additionally, although the SGC was designed to erode the discretion exercised by sentencers, it was not eliminated entirely since guidelines will not necessarily be followed in every case (Easton and Piper, 2008: 55).

The SGC is a non-departmental body chaired by the Lord Chief Justice. It has seven judicial members representing each tier of criminal courts in England and Wales who are appointed by the Lord Chief Justice following consultation with the Lord Chancellor. Four non-judicial members are also appointed by the Lord Chancellor after consulting the Lord Chief Justice and the Home Secretary. Parliament exercises a scrutinizing role through the Justice Committee in connection with the Council's draft guidelines. The Sentencing Advisory Panel is made up of judges, magistrates, academics, criminal justice practitioners and people from outside the criminal justice system. Members are appointed by the Lord Chancellor, in consultation with the Secretary of State and the Lord Chief Justice.

The 2009 Coroners and Justice Act makes provision to replace both the SGC and the SAP with a new Sentencing Council for England and Wales in order to enhance consistency and predictability of sentencing.

See also: discretion, judges, legal profession England and Wales

References and further reading

Easton, S. and Piper, C. (2008) *Sentencing and Punishment: The Quest for Justice.* Oxford: Oxford University Press, second edition.

Home Office (2004) *Reducing Crime – Changing Lives: The Government's Plans for Transforming the Management of Offenders.* London: Home Office.

Hudson, B. (2003) *Understanding Justice: An Introduction to Ideas, Perspectives and Controversies in Modern Penal Theory.* Buckingham: Open University Press.

Thomas, D. (2003) 'Judicial Discretion in Sentencing', in L. Gelsthorpe and N. Padfield, *Exercising Discretion: Decision-making in the Criminal Justice System and Beyond.* Cullompton, Devon: Willan Publishing.

sentencing tariff

The sentencing tariff stipulates the length of time a prisoner serving an indeterminate sentence should spend in custody in order to satisfy the requirements of general deterrence and retribution.

The tariff applies to all sentences where there is no automatic right of release. This encompasses mandatory and discretionary life sentences and also the sentence of Imprisonment for Public Protection (IPP) that was created by the 2003 Criminal Justice Act.

Following the abolition of the death penalty, the 1967 Criminal Justice Act gave the Home Secretary the power to release convicted murderers on licence if the newly created Parole Board recommended such a course of action.

Initially the period served by prisoners who received mandatory life sentences was set by the Home Secretary following advice received from the trial judge and the Lord Chief Justice. The Home Secretary frequently followed recommendations made by the judicary but occasionally departed from them and set a longer or shorter period than had been suggested. Once the tariff had been served, the Parole Board would make a recommendation as to whether the prisoner should be released or remain in prison.

The trial judge alone set the tariff for those receiving non-mandatory life sentences (as is also the case with the IPP sentence).

One danger with the involvement of the Home Secretary in sentencing decisions was that his or her judgment might be influenced by factors such as public opinion and the need to maintain public confidence in the system of criminal justice. This might result in injustice being done to the prisoner.

Accordingly, the Home Secretary's role in determining the tariff for mandatory life sentences was subject to legal challenge.

In December 1999 the European Court of Human Rights ruled (in connection with the decision of the Home Secretary to increase the tariff to be served by the killers of James Bulger that had been set by the Lord Chief Justice) that fixing a tariff was tantamount to a sentencing procedure and should have been exercised by an impartial judge and not a member of the executive branch of government (Slapper and Kelly, 2008: 47–8).

In 2002 the House of Lords ruled that the involvement of the Home Secretary in sentencing decisions contravened Article 6 of the European Convention on Rights and Fundamental Freedoms since a politician did not constitute an independent tribunal as was required by this provision.

Accordingly the power to determine the tariff to be served by a person serving a mandatory life sentence was henceforth set by the trial judge. However, the 2003 Criminal Justice Act imposed a set of principles (in the form of lengths of terms of imprisonment) that the trial judge, when setting the tariff, was required to follow.

See also: criminal court system England and Wales, human rights, punishment (aims of)

References and further reading

V *v.* UK [GC] No 24888/94 ECHR 1999-IX and T *v.* UK [GC] No 24724/94, 16 November 1999.

R *v.* Secretary of State for the Home Department ex parte Anderson [2002] UKHL 46, 2002.

Slapper, G. and Kelly, D. (2008) *The English Legal System.* London: Cavendish, seventh edition.

separation of powers

The separation of powers is a constitutional doctrine that defines the relationship that should exist between the three branches of government – the legislature, the executive and the judiciary.

This principle was put forward by Montesquieu (1748). His key concern was to avoid tyranny which he believed arose from the concentration of power in the executive branch of government. He asserted that tyranny was most effectively avoided if the three branches of government were separate in the sense of each performing a defined range of functions, each possessing autonomy from the other two and each being staffed by a separate set of personnel.

An important aspect of the application of the separation of powers is the independence of the judiciary. In the UK, once appointed, judges enjoy considerable freedom of action 'and are not in danger of losing their posts for decisions that displease the other branches' (Hodder-Williams, 1996: 122).

One difficulty with the separation of powers is that were it rigidly followed each branch of government would be accountable only to itself. This might result in insufficient restraints being imposed over their actions, enabling each the potential to act in an arbitrary manner, performing unreasonable or dictatorial actions. Accordingly, the separation of powers is subject to qualifications in liberal democratic states.

In the United States, the constitution provided for the fragmentation of political power through a system of checks and balances whereby the key functions and operations of one branch of government were subject to scrutiny by the others. Thus the President's power to appoint judges to the Supreme Court is restricted by the requirement that the appointee has to be approved ('confirmed') by the Senate before taking office. In the UK, law passed by the legislature should accord with the principles established by the 1950 European Convention for the Protection of Human Rights and Fundamental Freedoms. Since the enactment of the 1998 Human Rights Act UK judges have the responsibility to use this as a yardstick with which to judge actions undertaken by the government.

See also: accountability, human rights, judicial review

References and further reading

Hodder-Williams, R. (1996) *Judges and Politics in the Contemporary Age.* London: Bowerdean Publishing.

Montesquieu, Baron de C-L. (1748) *De L'Esprit des Lois*, reprinted in A. Cohler, B. Miller and H. Stone (1989) *Cambridge Texts in the History of Political Thought.* Cambridge: Cambridge University Press.

Serious Organized Crime Agency (SOCA)

The Serious Organized Crime Agency is a national body whose role is to combat those forms of criminal activity that have national or international organization.

SOCA was established by the 2005 Serious Organized Crime and Police Act. It is headed by a Director-General and its work is guided by a small board. The agency is accountable to the Home Secretary who is responsible to Parliament for its performance. The personnel of SOCA are not police officers, although they possess the powers, responsibilities and roles associated with those employed within the police service.

SOCA brought together under one organizational roof a number of bodies that were concerned with combating serious crime. These were the National Criminal Intelligence Service (established in 1992), the National Crime Squad (set up in 1997), the investigative and intelligence work performed by HM Customs and Excise in relation to serious drug trafficking and the recovery of criminal assets, and the responsibilities exercised by the Home Office for organized immigration crime. The Assets Recovery Agency joined SOCA on 1 April 2008.

This reform was designed to remedy existing defects that included overlapping responsibilities in areas such as combating drug trafficking (Home Office, 2004: 22). It was concluded that this new body would 'lead to a greater consistency of approach' and provide 'a critical mass in key skill areas, address current problems of duplication and coordination, limit bureaucracy, provide opportunities for economies of scale, and represent a "one stop shop" for our international partners (whereby SOCA became the UK's "first port of call" in relation to Europol). High quality intelligence was argued to be of utmost importance in the fight against organized crime, and SOCA was designed to address some of the key weaknesses in the generation, dissemination and use of intelligence material' (Home Office, 2004: 22 and 29).

The agency was provided with a number of important powers with which to tackle serious crime. These include compulsory powers (broadly similar to those given to the Serious Fraud Office in the 1987 Criminal Justice Act) whereby individuals are compelled (through the mechanism of a disclosure notice) to cooperate with investigations by answering questions, providing information or producing documents (Owen *et al.*, 2005: 20–3). The 2005 legislation also introduced statutory procedures to foster the more widespread use of 'Queen's evidence' to encourage defendants to testify against co-defendants.

However, the role performed by SOCA has been subject to criticism. One study branded it as 'a white elephant', characterized by ineffectiveness. It argued that the Metropolitan Police was the only credible force capable of leading on national and regional serious and organized crime using the model that had been developed to combat terrorism (Bassett *et al*, 2009: 5–6 and 22–3).

See also: Europol

References and further reading

Bassett, D., Haldenby, A., Thraves, L. and Truss, E. (2009) *A New Force*. London: Reform.

Home Office (2004) *One Step Ahead: A 21st Century Strategy to Defeat Organised Crime*. London: TSO, Cm 6167.

Owen, T. *et al*, (2005) *Blackstone's Guide to the Serious Organised Crime and Police Act 2005*. Oxford: Oxford University Press.

similar fact evidence

See **rules of evidence**

solicitors

See **legal profession England and Wales**

Solicitors' Regulation Authority

See **legal profession England and Wales**

soundings

See **judges**

Special Constabulary ('the Specials')

The Special Constabulary now consists of members of the general public who volunteer their services to perform a limited number of hours of police work in their spare time. They are given a limited amount of training delivered (since a recommendation made by a Police Advisory Board for England and Wales report in 1981) at weekend residential training courses. They exercise full police powers for the areas in which they are appointed.

The origins of the Specials date to the early years of the nineteenth century. The 1831 Special Constables Act permitted magistrates to enrol Special Constables in times of emergency. This Act built upon earlier measures in 1673 and 1820 providing for the temporary (but compulsory) enrolment of citizens to deal with specific emergencies. The 1831 Act retained the element of compulsion but this was abandoned in 1835 when legislation made membership of the Special Constabulary a voluntary choice.

It was observed, however, that in the early decades of the nineteenth century the Special Constabulary was hardest to recruit in the areas where it was most needed, a problem attributed to the lack of a substantial middle class in the manufacturing districts (Mather, 1959: 83). For this reason, the 1843 Enrolled Pensioners Act provided for the compulsory enrolment of out-pensioners of Chelsea hospital as special constables as a response to public order emergencies, and a further Act of 1846 made similar provisions for out-pensioners of Greenwich hospital (Mather, 1959: 87).

As originally conceived, the Special Constabulary was designed to 'beef up' policing in times of crisis (such as during the two world wars and at the time of the general strike in 1926). Accordingly, the state adopted a more sceptical view of its importance in 'normal' times and to a large extent the organization suffered from benign neglect after 1945. This was evidenced by the contracting size of the organization: in 1938 the Special Constabulary numbered in excess of 118,000 volunteers, but by 1989 this figure had shrunk to around 16,000 (Fielding, 1991: 87).

However, in the 1990s the Special Constabulary was reinvigorated to undertake routine patrol tasks. In 1993 the Home Secretary announced the establishment of the Parish Constable scheme in rural areas. This involved deploying Special Constables to provide a foot patrol presence and address nuisance and minor crime, and Parish Wardens (who were not members of police forces) to channel information and advice between the police and community. This scheme was subsequently extended throughout the country as part of the Neighbourhood Constable initiative and has become intimately involved with the development of neighbourhood policing in the early years of the twenty-first century, an important aspect of which is the provision of a visible police presence in localities.

See also: neighbourhood policing, Police Service England and Wales, reassurance policing

References and further reading

Mather, F. (1959) *Public Order in the Age of the Chartists.* Manchester: Manchester University Press.

Fielding, N. (1991) *The Police and Social Conflict: Rhetoric and Reality.* London: Athlone Press.

summary justice

See out of court disposals

summary offences

See criminal court system England and Wales

supergrass

See informants (grasses/super-grasses)

surveillance

Surveillance involves monitoring the population, objects or systems (House of Lords Constitution Committee, 2009: para. 18) in order to prevent or detect crime. It may be randomly directed at the public (known as 'mass' or 'undirected' surveillance) or it may be targeted at particular individuals or organizations in connection with a specific investigation.

Surveillance takes a number of forms. It may involve the use of covert techniques (including telephone tapping, the use of informants or bugging devices) or it may embrace the use of overt methods of monitoring such as CCTV. Surveillance also embraces the collection and processing of data on individuals by the state which can then be accessed in connection with criminal activities. The National DNA Database (NDNAD) is an example of this. Related forms of surveillance give the state access to data held by private bodies in forms that include bank accounts. Suspicious activity reports forwarded by organizations such as banks to SOCA's UK Financial Intelligence Unit are an example of this method of surveillance that is directed at terrorism and money laundering.

CCTV is an important aspect of surveillance. Most of these are owned by private organizations, although the government has made significant financial contributions to CCTV schemes operated by local authorities. During the 1990s around 78 per cent of the Home Office's crime prevention budget was spent on installing CCTV (House of Lords Constitution Committee, 2009: para. 70). However, it has developed since the 1970s on a piecemeal basis, resulting in problems that include incompatibility of systems. In 2007 the government announced the initiation of a national CCTV strategy to provide strategic direction to the future development of the public space CCTV infrastructure (Gerrard *et al.*, 2007).

Surveillance and the collection of data on individuals has reached considerable proportions in the UK whose governments have constructed 'one of the most extensive and technologically advanced surveillance systems in the world' (House of Lords Constitution Committee, 2009: para. 1). It is seen as an important method to counter serious crime and government ministers have made suggestions to extend the scope of the state through means that include a 'superdatabase' which would track an individual's emails, telephone calls, texts and Internet use and through the enhanced sharing of personal data across public sector bodies.

A significant issue raised by the use of surveillance is the threat this poses to personal privacy and individual freedom (House of Lords Constitution Committee, 2009: para. 100). There are a number of protections available to the public (that include the 1998 Human Rights Act, the 1998 Data Protection Act and the 2000 Regulation of Investigatory Powers Act) and the Information Commissioner's Office. The 2000 Regulation of Investigatory Powers Act, for example, provided a number of safeguards, requiring warrants to be issued to authorize intrusive surveillance such as telephone tapping and establishing the office of Chief Surveillance Commissioner to monitor the use of the legislation. The House of Lords has also called for judicial oversight of surveillance by public bodies (House of Lords Constitution Committee, 2009).

See also: crime prevention, National DNA Database, informants (grasses/supergrasses), Serious Organized Crime Agency

References and further reading

Gerrard, G., Parkins, G., Cunningham, I., Jones, W., Hill, S. and Douglas, S. (2007) *National CCTV Strategy*. London: Home Office and the Association of Chief Police Officers.

House of Lords Constitution Committee (2009) *Surveillance: Citizens and the State*. London: TSO, 2nd Report of the Session 2008–9, House of Lords Paper 18.

Lyon, D. (2007) *Surveillance Studies: An Overview*. Cambridge: Polity Press.

suspended sentence

See **sentences of the criminal courts**

T

thief takers

A thief taker was an eighteenth-/ early nineteenth-century private detective whose self-appointed role was to secure the return of stolen goods and/or bring criminals to justice.

Thief takers were paid either by the victim of a crime or from a reward offered by the government following a serious offence such as highway robbery. They thus filled a void in the old system of policing as the role of constables did not extend to the investigation and prosecution of crime.

However, this system of 'free- lance thief takers' (Rawlings, 2008: 65) was subject to abuse. They sometimes organized the theft of goods in order to obtain a payment for their return or they extorted money from a thief as the price for not handing him over to the author- ities. A particular abuse was to act as a go-between between thief and victim to secure the return of stolen property in return for a fee (Morton, 2002: 39–41). This latter situation resulted in a Receiving Act being enacted in 1717, usually termed the Jonathan Wild Act. This measure, named after the infamous thief taker Jonathan Wild, made it a capital offence to receive a reward under the pretext of helping an owner to secure the return of goods in cases which failed to lead to the prosecution of a thief.

Although the system of private thief takers was prone to serious abuse it helped to curb criminal activities. Contemporary accounts observed that far fewer criminals were brought to justice after Wild's execution in 1725 (Morton, 2002: 43). The role of thief takers was adversely affected by the develop- ment of the new policing system and by powers given to magistrates during the 1830s to deny thief takers a reward. However, they were the forerunners of informants.

The system of privately employed thief takers was supplemented in the eighteenth century by those who were financed through public funds. This system originated with the employment by individual magistrates of their own constables to supplement parish constables. An important example of this was the Bow Street Runners. This force was organized by the Fielding brothers who were the Chief Magistrates at Bow Street, Westminster, between 1748 and 1780. The role of the runner was to detect crimes reported to the magistrates' office.

The force was initially paid for by rewards obtained from apprehending criminals (which were sometimes provided by the government) and after 1753 by a central government grant. Its key significance to the development of policing was that it was outside the control of the parishes within which it operated (Rawlings, 2008: 56).

The main role performed by the 'runners' (whose correct name was 'principal officers') was to investigate crime. Patrol work (initially performed by the Night Patrol established in 1790 to which the horse patrol was added in 1805 and the day ('dismounted horse') patrol in 1821) also became a function of this police organization. The func-

tion of the 'runners' was also extended to include the dissemination of information regarding crime and criminals through publications that included the *Covent Garden Journal* and *Hue and Cry*.

The Bow Street model was more widely adopted throughout London (with the exception of the City of London) under the provisions of the 1792 Middlesex Justices Act whereby seven police offices (in Great Marlborough Street, Hatton Garden, Lambeth, Queen's Square, Union Hall, Westminster and Worship Street) were set up and staffed by stipendiary magistrates who supervised a small number of paid police officers.

See also: informants, magistrates, new policing system (development in nineteenth century), old policing system

References and further reading

Morton, J. (2002) *Supergrasses and Informers and Bent Coppers*. London: Time Warner.

Pringle, P. (1956) *Hue and Cry: The Story of Henry and John Fielding and the Bow Street Runners*. London: Museum Press.

Rawlings, P. (2008) 'Policing Before the Police' in T. Newburn (ed.) *Handbook of Policing*. Cullompton, Devon: Willan Publishing, second edition.

third sector

See **new public management**

triable either way offences

See **criminal court system England and Wales**

tripartite system of police governance

The tripartite system of police governance denotes that responsibility for the conduct of police affairs is shared between three bodies: police authorities, chief constables and the Home Secretary.

This structure (which had developed in a piecemeal fashion during the nineteenth century) was formalized by the 1964 Police Act which laid down the responsibilities each of these three parties should perform in connection with policing in England and Wales (outside of London).

The role of the police committee was to 'secure the maintenance of an adequate and efficient police force for their area'. Police authorities were given a number of powers in order to fulfil this responsibility, which included setting a budget for their force, appointing and dismissing its senior officers and the provision and maintenance of premises, vehicles, clothing and other equipment.

The Act placed each force under the operational 'direction and control' of its chief officer, whose prime responsibility was to enforce the law and maintain the Queen's peace. The legislation gave the chief constable a number of day-to-day functions in relation to the administration of the force, which included the appointment and dismissal of officers up to the rank of chief superintendent and the specific requirement to investigate all complaints made by the public against police officers.

The 1964 Police Act gave the Home Secretary a range of strategic and tactical responsibilities which were designed to promote the overall efficiency of the police service. These included powers to pay or withhold the government grant to particular police authorities, make regulations connected with the 'government, administration and conditions of service of police forces' and to supply and maintain a number of services available to the police service generally.

Additionally, the 1964 Act established a system of accountability whereby the actions undertaken by the Home Office, chief constables or police committees could be subject to scrutiny by one or both of the other bodies involved in policing. This system of checks and balances was latterly criticized for constituting an 'entanglement' of responsibilities which resulted in uncertain lines of accountability making it 'hard to find sufficient basis for calling any of the parties to account' (Home Office, 1993: 7).

The balance of power between the three parties to the tripartite structure has been subject to subsequent change. The Home Office has assumed greater control over the operations of the police service in particular following the enactment of the 1994 Police and Magistrates' Courts Act which enabled the minister to set national objectives for the police service and performance targets to assess their attainment. The 2002 Police Reform Act authorized the Home Secretary to publish National Policing Plans which set out the strategic priorities for the police service over a three-year period and the indicators against which the performance of the service would be judged.

Legislation and other developments derived from the new public management reform agenda have resulted in the Home Office 'setting detailed targets, prescribing policing strategies, inspecting performance and requiring the implementation of detailed action plans' (Loveday and Reid, 2003: 7). These changes have tended to reduce the role performed by police authorities in connection with police affairs which have become 'the weakest pillar in the tripartite structure' (Local Government Association, 2008: 6).

A further reform related to the tripartite system of police governance was the creation of the National Policing Board in July 2006. This contains representation from key stakeholders including the National Policing Improvement Agency (NPIA), Association of Chief Police Officers (ACPO), Association of Police Authorities (APA), HM Inspectorate of Constabularies (HMIC), the Home Office and the Metropolitan Police Commissioner.

Its main functions are to agree on the Home Secretary's annual national strategic priorities for policing and key priorities for the NPIA; set agreed priorities for the police reform programme; enable ministers, the professional leaders of the service and police authorities to monitor progress in implementing the reform programme and identify and overcome barriers to delivery and to provide a regular forum for debate and three-way communication between the tripartite partners on the opportunities and challenges facing policing. It has been argued that the National Policing Board has developed as the main national forum for tripartite discussions in policing (Home Office, 2008: 66).

See also: constabulary independence, new public management, police authority

References and further reading

Home Office (1993) *Police Reform: A Police Service for the Twenty-First Century.* London: HMSO, Cm 2281.

Home Office (2008) *From the Neighbourhood to the National: Policing our Communities Together.* London: Home Office, Cm 7448.

Jones, T. (2008) 'The Accountability of Policing' in T. Newburn (ed.) *Handbook of Policing.* Cullompton, Devon: Willan Publishing, second edition.

Local Government Association (2008) *Answering to You: Policing in the 21st Century. Police Accountability – an LGA Discussion Paper.* London: Local Government Association.

Loveday, B. and Reid, A. (2003) *Going Local: Who Should Run Britain's Police?* London: Policy Exchange.

U

UK Border Agency

See **political oversight of the criminal justice system**

V

verballing

See **Judges' Rules**

victim-blaming

See **crime prevention, victimology**

victimization surveys

Victimization surveys attempt to measure the amount of crime in society by asking respondents to record their personal experiences of being victims of crime.

Victimization surveys are used in a number of official studies such as the British Crime Survey, the first of which was first published in 1982. Figures relating to England and Wales have been published biannually since 1992 and annually since 2001/2. Each survey involves interviewing a randomly selected representative sample of adults (aged over 16) in private households in England and Wales in order to ascertain information relating their experience of being victims of personal and household crime during the previous year. Following a recommendation (Smith, 2006) the survey conducted in 2009 (to be published in 2010) was extended to those aged 10–15 in order to obtain a truer picture of the extent of victimization.

Since surveys of this nature are unaffected by changes to reporting and recording practices which affect official crime statistics, they provide a more accurate comparison of crime trends from one year to the next. Additionally, the existence of data derived from this source makes it possible to obtain information on crimes which are either not reported to or not recorded by the police. Historically, this difference has been significant. In 2008/9 the BCS indicated that

10.7 million crimes had been committed whereas the police had recorded only 4.7 million (Walker et al., 2009: 1).

One historic explanation for the discrepancy between official crime statistics and the information derived from victimization surveys was that official statistics counted incidents as opposed to victims. Until 1998, official statistics classified an episode with several victims as one incident, whereas victimization surveys would record it as several thus suggesting a higher level of crime. Additionally, victims of crimes such as racial or sexual violence may be more willing to reveal details of such incidents to researchers conducting victimization surveys than to the police as they lack confidence that the criminal justice system will deal with their complaint justly.

However, a number of problems affect the reliability of victimization studies. They exclude 'victimless crimes', are distorted by the impossibility of obtaining a representative sample of victims of different categories of crime and are influenced by 'forward and backward telescoping' (Coleman and Moynihan, 1996: 77–9). The latter refers to the reporting of an incident that occurred outside the period that is being surveyed, or a failure to remember minor incidents that took place during that time. Such studies also rely on the accuracy of a person's perception that a particular act constituted a crime.

It has thus been concluded that victimization studies provide only selective information on crime. They generate data on certain crimes but offences such as domestic violence or sexual assault which are often not reported to the police are also under-reported in these surveys (Walklate, 1989).

See also: crime statistics, field research, hate crime, self-report studies, victimology

References and further reading

Coleman, C. and Moynihan, J. (1996) *Understanding Crime Data: Haunted by the Dark Figure.* Buckingham: Open University Press.

Walker, A., Flatley, J., Kershaw, C. and Moon, D. (eds) (2009) *Crime in England and Wales 2008/09. Volume 1. Findings from the British Crime Survey and Police Recorded Crime.* London: Home Office, Home Office Statistical Bulletin 11/09.

Smith, A. (2006) *Crime Statistics: An Independent Review.* London: Home Office.

Walklate, S. (1989) *Victimology: The Victim and the Criminal Justice Process.* London: Unwin Hyman.

victimology

Victimology is concerned with the scientific study of those who have been victims of crime. This study embraces issues that include the characteristics of victims, the relationship between offenders and victims and the interactions between victims and agencies within the criminal justice system. It may also consider persons to be victims who have not suffered directly as the result of conventional criminal actions but who have experienced injustice arising from actions undertaken by the state or other bodies such as business corporations.

Traditionally, criminological theory was concerned with those who committed crime. Since the Second World War, however, increased academic attention has been focused on those who are victims of this activity. An early study (von Hentig, 1948) suggested that victims made some form of contribution to the offences to which they had been subjected, and this led to research into areas which included the role which victims played in precipitating crime and the extent to which certain categories of persons seemed prone to being on the receiving end of criminal behaviour.

Much of the initial research into victimology was founded on the presumptions of positivism. This suggested that victims possessed particular characteristics that made it possible to identify them from non-victims. These differences could be uncovered by social scientific investigation and the findings could be put to practical use to prevent future occurrences of victimization.

In addition to accounts of victimization founded on positivist principles, there are other approaches that have extended the focus of victimology. The liberal strand within victimology has extended research underpinned by positivist perspectives to embrace white-collar, middle-class and corporate abuses. Further accounts have been based on radical and critical criminological perspectives which extends beyond the consideration of conventional forms of criminal activity.

The radical-critical strand within victimology 'extends to all forms of human suffering and is based on the recognition that poverty, malnutrition, inadequate health care and unemployment are all just as socially harmful as, if not more harmful than, most of the behaviours and incidents that currently make up the official "crime problem"' (Carrabine et al., 2004: 118). This perspective has also embraced structural explanations of victimization, which seek to locate the study of victims within a broader economic, social and political context (Mawby and Walklate, 1994).

Victimization is an important aspect of victimology. This has focused attention on the lifestyles and routines of victims of crime (especially repeat victims), emphasizing how changes to routines can influence crime rates. One difficulty with victimization is that studies of those who are victim-prone may result in victim-blaming (Ryan, 1971) which shifts some of the responsibility for crime onto the victim and away from the offender. An alternative approach is that of victim facilitation which focuses on factors conducive to victimization that unavoidably derive from a victim's lifestyle as opposed to wilful actions or omissions on his or her part.

See also: re-balancing the criminal justice system, victimization surveys

References and further reading

Carrabine, E., Iganski, P., Lee, M., Plummer, K. and South, N. (2004) *Criminology: A Sociological Introduction*. London: Routledge.

Mawby, R. and Walklate, S. (1994) *Critical Victimology*. London: Sage.

Ryan, W. (1971) *Blaming the Victim*. New York: Pantheon Books.

von Hentig, H. (1948) *The Criminal and His Victim*. New Haven, CT: Yale University Press.

vigilante justice

See **self-policing society**

Violent and Sex Offenders Register (ViSOR)

See **Megan's Law**

voir dire

See **rules of evidence**

Voluntary Bill of Indictment

See **criminal court system England and Wales**

W

warnings (juvenile justice)

See **cautioning (formal)**

What works?

The concept of 'what works?' refers to the development of evidence-based policy to combat crime and offending behaviour. Typically initiatives are piloted, evaluated and if deemed to be successful are rolled out nationally to be implemented by crime control agencies within the context of a strategy that sets targets for crime reduction.

Rising crime rates during the 1970s and beyond suggested that traditional offender rehabilitation programmes were failing to combat crime. This view was articulated by the suggestion that 'nothing works' (Martinson, 1974). Although this pessimistic conclusion was not universally endorsed by academic research (and was subsequently qualified by Martinson himself, 1979), it provided impetus for the development of the 'what works' agenda which was especially driven by concerns of cost-effectiveness.

The commitment of post-1997 Labour governments to evidence-based interventions across a wide range of public policy was articulated in a number of policy pronouncements that affected agencies such as the Probation Service (Home Office, 1998 and Home Office, 2000).

The 'what works' approach is designed to ensure that interventions by crime control agencies (and by other bodies including those in the third sector) are based upon evidence of success in reducing rates of re-offending. This is secured through the use of accredited programmes whose effectiveness has been evaluated. Assessment tools such as

OASys are used to match offenders to programmes that are most likely to benefit them and address their offending behaviour. The 'what works' approach further requires that accredited programmes are delivered according to consistent standards throughout England and Wales and are readily available to all offenders.

The emphasis on 'what works' places evaluation at the centre stage of the crime-fighting agenda. There are various models that outline the processes which evaluation entails (such as SARA – scanning, analysis, response and assessment) and it is integral to both the formulation of programmes and monitoring them to assess performance.

However, evaluation raises a number of issues. Ideally the effectiveness of a particular programme will be assessed by comparing participants with a control group who did not take part in it. Their omission raises ethical issues. Also, evaluation is not an exact science. Rigorous evaluation is a complex and costly exercise which may result in short cuts being taken to save time and money. Additionally, because evaluation has shown an intervention to have worked in a particular area it cannot be automatically be assumed that it can be copied and used elsewhere. There may have been unique factors affecting the success of an intervention that will be difficult to repeat in other places. Nor can it be inferred from evaluation that a similar activity will consistently produce similar results or reactions. Finally, data may be manipulated by evaluators to produce the results desired by those who commissioned it.

See also: accredited programmes, assessment tool, desistance, new public management, Probation Service

References and further reading

Home Office (1998) *Effective Practice Initiative. National Implementation Plan for the Supervision of Offenders.* London: Home Office, Probation Circular 35/98.

Home Office (2000) *What Works Strategy for the Probation Service.* London: Home Office, Probation Circular 60/2000.

Martinson, R. (1974) 'What Works? Questions and Answers about Prison Reform', *The Public Interest*, 35: 22–54.

Martinson, R. (1979) 'New Findings, New Views: A Note of Caution Regarding Sentencing Reform', *Hofstra Law Review*, 7, Winter: 243–58.

White Paper

See **law-making process**

women's police department

A women's police department was the separate organizational structure that existed within each police force in England and Wales within which female police officers were employed. These departments were phased out during the 1970s when women were fully integrated into the organizational structure of police forces.

The existence of women's police departments evidenced historical scepticism regarding the role of women in police work. The police service was historically an occupation for males and the employment of women police officers did not occur until the First World War when a number of independent organizations (such as the Women's Auxiliary Service) were set up.

Following the end of the war women police patrols were set up within the Metropolitan Police, although the women were not sworn in as constables. An attempt to regularize the employment of women was subsequently made when a select committee argued that women should be fully attested and trained and become an integral element of police forces in England and Wales (Baird, 1920).

Further pressures to secure the employment of women officers included the Bridgeman Committee (1924) and the Royal Commission on Police Powers and Procedure (1929). In 1930 the Home Secretary standardized the pay and conditions of service for women officers and specified that their main purpose was to perform functions related to children and women. The 1933 Children and Young Persons Act gave legal recognition to the status of female officers by requiring that female officers should be available to deal with juveniles.

However, the number of women police officers remained low: by 1971 only 3,884 were employed throughout England and Wales. They were organized in their own departments, had their own rank and promotion structures and their work was supervised by their own inspectorate. Their pay was only nine-tenths of that of their male counterparts.

The recruitment and conditions of work of female police officers was affected by the 1970 Equal Pay Act and the 1975 Sex Discrimination Act. These measures (and other related reforms undertaken by individual forces) were designed to boost the recruitment of women officers and secure their full integration into police forces. Separate women's police departments were abolished and female officers received the same pay as their male counterparts.

However, the abolition of women's police departments had unintended consequences. These departments adopted a victim-oriented approach to police work and the expertise that had been developed within them in connection with female victims of crime was lost when work of this nature became performed by detectives, most of whom were male. This meant that female victims of crime were often handled unsympathically. In 1982 a television documentary, *Police*, made public this problem by publicizing the insensitive and inappropriate manner with which detectives from the Thames Valley force responded to a complaint of rape. This highlighted the important role that female officers had to play in contemporary police work.

However, although the number of women police officers has subsequently increased (rising to 33,177 or 23 per cent of the total strength of police forces in England and Wales in 2007), their progress has been impeded by the entrenched nature of 'cop culture' that made the service resistant to any changes that conflicted with long-established practices and attitudes (Gregory and Lees, 1999: 199). The proportion of female officers in the senior ranks of the service remains relatively low: in 2008 only 12 per cent of senior police officers (Chief Inspector level and above) were women and only five forces in England and Wales were led by female chief constables.

This situation has been attributed in part to the length of time it takes to progress through the ranks which means that increased intakes of female officers in recent years will take a while to penetrate the highest echelons. Additionally, the resignation rates of female police officers is twice as high as their male counterparts, a situation that frequently arises for domestic reasons.

A national policy on police career breaks was agreed by the Secretary of State in 2000 to help remedy problems of this nature.

See also: domestic violence, Police Staff Associations

References and further reading

Baird, L. (1920) *Report of the Committee on the Employment of Women in Police Duties.* London: HMSO, Cm 877.

Bridgeman, W. (1924) *Report of the Departmental Committee on the Employment of Police Women.* London: HMSO, Cm 2224.

Gregory, J. and Lees, S. (1999) *Policing Sexual Assault.* London: Routledge.

Royal Commission on Police Powers and Procedure (1929) *Report of the Royal Commission on Police Powers and Procedure.* London: HMSO, 3297.

Silvestri, M. (2003) *Women in Charge: Policing, Gender and Leadership.* Cullompton, Devon: Willan Publishing.

World Court

See **International Court of Justice**

Y

youth justice system

The youth justice system refers to the criminal justice procedures that are used in connection with persons aged 10–20 who have broken the law. These constitute 'children' (aged 10–13), 'young persons' (aged 14–17) and 'young adults' (aged 18–20).

Historically, children were treated as 'small adults' and subject to the same criminal justice procedures. The age of criminal responsibility (below which a child cannot be charged with a criminal offence regardless of seriousness) was set at 8 years by the 1933 Children and Young Persons Act. It was subsequently raised to 10 years by the 1963 Children and Young Persons Act.

Historically the presumption of *doli incapax* applied, whereby in connection with crimes committed by children aged 10–13 it was necessary for the prosecution to prove that they knew right from wrong. This presumption was ended by the 1998 Crime and Disorder Act and henceforth the onus was on the defence to prove that the child was not responsible for his or her criminal actions.

The purpose of a separate system is contentious and tension has historically existed as to whether its main concern was to serve the interests of society by ensuring that young offenders were punished for their crimes or to safeguard the welfare of the young person by providing interventions that would avoid a repetition of the offending behaviour in adult life.

The key features of the juvenile justice system historically comprised of a separate sentencing procedure and a discrete custodial regime.

The 1908 Children Act set up a system of Juvenile Courts to deal with offenders aged 15 and below. These courts were renamed Youth Courts by the 1991 Criminal Justice Act and their jurisdiction was extended to deal with those aged 10–17. Magistrates who serve on these courts are drawn from a specialist Youth Court Panel.

Specific custodial regimes for young offenders initially took the form of borstals that were set up by the 1908 Crime Prevention Act to provide training within a strictly disciplined regime. These catered for offenders aged 16–20 (raised to 21 in 1936). Borstals were replaced by Youth Custody Centres by the 1982 Criminal Justice Act and by Young Offender Institutions (YOIs) in the 1988 Criminal Justice Act (catering for those aged 15–20).

In addition to YOIs there are other institutions for those below the age of 18 whose crimes merit a custodial sentence. These are Secure Training Centres (for young offenders up to the age of 17) and local authority Secure Children's Homes. The latter are for boys aged 12–14 and girls aged 12–16, although some vulnerable boys aged 15 and 16 may be accommodated within them.

An important development affecting the youth justice system came with the establishment of Youth Offender Teams (YOTs) in the 1998 Crime and Disorder Act. These provided a multi-agency (or partnership) approach towards juvenile crime whereby staff from a range of agencies that included social workers, probation officers, police officers, education and health authority staff were placed under a statutory obligation to participate in local arrangements for YOTs, whose role included assessing young persons and their offending behaviour, determining what intervention was required and developing and supervising intervention programmes. They also prepare pre-sentence reports in connection with criminal proceedings against juveniles.

The introduction of YOTs was a response to a criticism that the work of the different agencies that dealt with juveniles was poorly coordinated and their performance objectives were frequently dissimilar (Audit Commission, 1996: 59). In particular, school exclusions (which had risen threefold between 1990/91 and 1994/5) were stated to have had a significant bearing on juvenile offending (Audit Commission, 1996: 66–7).

Additionally, each local authority was required – in consultation with other agencies – to draw up a strategic plan for youth justice work in its area. The youth justice system is coordinated by a Youth Justice Board (YJB) whose role includes monitoring the standards of YOTs in connection with YJB Performance Targets.

YOTs are responsible for supervising community penalties imposed by the courts. The 2008 Criminal Justice and Immigration

Act replaced a number of existing community sentences that were available for young offenders with a generic sentence, the youth rehabilitation order. This was available for young offenders below the age of 18 who had committed an offence for which an adult could get a custodial sentence or to those aged below 15 who were persistent offenders. This order was similar to the community order that was made available to sentencers for adult offenders by the 2003 Criminal Justice Act and enabled a 'pick and mix' approach to be adopted from a long list of interventions (or 'requirements') to tackle juvenile offending. These included activity, curfew and exclusion requirements and, for the more serious offences, embraced intensive supervision and surveillance provisions.

Some existing community penalties remained, including referral orders. These were introduced by the 1999 Youth Justice and Criminal Evidence Act (consolidated by the 2000 Powers of the Criminal Courts (Sentencing) Act) and established Youth Offender Panels (YOPs) to which first-time offenders aged between 10 and 17 years old who pleaded guilty – and whose crime was sufficiently serious not to warrant an absolute discharge but which did not justify a custodial (or a hospital) sentence – would be referred through the mechanism of a referral order issued by a youth court. It is a mandatory sentence

that lasts between three and twelve months, one advantage of which is that many young offenders who would previously have been given a conditional discharge (or perhaps a fine) would now receive a programme designed to help prevent re-offending.

YOPs contain one member from the YOT and at least two other participants drawn from the local community (termed 'community panel members' or CPMs), one of whom acts as a facilitator. Meetings of the YOP must include the offender, his or her parents and, ideally, the victim or a representative of the community. Referral orders envisage that YOPs will operate according to the principles of restorative justice (Young and Hoyle, 2003: 203).

A key function of YOPs is to formulate a programme of action (termed a 'youth offender contract') that must include reparative provisions (such as community reparation or written apologies). If it proves impossible to reach an agreement on an appropriate contract, the offender will be referred back to the court for sentencing. Re-sentencing by the courts will also occur if the offender fails to comply with the requirements imposed on him or her by the referral order.

The 2008 Act extended the use of referral orders, giving sentencers the ability to impose one on a young offender who was convicted for a second time, who pleaded guilty and who had not previously been subject to a referral order. Additionally, under exceptional circumstances a YOT could request that an offender should be subject to a second referral order.

A distinct system is used in connection with juvenile crime in Scotland. Here the age of criminal responsibility is 8, but offending by young people below the age of 16 is primarily treated as a welfare issue. The procedure is governed by the 1995 Children (Scotland) Act and the 1996 Children Hearings (Scotland) Regulations. Offenders aged 8–15 are referred by the police to the Children's Reporter Administration which determines whether to refer the matter to the Children's Hearings System. This forum can decide to take no further action or it may impose a Supervision Requirement to which a wide range of conditions can be attached. Offenders aged 16–17 are referred by the police to the Procurator Fiscal who decides whether to refer the matter to the criminal courts. The case may, however, alternatively be referred to the Children's Hearing which has the power to impose a range of penalties including fines, probation and custody (Utting and Vennard, 2000: 14–15).

See also: boot camps, joined-up government, non-custodial sentences, restorative justice

References and further reading

Audit Commission (1996) *Misspent Youth.* Abingdon: Audit Commission.

Muncie, J. (2009) *Youth and Crime.* London: Sage.

Souhami, A. (2007) *Transforming Youth Justice: Occupational Identity and Cultural Change.* Cullompton, Devon: Willan Publishing.

Utting, D. and Vennard, J. (2000) *What Works with Young Offenders in the Community?* Ilford, Essex: Barnardo's.

Young, R. and Hoyle, C. (2003) 'Restorative Justice and Punishment' in S. McConville (ed.) *The Use of Punishment.* Cullompton, Devon: Willan Publishing.

Youth Offender Panel (YOP)

See **youth justice system**

Youth Offending Team (YOT)

See **youth justice system**

Z

zero tolerance

Zero tolerance is a phrase used to describe the total unacceptability of a particular form of action and to denote that any manifestations of it will invoke a coercive response by the state. It has particular significance as a style of policing embracing a reactive response to crime based on enforcement procedures.

Zero tolerance policing was launched on the back of the 'broken windows' thesis that was put forward in the 1980s (Wilson and Kelling, 1982). It entailed strenuously addressing petty offending (such as broken windows, graffiti or abandoned cars, which gave the impression that nobody cared about the area) through policing that was delivered in a 'hard-edged' or 'confident' manner (Dennis and Mallon, 1997). This approach sought to nip criminal activity in the bud to stop petty criminals becoming serious offenders and to prevent an area slipping into a haven for the commission of serious criminal activity. It was in the latter sense that zero tolerance policing has an aim akin to that of a moral crusade – regaining control of the streets on behalf of law-abiding people and seeking to overcome the 'culture of fear' that existed within them (Furedi, 1997). It was adopted in American cities such as New York where it seemed to have a major impact on the level of crime.

However, there were shortcomings identified with zero tolerance policing. Its imperative to demonstrate success in the war against crime might lead to the use of improper practices in the belief that the end justified the means. Its effectiveness was uncertain: zero tolerance policing might reduce crime in selected areas by displacing it elsewhere. The approach relied on the 'short, sharp shock' working over a brief period of time which might not be sustainable as a longer-term police method. It has also been argued that the success of this method of policing in New York might have been due to the large increase in the number of police officers rather than the tactic itself.

Supporters of the 'broken windows' approach were sceptical of the concept (Kelling and Coles, 1998: 9) since it relied on law enforcement to the detriment of other approaches designed to tackle the root causes of crime. However, zero tolerance policing may have a legitimate role to play in conjunction with other methods of policing such as problem-oriented policing in which inflexible law enforcement directed at a particular form of crime (especially one of a short-term nature) may be conducted alongside other longer-term approaches that are designed to remedy its deeper-rooted causes.

See also: 'broken windows', neighbourhood policing, reassurance policing

References and further reading

Dennis, N. and Mallon, R. (1997) 'Confident Policing in Hartlepool' in N. Dennis, *Zero Tolerance Policing in a Free Society*. London: Institute of Economic Affairs.

Furedi, F. (1997) *Culture of Fear*. London: Cassell.

Kelling, G. and Coles, C. (1998) 'Policing Disorder', *Criminal Justice Matters*, No. 33, Autumn: 8–9.

Wilson, J. and Kelling, G. (1982) 'Broken Windows', *Atlantic Monthly*, March: 29–38.

Section Two

Key Acts affecting criminal justice

Magna Carta (1215)

Magna Carta (also referred to as Magna Carta Liberatum, the Great Charter of Freedoms) was the first of a number of similar-titled measures that had as their objective the preservation of the rights of the subject against the wielding of arbitrary power by the monarch. The amended version of 1297 endured longest on the statute books of England and Wales. The initial concession of 1215 (signed at Runnymede) was forced upon King John by a number of his of barons (whose main gripe was increased taxation levied by the Crown) and required him to endorse a number of rights and privileges possessed by freemen, respect certain legal procedures and accept that his will could be overruled by a committee of 25 barons. It also provided a defence against illegal detention that became known as habeas corpus, applying to all citizens, and aided the development of the principles and practices of the legal system.

Although Magna Carta did not significantly fetter the powers of the monarch in the immediate future (many of its key provisions being omitted from subsequent versions of the 1215 document), it provided the foundations of constitutional rule whose content and principles were developed by subsequent events, including the English Civil War of 1641–1651.

The Statute of Winchester (1285)

There were several Statutes of Winchester, the first being in 1275 which codified a number of laws, some of which originated in Magna Carta. The 1285 Statute of Winchester, whose key purpose was 'to abate the power of felons', was passed in the reign of Edward I. It was especially important in developing the principle of local self-policing (which derived from the Anglo-Saxon period).

Under its provisions, all towns (initially in the summer months) were required to appoint a night watch to guard the entrances to the town and arrest suspicious strangers. This new system was referred to as 'watch and ward' (watch by night and ward by day). The duty to participate in the watch was placed on all householders (serving on a rota basis) and its role was subsequently developed to that of keeping good order in the town at night. The constable was responsible for supervising these arrangements and the measure also incorporated improvements in day policing through the appointment of two high constables in each Hundred, below which were the petty constables in each tything. The Statute of Winchester also introduced the procedure of the hue and cry whereby all able-bodied citizens were required to help arrest a criminal and required the

Hundred to compensate the victim of a robbery when the hue and cry had been raised but the offender had escaped.

The Justices of the Peace Act (1361)

Following the Norman Conquest attempts were made to enhance the degree of central control over the system of policing and law enforcement. Officials termed 'Keepers of the Peace' were appointed by King Richard I in 1195 to preserve the peace in disturbed areas and in 1327 Conservators of the Peace were appointed in each county to help preserve law and order. In 1361, King Edward III appointed 'a good and lawful man' in each county whose role was to maintain the peace and whose functions subsequently expanded into more general forms of law enforcement. These adopted the title given to them in the 1361 legislation as 'Justices of the Peace' and they later assumed the title of Magistrate in the sixteenth century.

Justices were appointed by the monarch and owed their allegiance to him. The 1361 Act required that the justices should meet four times a year to transact business, providing the origins of the Quarter Sessions. Subsequently, in 1605, provision was made by the holding of local sessions to conduct minor affairs where no jury was required. This was the origin of Petty Sessions, although this procedure was not given statutory recognition until 1828. This measure helped to erode the feudal power structure, since those who were appointed as justices tended to be members of the land-owning gentry rather than of the feudal elite. The power of the justices was exerted through their local manorial courts (or Courts Leet), one of whose functions was to appoint the constables. This procedure helped to assert the pre-eminence of the justices over the constables and provided the backbone for the 'old' policing system that was in place until the early decades of the nineteenth century.

The Bill of Rights (1689)

Although titled a 'Bill' this measure (whose full title was An Act Declaring the Rights and Liberties of the Subject and Settling the Succession of the Crown) was an Act of Parliament which originated from the 1688 Declaration of Rights which Parliament had presented to William and Mary when inviting them to assume the throne of England following the flight of James II after the 'Glorious Revolution'. The Bill of Rights set out a number of basic entitlements that all 'Englishmen' should be able to exercise and sought to delineate the powers of Parliament in relationship to the monarch, thereby providing the basis of a constitutional monarchy. The main provisions of the Bill of Rights were:

- The monarch could not suspend the execution of laws passed by Parliament or govern through the use of the royal prerogative.
- Parliament was required to authorize taxation which should not be based upon a demand issued by the monarch based upon the royal prerogative.
- All subjects should possess the right to petition the monarch.
- There should be no standing army in time of peace and Parliament's agreement was required in order to use the army against the civil population when the country was not at war.
- Protestants should be able to bear arms for their self-defence.
- The monarch should not interfere in elections to return members to Parliament.
- Parliaments should be held frequently in order to redress grievances and to amend, strengthen and preserve the laws.
- Members of Parliament should enjoy the rights to freedom of speech and debate and the proceedings of Parliament should not be impeached or questioned in any court or place outside of Parliament.
- The monarch could not unilaterally establish new courts capable of inflicting penalties on the population.
- Excessive bail or fines should not be imposed and 'cruel and unusual punishments' should not be inflicted.
- The importance of the system of trial by jury was affirmed and jurors trying cases of high treason were required to be freeholders.
- There should be no fines or forfeiture without a preceding trial.

The Penitentiary Acts (1779 and 1794)

The 1779 measure was inspired by the penal reformer John Howard and its aim was to institute a nation-wide system of state-administered prisons. This would enable the existing penalties of execution and transportation to be replaced by terms of imprisonment.

Prior to the 1779 Act, prisons were locally controlled and their operations were often in private hands. Conditions were squalid, disease-ridden and overcrowded. Howard's ideal was to institute a system of prisons that were clean and secure and subject to a system of outside inspection. Inmates would be classified by sex, age and the severity of the crimes they had committed. Gaolers would be paid a wage rather than having to rely on fees that they exacted from inmates.

Howard devoted particular attention to the role of prisons, viewing them as institutions capable of reforming offenders. This would be achieved by a prison regime built around solitary confinement and hard labour with inmates being subjected to a disciplined regime enforced by rules and regulations and in which they would receive religious instruction. It was assumed that this would make the offender conducive to a process of self-examination, penitence and a desire to reform.

The 1779 Act did not, however, achieve its full potential and only two prisons (both in London, one for male prisoners and the other for females) were constructed under its provisions. One reason for this was that the views of Howard and other evangelical prison reformers were challenged by the utilitarian views advocated by Jeremy Bentham which gave rise to the 1794 Penitentiary Act. This provided for the construction of a prison at Millbank based on Bentham's panopticon principles which emphasized the importance of surveillance. The project was abandoned in 1803 although Millbank was completed (without Bentham's involvement) in 1821.

The Vagrancy Act (1824)

This legislation was introduced to deal with 'idle and disorderly persons, rogues and vagabonds' (especially soldiers who had fought in the Napoleonic Wars) whose lack of employment and accommodation forced them to live on the streets and beg.

One provision of this Act (section 4) made it illegal for a suspected person or a reputed thief to loiter in a public place with the intention of committing an arrestable offence. Under these circumstances a police officer was empowered to stop and search persons in order to prevent the commission of a crime. In theory the person who was stopped and searched was required to have performed two actions to justify the police intervention.

The stop and search provisions of the 1824 legislation (popularly referred to as 'sus') were used in connection with police crackdowns on street crime ('mugging') during the 1970s and 1980s. The requirement that the suspected person should have performed actions to justify his or her stop and search was widely ignored and it was alleged that 'sus' was used on a random basis by police officers, based on stereotypical assumptions that linked young black males to crime.

The 'sus' provision was repealed following the 1981 urban disorders and was replaced by the 1981 Criminal Attempts Act. Further reforms to police stop and search powers were provided for in the 1984 Police and Criminal Evidence Act and the accompanying PACE Codes of Practice.

The Metropolitan Police Act (1829)

This Act established the first 'new' police force on mainland Britain, the Metropolitan Police Force (now termed Metropolitan Police Service). It replaced the 'old' system of policing that existed in London based upon parish constables and watchmen with a professional organization in which constables were paid a wage to perform their functions. The legislation was promoted by the Home Secretary, Sir Robert Peel.

The police force set up by the 1829 measure covered the Metropolitan Police District which included all of London (with the exception of the City of London) and parts of the neighbouring counties of Middlesex, Surrey and Kent. It was funded by a Police Rate, levied in each parish on those eligible to pay the Poor Rate. It was initially under the day-to-day control of two commissioners (Charles Rowan and Richard Mayne) who were accountable to the Home Secretary. When Rowan retired in 1850 a second Commissioner was not appointed and control of the force was henceforth vested in one Commissioner.

The County and Borough Police Act (1856)

This legislation laid the foundations of the modern-day police service. The Act imposed a requirement on watch committees in towns and magistrates in rural areas to establish new police forces in their localities – previously this action had been discretionary in rural areas. As an inducement for them to do this, central government offered a financial contribution towards the costs incurred by local forces (which was initially equivalent to one-quarter of the costs of pay and clothing). However, this money would be paid only if they obtained a certificate to vouch that they were conducted in an efficient manner. This certificate was issued by an inspector who visited each force and reported back to the Home Office – the origins of Her Majesty's Inspectorate of Constabulary.

The Prison Act (1878)

The main purpose of this legislation was to bring prisons in England and Wales under a national form of control administered by the Prisons Commission. Prior to its enactment, the control of prisons was divided. Local prisons were administered locally by a variety of bodies that included local authorities and private sector bodies with magistrates customarily playing an important role. Some prisons, however, were subject to central direction by the Convict Prison Service which was established in 1850 under the control of the Home Office.

The 1878 measure was responsible for closing some of the worst of the local prisons and also for introducing new approaches towards punishment. However, in both local and convict prison regimes, conditions were harsh, based upon the system of separate confinement.

The Prison Act (1898)

This measure was based upon recommendations contained in the 1895 Gladstone Report and sought to provide for a prison environment in which the reform of inmates was promoted alongside their punishment. In this sense it was responsible for the introduction of a modern penal system. The use of the treadmill solely as a form of hard labour was abolished and the containment of prisoners in isolation could last no longer than one month. The association of prisoners whilst performing labour was provided for when this was practicable and the Act also enabled the courts to classify in three divisions prisoners whose sentence was that of imprisonment without hard labour.

The Probation of Offenders Act (1907)

A number of initiatives designed to aid the rehabilitation of persons convicted by the courts had been pursued during the nineteenth century. The 1907 measure placed work of this nature on a statutory footing by empowering the courts to appoint and pay probation officers whose role was to 'advise, assist and befriend' those who had been convicted. Probation was available to all courts and for almost all offences provided the offender agreed and also consented to adhere to conditions that included keeping in touch with the probation officer, leading an honest and industrious life, being of good behaviour and keeping the peace. This Act was the basis of the modern Probation Service. In 1925 the appointment of at least one probation officer to each court became a mandatory requirement.

Murder (Abolition of the Death Penalty) Act (1965)

Prior to 1965 the offence of murder carried a mandatory sentence: death. Concerns about the morality of state executions and worries as to whether the guilty person deserved such a penalty (or was even guilty of the offence for which they might have been wrongfully convicted) resulted in the abolition of the death penalty. The campaign to do this in Parliament was spearheaded by Labour MP Sydney Silverman. Initially the Act provided for a five-year ban, but this was made permanent in 1969. In 1973 permanent abolition was extended to Northern Ireland. The UK became totally abolitionist when the government signed the Sixth Protocol of the European Convention on Human Rights in 1999.

The Police and Criminal Evidence Act (1984)

The legislation emerged as a response to Lord Scarman's inquiry into the 1981 urban disorders and the 1981 Royal Commission on Criminal Procedure which had been chaired by Sir Cyril Philips.

The legislation gave the police a number of key powers, which included the ability to:

- stop and search a person or a vehicle in a public place;
- enter private property, search the premises and seize material found there (with or without a warrant);
- arrest;
- take fingerprints and other non-intimate samples;
- detain a person in custody.

Additionally the Act rationalized these powers across England and Wales, thus providing a national raft of police powers.

These powers frequently brought the police into abrasive forms of contact with members of the general public. In an attempt to guard against abuses that might undermine public support for the police, a number of safeguards were introduced that were designed to regulate the manner in which these powers were exercised and to specify the rights of the public when on the receiving end of them. These safeguards were either contained in the Act itself or in detailed Codes of Practice issued under the authority of PACE which provided guidance to police officers as to how their powers should be used. Codes of Practice are reissued periodically and redefine police responsibilities in relation to those suspected of having committed a crime.

In addition to police powers, other reforms were introduced by the 1984 legislation. The Police Complaints Board was abolished in favour a new body, the Police Complaints Authority, which had the ability to supervise the investigation of complaints made by members of the public against the police. Police forces were also required to establish mechanisms whereby they would consult with the general public on the policing of an area.

The Prosecution of Offences Act (1985)

This measure (which was based upon proposals contained in the report of the 1981 Royal Commission on Criminal Procedure) established an independent service – the Crown Prosecution Service (CPS) – to prosecute on behalf of the state persons who were charged with criminal offences. This task had formerly been carried out by the police (with the exception of a handful of prosecutions brought by private citizens). The role of the new service was to review files of evidence arising from a police investigation and determine whether to proceed with a prosecution (and if so, what the accused person should be charged with).

In arriving at decisions of this nature CPS lawyers are guided by the Code for Crown Prosecutors which gives guidance concerning the general principles to be followed when making decisions concerning whether or not to prosecute. These emphasize the need for there to be a realistic prospect of securing a conviction (the evidential test) and whether the public interest is served by pursuing a prosecution. The Code is prepared by the Director of Public Prosecutions (DPP), the most recent edition of which was issued in 2004.

Additionally, lawyers employed by the CPS frequently conduct the prosecution of cases, especially in Magistrates' Courts.

The CPS has undergone a number of important changes since its formation, including to its organization and powers. An example of the latter has included the introduction of statutory charging by the 2003 Criminal Justice Act. This has resulted in charging decisions for some offences being transferred from the police to the CPS.

The Police and Magistrates' Courts Act (1994)

This legislation introduced a number of innovations to the governance of the police. It was founded upon the principles of new public management and significantly increased the powers of the Home Office over policing in areas that were formerly the responsibility of chief constables, thereby eroding the historic principle of constabulary independence.

The main provisions of this Act were to enable the Home Secretary to set national objectives (later termed 'ministerial priorities' and now 'ministerial objectives') for the police service and to devise performance targets to assess the attainment of these objectives. The Act introduced cash-limited budgets, thereby enhancing the government's control over expenditure and provided for simplified procedures for amalgamating forces. Police authorities became free-standing bodies under the legislation to which the Home Office directly paid central government's financial allocation for local police work. The key role of these bodies became the drawing up of an annual costed local policing plan which contained a statement of national and local objectives, performance indicators and finances available. The composition of police authorities was also amended by this Act, the main innovation being the introduction of independent members to supplement the councillors and magistrates who served on these bodies.

The Crime and Disorder Act (1998)

This measure initiated a number of developments affecting the operations of the criminal justice system. These included the provision of a range of new court disposals that included Anti-social Behaviour Orders, parenting orders, child safety orders, curfew notices, reparation orders, supervision orders, reprimand and warning for offenders aged 10–17, action plan orders and detention and training orders.

An important aspect of this legislation was to require a joined-up (or partnership) approach to be adopted by a number of public agencies to combat crime.

The 1998 Act imposed a statutory duty on 'responsible authorities' (initially police forces and local authorities, to which other bodies were subsequently added) to act in cooperation with police authorities, health authorities and probation committees in multi-agency bodies which became known as Crime and Disorder Reduction Partnerships (CDRPs), although this designation did not appear in the legislation. In Wales CDRPs are termed Community Safety Partnerships (CSUs). The role of these partnerships was to develop and implement a strategy for reducing crime and disorder in each district and unitary local authority in England and Wales.

The 1998 legislation provided local government with a major role in the area of crime prevention (or what now became known as 'community safety'). This was accomplished through their involvement with CDRPs and was re-enforced by section 17 of the legislation which imposed a statutory duty on agencies which included local government and police authorities to 'do all that it reasonably can do to prevent crime and disorder in its area' in relationship to the performance of its other responsibilities.

Additionally, the Act provided for the establishment of multi-agency Youth Offending Teams (YOTs). These embraced local authority education and social services departments, the probation and health service and the police; they were required to work together in connection with youth offending. They perform a number of functions in relation to young offenders aged between 10 and 17 that include determining whether intervention is required in support of the police Final Warning Schemes and YOTs are responsible for the development and supervision of intervention programmes with the support and cooperation of other agencies. They prepare pre-sentence reports and other information required by the courts in connection with criminal proceedings against juveniles, liaise with victims and supervise community sentences imposed by the courts.

The Human Rights Act (1998)

The 1998 Human Rights Act incorporated the provisions of the European Convention on Human Rights into UK domestic law. The practical impact of this was that complaints by UK citizens alleging that their human rights had been flouted by public authorities in the UK could be determined by domestic courts rather than requiring the citizen to approach the European Court of Human Rights.

The European Court of Human Rights has always possessed the ability to influence the operations of agencies within the criminal justice system when aggrieved citizens have successfully referred their case to Strasbourg. However, the ability of UK citizens to refer their complaints to domestic courts since the enactment of the 1998 Act has tended to provide for the increased use of attempts to secure legal recourse regarding alleged human rights violations.

An important significance of this legislation has been on the power of the judiciary which has subsequently been able to use this Act as a standard with which to judge other Acts passed by Parliament. This judgment can be applied retrospectively in connection with old legislation as well as with new Acts. (See: European Convention on Human Rights, especially for the manner in which Parliament responds to pronouncements of the courts.)

The Police Reform Act (2002)

The 2002 Police Reform Act contained a number of important provisions that related to the performance culture of the service. These served to enhance the power of central government through mechanisms that included the requirement to produce a national policing plan and to issue Codes of Practice for chief constables that were designed to promote the efficiency and effectiveness of police forces.

The Act provided the Home Secretary with the power to require HMIC to inspect a force and to direct police authorities to institute remedial measures where the inspection indicated the force was not effective or efficient. The Home Secretary was empowered to direct the police authority to submit an action plan as to how deficiencies of this nature would be addressed. The legislation also gave the Home Secretary the reserve power to compel police authorities to require their chief constable to retire or resign in the interests of force efficiency or effectiveness.

The 2002 Act also provided for the establishment of a new body, the Independent Police Complaints

Commission (IPCC), to investigate complaints made by members of the public against police officers. Unlike earlier machinery of this nature, the IPCC has the ability to appoint non-police personnel to conduct some investigations.

The Criminal Justice Act (2003)

The 2003 Criminal Justice Act promoted a wide range of reforms to the operations of the criminal justice system. Many of these had been proposed in the Halliday Report (2001).

Its key provisions included amending powers affecting police interactions with persons suspected of having committed a crime in areas that included the taking of fingerprints and non-intimate samples without consent. Conditional cautions (that is, cautions to which conditions could be attached) were introduced for offenders aged 18 and over and statutory charging was initiated whereby the CPS (usually working in police stations) assumed total responsibility for deciding whether to charge a person and with what offence.

The legislation permitted juries to be dispensed with when there was a serious concern of jury tampering and overturned double jeopardy to enable a person to be re-tried of an offence of which he or she had been acquitted when new

and compelling evidence emerged that was reliable, substantial and appeared to be highly probative of the case against the previously acquitted person. The legislation also permitted courts to accept evidence of a person's previous 'bad character' that was relevant to a new offence that he or she was charged with and allowed for the admissibility of hearsay evidence under certain circumstances.

The 2003 legislation made a clear distinction between dangerous and non-dangerous offenders and sought to increase the use of non-custodial penalties by replacing existing community sentences with a new generic sentence, the community order. This enabled sentencers to adopt a 'pick and mix' approach and impose a number of requirements on offenders.

Other changes to sentencing introduced by the 2003 Act included the introduction of a suspended sentence order (otherwise known as custody minus). This applied to cases where a court considered that a custodial sentence of below 12 months was appropriate and enabled it to give the offender one last chance and impose requirements derived from a community order on the offender. The legislation also made changes to the deferred sentence order whereby the offender was required to undertake any requirements imposed by the court, compliance with which was monitored by the Probation Service. A new penalty, Imprisonment for Public Protection, was introduced to enable courts to sentence those aged 18 or over who had committed a serious crime to an indeterminate prison sentence where there was a serious risk that the offender would commit further offences of this nature if released into the community.

The legislation also provided for the establishment of a Sentencing Guidelines Council that sought to promote consistency of sentencing by the criminal courts.

The Constitutional Reform Act (2005)

This measure introduced a number of reforms to the operations of the judicial system in England and Wales. The Lord Chancellor was no longer required to be a member of the House of Lords. The Act established a Judicial Appointments Commission whose role was to nominate candidates for judicial office to the Lord Chancellor. It also set up the Judicial Affairs and Conduct Ombudsman to investigate complaints made by applicants for judicial posts. The Act was also responsible for establishing the Supreme Court as the highest court in England and Wales, replacing the role previously carried out by the Judicial Committee of the House of Lords.

The Private Security Industry Act (2005)

This legislation was the first Act to provide for a comprehensive system of regulation of the security industry. After 1945 the security industry performed an increased range of responsibilities in connection with security functions that included installing crime prevention measures such as burglar alarms and providing doormen at clubs and public houses and patrol personnel in shopping malls. Concern regarding the calibre and background of some of those employed within this sector resulted in the creation of a Security Industry Authority (SIA) whose role is to license persons seeking employment in the various sectors of the security industry. A licence will be provided only after the SIA has conducted a background check into the person who has applied to them to verify that their employment in the security industry is appropriate.

Section Three

Key documents affecting criminal justice

The Gladstone Report (1895): prison reform

The Gladstone Report was responsible for extending the role of prisons beyond that of deterrence and punishment to that of deterrence and reformation. The report argued that the main fault of prison was that 'it treats prisoners too much as irreclaimable criminals, rather than reclaimable men and women'.

Accordingly, the report argued that prison discipline and treatment should be designed to maintain, stimulate or awaken the higher susceptibilities of prisoners, to develop their moral instincts, to train them in orderly and industrial habits, and whenever possible to turn them out of prison better men and women, both physically and morally, than when they came in.

The emphasis placed by the report on the role of prisons to reform inmates resulted in considerable attention being devoted to the conditions within prison. It asserted that prisoners were sent to prison *as* rather than *for* punishment and recommended such changes as the abandonment of methods of unproductive labour, especially the use of crank and treadmill. In its place the use of industrial labour was proposed. This should be regarded as a privilege and so could be withdrawn and thus used as a mechanism of control.

The report also supported new initiatives to classify prisoners and sought the extension of educational facilities within prisons. It also advocated support for prisoners upon their release which would be facilitated by voluntary bodies being given access to inmates whilst in prison. It proposed reduced periods of solitary confinement for convicts.

The Gladstone Report inspired future thinking on the role of prisons. Some of its ideas (especially in connection with prison conditions) were incorporated into the 1898 Prison Act.

Reference

Gladstone, H. (1895) *Report from the Departmental Committee on Prisons.* London: HMSO, Sessional Paper 1895, c. 7702.

Royal Commission on the Police (1962): police reform

The appointment of a Royal Commission on the Police was prompted by a court case in 1959 when the Metropolitan Police Commissioner settled an action for assault and false imprisonment against one of his officers (PC Eastmond) without accepting liability and without disciplining the officer involved. Public concern about this incident resulted in the appointment of a royal commission.

The role of the commission was to examine the constitution and function of police authorities, to consider the status and accountability of police officers (including chief constables), to review the relationship between the police and public (especially in connection with ensuring that complaints by the public against the police were effectively dealt with) and to consider the broad principles that should govern the remuneration of constables.

The Commission's recommendations took into account a number of considerations that included claims by chief constables that they should exercise complete independence from local control in connection with law enforcement and claims from police authorities that it was possible for them to issue general instructions to the police in connection with general issues of this nature. The Commission discussed the case for creating a national police force under the control of the Home Secretary but failed to endorse this, instead recommending that future police administration should be based upon a partnership between central and local government with an enhanced degree of control by central government.

The report provided for the tripartite division of responsibilities for police affairs shared between police authorities, central government and chief constables which was provided for in the 1964 Police Act.

Reference

Royal Commission on the Police (1962) *Report of the Royal Commission on the Police.* London: HMSO, Cmnd 1728.

The Mountbatten Report (1966): prison security

The Mountbatten Report was commissioned by the Home Secretary following the escape of the convicted spy, George Blake, from Wormwood Scrubbs prison in 1966.

The main suggestion made by the report was in connection with the classification of prisoners according to the level of security that was needed to keep them in prison. Instead of a classification system that distinguished only between first-time prisoners ('stars') and those who had served one or more previous sentences ('ordinaries'), an A, B, C, D categorization was proposed. Category A prisoners were those requiring the most stringent form of security arrangements arising from the risks they posed, should they escape, either to national security or to members of the police service or general public arising from their violent behaviour. At the other end of the scale, category D prisoners were those who could be reasonably trusted to serve their sentences in open conditions.

This new system of categorization was implemented and remains in use today. However, Mountbatten's other key suggestion (that of building a special maximum security prison ('Vectis') to house Category A prisoners) was not acted upon in part because of issues relating to the staffing and control of these institutions. Instead these prisoners are spread around the prison estate in prisons housing Categories B and C prisoners.

Reference

Mountbatten, Earl (1966) *Report of the Inquiry into Prison Escapes and Security*. London: Home Office, Cmnd 3175.

The Scarman Report (1981): urban disorders

This report was prepared on the orders of Home Secretary Lord Scarman under the provisions of the 1964 Police Act following the disorders that initially occurred in Brixton, South London, in April 1981, and in other English cities during that summer. It examined the extent to which policing methods (in particular perceptions that stop and search was used in a racially discriminatory fashion) were responsible for these riots.

Although Lord Scarman drew attention to the social and economic problems faced by residents of Brixton, he also put forward recommendations regarding policing that included the need to introduce safeguards concerning police interventions with the public (especially stop and search), the reform of the complaints machinery and Police Disciplinary Code, the introduction of police–public consultative machinery, the recruitment of increased numbers of officers from minority ethnic communities and the initiation of changes to police training programmes to equip officers to more effectively meet the challenges posed by policing a multi-racial society. Many of these changes were incorporated in the 1984 Police and Criminal Evidence Act and others were introduced by the police service.

Reference

Home Office (1981) *The Brixton Disorders 11–12 April 1981: Report of an Inquiry by the Rt Hon The Lord Scarman OBE*. London: HMSO, 1981, Cmnd 8427.

The Royal Commission on Criminal Procedure Report (1981): reform of the criminal process

This inquiry arose against the background of disquiet arising from revelations contained in the Fisher Report into police practices in connection with their investigation into the murder of Maxwell Confait which resulted in the conviction of three youths being quashed by the Court of Appeal. It examined a wide range of issues related to the investigation and prosecution of crime which included police investigative powers (including stop and search, surreptitious surveillance and rules relating to arrest, detention and search of a suspect), the questioning by the police of a suspect and the suspect's rights and the procedures involved in the prosecution of offenders.

The Royal Commission put forward a wide range of proposals for reform. These included the rationalization of police stop and search powers across England and Wales and the introduction of safeguards in connection with their use. Strict time limits were proposed as to how long a suspect who had been brought to a police station under arrest could be detained for questioning before being either charged or released. These would be enforced by a newly created post of custody officer (usually a uniformed sergeant). It was proposed that interviews held in a police station should be tape-recorded and that the responsibility for prosecution should be removed from the police and placed in the hands of an independent prosecution service. In justification of this reform, the Royal Commission pointed out that police advocacy in cases heard in Magistrates' Courts had been to a large extent replaced in most forces by the establishment of prosecuting solicitors' departments.

Key reforms proposed by this report (and also by Lord Scarman's report of the same year) were incorporated into the 1984 Police and Criminal Evidence Act and the 1985 Prosecution of Offenders Act.

References

Fisher, Sir H. (1977) *Report of an Inquiry into the Circumstances Leading to the Trial of Three Persons Arising out of the Death of Maxwell Confait and the Fire at 27 Doggett Road, London, SE6*. London: House of Commons, House of Commons Paper 80.

Philips, Sir C. (1981) *The Royal Commission on Criminal Procedure. Report*. London: HMSO, Cmnd 8092.

The Morgan Report (1991): crime prevention

A major catalyst to increase the involvement of local government in the area of crime prevention was the publication of a report prepared by the Home Office Standing Conference on Crime Prevention, which was chaired by James Morgan, in 1991. This was set up to monitor the progress that had been made in the local delivery of crime prevention through the multi-agency approach.

The report argued that the local authority was a natural focus for coordinating, in collaboration with the police, the broad range of activities directed at improving community safety but asserted that the absence of a clear statutory responsibility for local government to play its part fully in crime prevention had inhibited progress.

The Morgan Report was responsible for introducing the concept of 'community safety' as opposed to crime prevention, arguing that the latter term suggested that crime prevention was solely the responsibility of the police. Partnership was thus seen as the appropriate direction on which future policy of this nature should be based. The new designation asserted the important role that communities should play in crime prevention strategies and sought to stimulate greater participation from all members of the general public in the fight against crime. It would also enable fuller weight to be given to activities that went beyond the traditional police concentration on 'opportunity reduction' methods of crime prevention, and would encourage greater attention to be paid to social issues.

The negative views held by Conservative governments towards local government made it unlikely that they would seek to increase its role in community safety issues. Therefore there was no central funding made available to implement any of the proposals contained in the Morgan Report. However, a number of local authorities began to implement them on a discretionary basis.

The ideas contained in the report subsequently exerted influence over actions pursued by post-1997 Labour governments to promote community safety, in particular through the partnership provisions of the 1998 Crime and Disorder Act.

Reference

Home Office Standing Conference on Crime Prevention (1991) *Safer Communities: The Local Delivery of Crime Prevention Through the Partnership Approach*. London: Home Office.

The Woolf Report (1991): prison conditions

This report was written following a severe prison riot in Manchester's Strangeways prison which lasted for a period of 25 days.

Lord Woolf identified overcrowding and idleness as the two main causes of this disturbance; to avoid problems of this nature in the future he stated that there was a need for a balance to be struck within prisons between security, control and justice.

Lord Woolf argued that justice required prisoners to be treated fairly and humanely. To ensure this he proposed a number of reforms that included the introduction of a national system of accredited standards for prisons, the establishment of a prison ombudsman to safeguard the interests of prisoners, the end of the practice of 'slopping out' through the provision of access to sanitation by all inmates by 1996, improved links with families coupled with more prison visits and the liberalization of home leave and temporary release provisions, the introduction of contracts for each prisoner outlining their expectations and responsibilities and improved conditions for remand prisoners.

The significance of this report concerned the changes that it introduced into the prison environment. The government endorsed some of these recommendations in their 1991 White Paper *Care, Custody and Justice: The Way Ahead for the Prison Service in England and Wales*. These included the introduction of accredited standards and a prison ombudsman. Following the publication of the report prisoners were given increased access to telephones in order to maintain contact with their families and the practice of 'slopping out' was ended in most institutions by April 1996.

Reference

Home Office (1991) *Prison Disturbances 1990: Report of an Inquiry by the Rt Hon Lord Justice Woolf (part I and II) and his Honour* *Judge Stephen Tumim (part II).* London: HMSO, Cm 1456.

The Learmont Report (1996): prison security

The escape of six high security prisoners from Whitemoor Prison in September 1994 resulted in an inquiry carried out by Sir John Woodcock. The findings of this report prompted the Home Secretary to commission a review of security throughout the entire prison service to be conducted by General Sir John Learmont. The terms of reference of this inquiry were extended following the escape of three prisoners from Parkhurst Prison in January 1995.

The report argued that the Parkhurst escape revealed 'a chapter of errors at every level and a naivety that defies belief' and referred to the existence of 'a multitude of security lapses and unacceptable practices'.

It put forward a number of recommendations that highlighted the need for improved methods of security. These included reforms to the organization and management of the prison service, the need to reduce the proliferation of paperwork, the devising of new Key Performance Indicators affecting areas such as staff morale and rates of recidivism, the need for the Director General to have regular contact with those who have operational responsibilities and to devote less time to Parliamentary matters, the more effective control over prisoner movements by prison staff, the provision of sufficient work and wages or educational facilities and the enhanced use of privileges and incentives. The report also proposed that a high security prison should be built for prisoners in the highest security categories.

The immediate significance of this report was that the Home Secretary dismissed Derek Lewis, the Director General of the Prison Service (although in March 1996 the High Court ruled this action had been wrongful). Aspects of this report were compatible with the 'decent but austere' regime promoted by Home Secretary Michael Howard whose provisions included the introduction of the Incentives and Earned Privileges Scheme and random Mandatory Drug Tests.

Reference

Home Office (1996) *Review of Prison Service Security in England and Wales and the Escape from Parkhurst Prison on Tuesday 3rd January 1995.* London: HMSO, 1996, Cm 3020.

Misspent Youth (1996): reform of the youth justice system

In 1996 the Audit Commission published a report, *Misspent Youth*, that was highly critical of the operations of the youth justice system.

It queried the effectiveness of existing arrangements, arguing that the low detection rates for juvenile offences meant that very few offenders were processed by Youth Courts, and thus the vast majority of them received neither help nor punishment. It also questioned the effectiveness of custodial sentences. Although the use of this form of punishment declined between 1984 and 1994 (and the average length of sentence was shorter), around 90 per cent of young males who were sentenced to custody for less than one year were re-convicted within two years of release.

Arguments relating to efficiency needed to be placed within the context of cost. The report pointed out that it cost the police £1,200 to identify a young offender, and a further £2,500 to prosecute him or her successfully. The total cost of dealing with offending by young people was around £1 billion a year. These figures suggested that the system provided poor value for money and that resources that were focused on processing offenders could be used more efficiently in particular in connection with preventing offending behaviour and changing the future behaviour of those who had offended.

The report further drew attention to the considerable period of time that frequently elapsed between arrest and sentence, stating that on average, the whole process could take from 70 days in some areas to 170 in others. Excessive delay meant that the crime was not fresh in the mind of the juvenile offender who was thus less likely to be amenable to suggestions to mend his or her ways.

The report also drew attention to the lack of coordination of the different agencies which dealt with juveniles whose performance objectives were frequently dissimilar. It was argued that lack of jobs, inadequate nursery education and family centres to help young isolated mothers contributed to the level of youth crime. In particular, school exclusions (which had risen threefold between 1990/91 and 1994/5) were stated to have had a significant bearing on juvenile offending.

This report formed the basis of a number of reforms promoted by post-1997 Labour governments in connection with the operations of the youth justice system, including the emphasis placed on joined-up government through mechanisms that included Youth Offending Teams provided for in the 1998 Crime and Disorder Act. A further report was published in 1998 which focused on changes required to implement requirements in the 1998 legislation in areas that included information-sharing between agencies and the development of local strategies to combat youth crime.

References

Audit Commission, (1996) *Misspent Youth*. Abingdon: Audit Commission.

Audit Commission (1998) *Misspent Youth '98: The Challenge of Youth Justice: Audit Commission Update*. Abingdon, Audit Commission.

The Macpherson Report (1999): the criminal justice system and racism

This report was ordered by Home Secretary Jack Straw following the failure of the Metropolitan Police Service to convict those responsible for the racist killing of the black teenager Stephen Lawrence in 1993. Sir William was asked to identify the lessons to be learned for the investigation and prosecution of racially motivated crimes.

The report concluded that the investigation had been affected by fundamental errors and attention was drawn to incompetence and institutional racism as key explanations. The report put forward 70 recommendations for reforms to the operating practices of the criminal justice system especially the police service in order to avoid recurrences of this situation. These included introducing a ministerial priority under the provisions of the 1994 Police and Magistrates' Courts Act for the improvement of trust and confidence in policing amongst minority ethnic communities (which would be measured by a range of indicators including the recruitment of officers from minority ethic backgrounds), redefining the term 'racist incident' to make the police service more victim-oriented in their approach to such issues, the review and revision of racism awareness training for police officers, providing a sanction (usually dismissal) for police officers using racist words or actions, the recording of stops and search and stop and account procedures and amending the Race Relations Act to place all members of the police service under its provisions.

The majority of Sir William's recommendations were adopted by the government and form the basis of attempts to improve police relationships with minority ethnic communities in the early years of the twenty-first century.

Reference

Home Office (1999) *The Stephen Lawrence Inquiry: Report of an Inquiry by Sir William Macpherson of Cluny.* London: TSO Cm 4262.

The Patten Report (1999): policing in Northern Ireland

The Patten Report was the product of an independent commission on Policing for Northern Ireland which stemmed from the 1998 Belfast (or Good Friday) Agreement. It put forward 175 recommendations regarding the future policing arrangements for Northern Ireland.

It emphasized the importance of human rights as an underpinning of these new arrangements and recommended that the new service should be accountable to a Policing Board which would set objectives and priorities for policing over a 3–5 year period and adopt an annual policing plan against which it would monitor the performance of the service. The Board would also negotiate an annual budget with the Northern Ireland Office until policing was devolved to the Northern Ireland Executive. The Board would consist of 19 members, 10 from the Assembly and 9 independents.

It proposed that District Policing Partnership Boards should be established by the District Councils to discuss local policing matters with the Police District Commander and also recommended that each neighbourhood should have its own dedicated policing team.

The report recommended that the new force should be named the Northern Ireland Police Service and consist of around 7,500 officers. It should adopt a badge and symbols that were free from any association with either the British or Irish states and that the Union flag should cease to fly from police buildings, being replaced by the Service's own flag.

The report noted that only 8 per cent of the existing Royal Ulster Constabulary were Catholics compared to in excess of 40 per cent of the overall population. In order to make the service more representative of the society that it policed, the report suggested that recruitment should be on the basis of 50 per cent Catholics and 50 per cent Protestant for the next ten years, by which time the overall number of Catholics would exceed 30 per cent of the entire composition of the force. At that stage further consideration could be given as to whether special measures of this nature were still required.

The report provided the basis for police reform in Northern Ireland. The new force (termed 'Police Service for Northern Ireland') and the Police Board were created by the Police (Northern Ireland) Act of 2000 (which was amended in 2003). The recommendations regarding recruitment were commenced in April 2002.

Reference

Independent Commission on Policing for Northern Ireland (1999) *A New Beginning: Policing in Northern Ireland. The Report of the Independent Commission on Policing for Northern Ireland.* London: TSO.

The Auld Report (2001): reorganization of the court system in England and Wales

The Auld Report was commissioned by the three criminal justice ministers to examine the practices and procedures of, and the rules of evidence applied by, the criminal courts at every level, with a view to ensuring that they delivered justice fairly, by streamlining their processes, increasing their efficiency and strengthening the effectiveness of their relationships with others across the criminal justice system, and having regard to the interest of parties that included victims and witnesses, thereby promoting public confidence in the rule of law.

One of the key recommendations contained in the report was to create a unified Criminal Court consisting of three divisions: the Crown Division (constituted as the present Crown Court) which would exercise jurisdiction over all indictable crimes and the more serious ones which were 'triable either way'; the District Division (constituted by a judge – normally a District Judge or Recorder who would be solely responsible for sentencing decisions – and at least two magistrates) which would exercise jurisdiction over a mid range of 'either way' cases, the penalty for which was a maximum of two years imprisonment; and the Magistrates' Division (constituted by a District Judge or magistrates as was currently the case with Magistrates' Courts) which would exercise jurisdiction over the less serious 'either way' cases and over all summary cases.

Juries would be used only in the Crown Division, although it was proposed that a defendant in a case heard before either the Crown or the District Division could opt for trial before a judge alone. The decision as to which court would hear 'either way' cases would be taken away from the defendant and instead would be vested in the Magistrates' Division courts (with the possibility of an appeal from the defendant which would be heard by a District Judge).

Although the government failed to implement the reforms that were proposed to the structure of the criminal courts, the 2003 Courts Act unified the administration of Magistrates' Courts (which had previously been conducted locally) with the administration of other courts through the creation of Her Majesty's Courts Service. This replaced the existing management structure that consisted of Magistrates' Courts Committees and the Court Service. It was intended that the new management structure would be locally accountable and was designed 'to enable management decisions to be taken locally by community focused local management boards, but within a strong national framework of standards and strategy direction'. The new

service operated on the basis of 42 areas, in line with the organizational structure utilized by other agencies in the criminal justice process, and was accountable to Parliament through the Lord Chancellor's Department.

Other proposals that were acted upon included the establishment of a National Criminal Justice Board to provide overall direction for the criminal justice system. Decisions of the Board would be implemented by Local Criminal Justice Boards who would also manage the operations of the criminal justice system in their area. The report introduced reforms to the jury system which included removing ineligibility or excusal as of right from jury service.

Reference

Auld, Rt. Hon. Lord Justice R. (2001) *Review of the Criminal Courts of England and Wales.* London: TSO.

The Halliday Report (2001): sentencing reform

The Halliday Report was commissioned to investigate whether the sentencing framework for England and Wales could be changed to improve results, especially by reducing crime. In particular it was charged with considering the introduction of a more flexible sentencing structure providing a 'seamless sentence' in which the boundaries between custodial and community penalties became less rigid.

The report put forward a number of proposals which included replacing custodial sentences of below 12 months with a 'Custody Plus' sentence in which a brief period of custody would be followed by supervision in the community. It recommended that custodial sentences of more than 12 months should be served on the basis of 50 per cent in prison and 50 per cent in the community under supervision, with Home Detention Custody abolished.

The report also argued in favour of replacing existing community penalties with a single community punishment order and recommended that comprehensive sentencing guidelines should be produced for all criminal courts. This work could be performed either by the Court of Appeal sitting in a new capacity or by a new, independent body.

Many of the reforms proposed by the Halliday Report were incorporated as provisions of the 2003 Criminal Justice Act.

Reference

Halliday, J. (2001) *Making Punishment Work. A Review of the Sentencing Framework for England and Wales.* London: Home Office.

The Cantle Report (2001): community cohesion

A series of riots occurred in a number of towns in northern England (including Burnley, Bradford and Oldham) in the spring and summer of 2001. These events prompted ministers to commission studies to investigate their causes. One of the most influential of these was chaired by Ted Cantle.

One of the key findings of his report was the existence of segregation in areas affected by these disorders, in which communities defined in racial terms were living in adjacent areas but failed to have any contact with each other. The report argued that 'separate educational arrangements, community and voluntary bodies, employment, places of worship, language, social and cultural networks, means that many communities operate on the basis of parallel lives. These lives often do not seem to touch at any point, let alone overlap and promote any meaningful interchanges'.

This absence of contact may lead to misunderstandings between communities. These create tensions capable of being exploited by outside extremist political organizations.

This report was published alongside others that included one by a ministerial group. Their main significance was to project community cohesion as a key policy objective which, according to the ministerial report, required 'a shared sense of belonging based on common goals and core social values, respect for difference (ethnic, cultural and religious), and acceptance of the reciprocal rights and obligations of community members working together for the common good'. Agencies operating in the criminal justice system were henceforth required to pursue activities that would contribute towards healing community fragmentation and promote social cohesion.

References

Home Office (2001) *Community Cohesion: A Report of the Independent Review Team, Chaired by Ted Cantle*. London: Home Office.

This was accompanied by Home Office (2001) *Building Cohesive Communities: A Report of the Ministerial Group on Public Order and Community Cohesion*. London: Home Office.

Local studies included:

Burnley Task Force (2001) *Burnley Speaks, Who Listens? Burnley Task Force Report on the Disturbances in June 2001*. Burnley: Burnley Task Force.
Oldham Independent Review (2001) *One Oldham, One Future*. Manchester: Government Office for the North West.

The Carter Report (2003): the formation of the National Offender Management Service (NOMS)

The Carter Report was commissioned to consider the future direction of the correctional services in England and Wales.

One of its key aims was to 'break down the silos of prison and probation and ensure a better focus on managing offenders'. Arguments that were put forward to support this proposal included the allegations that information-sharing between the two services was often poor (a difficulty compounded by organizational boundaries raising data protection issues), that programmes and interventions delivered in prison were not always followed up in the community and that no single organization was ultimately responsible for the offender which meant 'there is no clear ownership on the front line for reducing re-offending'.

To redress these deficiencies the report called for the formation of a new body embracing the prison and probation service, the National Offender Management Service (NOMS), which would focus on the management of offenders throughout the whole of their sentence, 'driven by information on what works to reduce offending'. The new service would be charged with a clear responsibility to reduce re-offending (which would be measured two years after the end of the sentence), making use of a system based on improved information to provide for the risk-assessed use of scarce resources. It was also suggested that improved service delivery could be achieved through greater contestability, whereby contracts for programmes to prevent re-offending could be made the subject of competition by the public, private and voluntary sectors.

In order to achieve this reform, it was proposed that the prison and probation services should be restructured with a single chief executive accountable to ministers for the delivery of outcomes. One person (the National Offender Manager) would be responsible for the target to reduce re-offending and would have complete control over the budget for managing offenders. Under the new arrangements there would be a head of public sector prisons and an operational head in charge of community interventions and punishment who would report directly to the chief executive.

It was proposed that Regional Offender Managers (nine in England and one in Wales) should be appointed to exercise responsibility for the end-to-end management of offenders in their region. Their main work would be contracts with the providers of prison places, community punishment and interventions such as basic skills or health whether in the public, private or voluntary sectors.

The conclusions of this report were endorsed by the government which established NOMS with the dual aims of punishing offenders and reducing re-offending. Its role was to provide for the 'end-to-end management' of offenders, regardless of whether they were serving their sentences in prison, the community or in both.

Reference

Carter, P. (2003) *Managing Offenders, Reducing Crime: A New Approach*. London: Cabinet Office Strategy Unit.

The Bichard Inquiry (2004): information-sharing between police forces

The Bichard Inquiry was set up to investigate child protection procedures in the Humberside Police and Cambridgeshire Constabulary following the murders of Jessica Chapman and Holly Wells at Soham in 2003. Specifically it examined the effectiveness of the relevant intelligence-based record-keeping, the vetting practices in those forces since 1995 and information-sharing with other agencies.

One of the key issues that emerged in relation to this event was that information possessed by the Humberside Police that detailed allegations of sexual offences by the person convicted of these murders had not emerged in the vetting carried out by the Cambridgeshire Constabulary prior to him taking up a post as a school caretaker.

The inquiry discovered evidence of errors, omissions, failures and shortcomings which it deemed to be 'deeply shocking'. It highlighted the failure to appreciate the value of intelligence within the Humberside Police and drew attention to the absence of a national information technology system on which intelligence could be recorded.

A number of developments relating to information-sharing were initiated in response to deficiencies in these areas that were highlighted by the Bichard investigation. These included the IMPACT Nominal Index (INI) that enabled individual police forces to share information they had gathered locally. The INI provided pointers as to the location where those looking for information could find it. It was intended to develop this to provide direct access to material of this nature through the mechanism of a Police National Database. However, problems with the nature of data stored by individual forces have impeded the progress of this reform.

A key factor that impedes progress in information-sharing between police forces is that they have traditionally been highly insular in their adoption of technology of this nature. The National Police Improvement Agency has been given a remit to remedy such problems.

Reference

Bichard, Sir M. (2004) *The Bichard Enquiry Report.* London: TSO, House of Commons Paper 653.

The O'Connor Report (2005): police force amalgamations

In 2005 a report by Her Majesty's Inspectorate of Constabulary written by Denis O'Connor put forward proposals for the fundamental reform of the structure of police forces in England and Wales. This would be secured by a programme of amalgamations that would drastically reduce the number of police forces in England and Wales.

One of the most important reasons justifying such reform concerned the need to deliver the 'protective services' more efficiently. These embraced activities that crossed Basic Command Unit (BCU) and – usually – force boundaries and were designated as Level 2 Services by the National Intelligence Model. These were grouped under seven headings:

* counter terrorism and extremism;

- serious organized (including that committed by criminal gangs) and cross-border crime;
- civil contingencies and emergency planning;
- critical incident handling;
- major crime investigations homicide;
- public order; and
- strategic roads policing

(to which an eighth, protecting vulnerable people, was subsequently added).

The report argued that these services were not performed to a consistently high standard across the board. Intelligence was viewed as essential in combating serious crime and was singled out as an area of work that required particular improvement.

Other reasons were also advanced to justify police force amalgamations. Economic considerations figured prominently in the report which argued that merger savings might amount to £70 million a year and that the net present value of merger savings and productivity gains could amount to £2,250 million over ten years. One aspect of savings was that arising from economies of scale in areas that include shared information technology and other services and estate rationalization.

The thrust of the O'Connor Report was that 'size mattered' when it came to enabling all forces to deliver the 'protective services'

to an acceptable standard. The aim of the reform was to create organizations that were large enough to provide a full suite of sustainable services, yet small enough to be able to relate to local communities. It was argued that the minimum size of a force should be 4,000 officers.

To achieve this objective the report endorsed what was termed the 'strategic force' proposal which entailed forces being re-grouped against a framework of design considerations, which included exceeding critical mass, criminality and geography. The report argued that this proposal was the best option for improving the level of protective services and providing enhanced value for money.

Although this report had the backing of the then Home Secretary, Charles Clarke, opposition mounted by chief constables and police authorities was able to prevent its implementation and the amalgamation proposals were dropped by Clarke's successor as Home Secretary, John Reid, in 2006. Inter-force collaboration was henceforth viewed as the best way to improve the delivery of the protective service. However, the impact of recession on public sector services is likely to resurrect interest in amalgamations if these can be shown as a means to save money in a period of financial restraint.

Reference

Her Majesty's Inspectorate of Constabulary (2005) *Closing the Gap – A Review of 'Fitness for Purpose' of the Current Structure of Policing in England and Wales.* London: Home Office.

The Corston Report (2007): women and the criminal justice system

The Corston Report called for a radical change based upon a woman-centred approach in the way in which women were treated throughout the criminal justice system including those at risk of offending in addition to those who had offended.

The report put forward 43 recommendations. These included the suggestion that the government should announce a strategy to replace within ten years existing women's prisons with geographically dispersed, small, multi-functional centres and the proposal that the government should establish an inter-departmental ministerial group for women who had offended or who were at risk of doing so which would govern a Commission for Women in these categories with a remit to provide care and support. The report urged improved co-ordination of the seven pathways to resettlement and suggested a further two should be added to provide support to women who had been abused, raped or who suffered domestic violence and for women who had been involved in prostitution. It was also urged that higher priority should be placed on life skills in the education, training and employment pathway.

The report urged that custodial sentences for women should be confined to serious and violent offenders who posed a threat to the public with community sentences being the normal penalty imposed on women offenders. The government was urged to take the lead to convince the public that prison was not the right place for women offenders who posed no risk to the public.

The government responded positively to a number of these proposals. The Reducing Re-offending Inter-Ministerial Group was charged with advancing the proposals in the report and a new cross-departmental Criminal Justice Women's Unit would be created with responsibility for women and criminal justice that would drive forward and monitor the work on behalf of the Ministry of Justice. It would report to the Inter-Ministerial Group. Additionally, a short project – the Future of the Women's Custodial Estate – would be set up to explore the recommendations in the report relating to the establishment of small custodial centres.

The government accepted the report's proposals regarding the pathways to resettlement and also accepted in principle that custodial sentences for women should be confined to those who were serious and violent offenders who posed a threat to the public. However, it failed to fund the Women's Commission that was designed to drive forward the recommendations contained in the report.

Reference

Corsten, Baroness J. (2007) *A Review of Women with Particular Vulnerability in the Criminal Justice System.* London: Home Office.

The Carter Review (2007): prison policy

The Carter review was concerned with the efficient and sustainable use of custody in England and Wales. It was charged with considering options for improving the balance between the supply of prison places and the demand for them, to assess the pace, scale and value for money of the current building programme in the light of likely future demands for prison places, to assess the management and efficiency of public sector prisons, to assess the potential for further cost-effective renewal of the prison estate by replacing expensive and poor quality prisons with state-of-the-art penal establishments, to assess the impact of recommendations concerning the prison estate on other parts of the criminal justice system and to assess changes in sentencing framework and remand policy that would enable the supply of and demand for prison places to be aligned.

The report pointed out that the cost of penal policy had risen from £2.843 billion in 1995 to £4.325 billion in 2006. The prison service had an overall capacity of 81,500 places spread over 139 institutions (128 of which were operated by HM Prison Service and 11 by private sector companies).

The report called for the development of a transparent mechanism that would reconcile prison capacity with criminal justice policy. Its recommendations included an expansion of the current building programme to provide for an additional 6,500 places by the end of 2012 (on top of the additional 8,500 places already planned for). It was argued that state-of-the-art ('titan') prisons should be planned and developed to enable a programme of prison closures starting in 2012 affecting old, inefficient and ineffective prisons. It also argued that there was scope to increase the efficiency of the prison system by improved service specifications and monitoring and streamlined overheads.

The report also called for a structured sentencing framework to be developed and a permanent Sentencing Commission to be established in order to secure transparency, predictability and consistency of sentencing across England and Wales. Its role would include assessing proposed legislation that could impact on the factors that contributed to the prison population.

The report suggested the establishment of an Implementation Board that would drive forward the report's recommendations concerning the management and running of prisons.

In 2009 the government announced that it had abandoned plans contained in the report to construct three 'titan' prisons.

Reference

Carter, Lord (2007) *Securing the Future: Proposals for the Efficient and Sustainable Use of Custody in England and Wales.* London: Ministry of Justice.

The Casey Review (2008): reform of the criminal justice system

The Casey Review was concerned with the gap that existed between what the public wanted in connection with crime and the services with which they were provided. This divergence manifested itself in ways that included public perceptions that crime had not fallen and that sentences were too lenient, despite the existence of much official evidence to the contrary.

Such fears and perceptions had an adverse impact on the public's confidence and its willingness to engage which resulted in the decline of community spirit.

The key proposal to remedy these problems was that of empowerment, whose key objective was to give communities much more power to say what matters most to them and to ensure that local agencies focus on delivering the services and improvements their communities want – 'Power should lie with the people, not with institutions' (Casey, 2008: 84).

The improved flow of information was at the heart of proposals to secure empowerment. This would align the public and criminal justice agencies in combating crime. Key recommendations included the publication of local monthly information on crime and the action that was being taken to tackle it and the provision of information on a regular and consistent basis by HM Courts Service on court cases, sentencing decisions and the subsequent progress of offenders.

The review suggested the need for 'signal justice', involving high-profile action to challenge and punish offenders and advocated a level of greater visibility in matters such as community sentences (which should be renamed 'Community Payback' and entail more demanding tasks to be performed by offenders). It also recommended the standardization of neighbourhood policing across England and Wales and its future development within the context of neighbourhood management.

The Casey Review exerted an important influence on subsequent developments affecting the criminal justice system. The relaxation of Home Office targets for the police service and reductions in the volume of paperwork required to be completed by police officers in order to enable policing to deliver what local communities wanted were influenced by suggestions made by this review (and also by other contemporary reports). The review also influenced the introduction of the policing pledge towards the end of 2008 which established a set of national standards as to what the public could expect from the police service (covering issues such as the time taken to answer emergency and non-emergency calls and information to victims of crime regarding the progress of their case).

Reference

Casey, L. (2008) *Engaging Communities in Fighting Crime: A Review by Louise Casey.* London: Cabinet Office.

The Flanagan Reports (2007 and 2008): police reform

The Flanagan Reports were concerned with a wide range of issues affecting the future direction of policing. An interim report was published in September 2007 in which prominent attention was given to neighbourhood policing and the need to reduce the volume of bureaucracy that was imposed on the police service. The full report was published in February 2008 which put forward 33 recommendations.

The final report asserted that policing in England and Wales was at a crossroads and there was a need for a radically new approach towards policing. It called for a national debate on the future of policing.

The report made a number of suggestions which included reducing the bureaucracy in connection with stop and account and stop and search procedures, including the use of mobile technology to reduce the volume of paperwork produced by stop and search encounters. It was proposed that civilian staff could assume responsibility for additional functions that were currently carried out by police officers and that the number of criminal offences that required comprehensive recording should be reduced in number. An enhanced system of accountability of the police to local communities was recommended in order for the police service to understand local needs and respond to them and it was argued that the government should facilitate the voluntary mergers of police forces where a sound business case could be put forward to justify such a course of action. Chief constables were urged to adopt an entrepreneurial approach to policing in order to exploit available business opportunities and the report suggested that the government should examine the role of risk in the police service and initiate a national debate on risk aversion and culture change. The objective of advancing joined-up government through the mechanism of Integrated Prosecution Teams was also advocated.

A number of suggestions were made regarding neighbourhood policing. The interim and final reports expressed the desire to build upon the advances that had been made in connection with neighbourhood policing by integrating it into a broader neighbourhood management approach that would secure the coordinated delivery of a range of local services.

The Flanagan Report exerted a considerable impact on the police reform agenda. The Home Secretary agreed to implement a number of proposals which included scrapping the existing stop and account form, streamlining the documentation associated with stop and search and reducing the length of the form on which crime was recorded. Further reforms were contained in a Green Paper that was issued in 2008.

References

Flanagan, Sir R. (2008) *Independent Review of Policing by Sir Ronnie Flanagan – Interim Report.* London: Review of Policing.

Flanagan, Sir R. (2008) *Independent Review of Policing by Sir Ronnie Flanagan – Final Report.* London: Review of Policing.

Home Office (2008) *From the Neighbourhood to the National: Policing our Communities Together.* London: Home Office, Cm 7448.

Section Four

Internet sources

Acts of Parliament

(www.opsi.gov.uk/acts)

Much of the work performed within the criminal justice process is governed by Acts of Parliament. Legislation affecting the criminal justice process is contained in Public General Acts and all are available online from 1988 onwards in HTML and PDF format. Some Acts are also available in PDF format from 1832 to 1987.

Association of Chief Police Officers (ACPO)

(www.acpo.police.uk)

ACPO's website contains online copies of the annual report since 2000 and ACPO policies on a very wide range of activities and issues concerned with the internal and external operations of the police service.

Association of Police Authorities (APA)

(www.apa.police.uk/apa)

The APA's website provides up-to-date statements on contemporary police issues and the APA's annual report is available from 2002/3.

Attorney General's Office

(www.attorneygeneral.gov.uk)

The Attorney General's Office website contains material that includes consultation documents, guidelines issued by the Attorney General, key speeches, statistical information on matters such as unduly lenient sentences and the Office's annual report.

Audit Commission

(www.audit-commission. gov.uk)

The Audit Commission website contains a range of online reports relevant to criminal justice matters. The website also has a community safety section that contains information on issues such as inspections of local community safety services and the police use of resources.

Bar Council

(www.barcouncil.org.uk)

Much of the work of the Bar Council is discharged by committees and reports by these (covering issues such as equality and diversity) are available on line. The website also contains a link to the Bar Standards Board (www.barstandardsboard. org.uk) that deals with the regulation of barristers.

Commission for Equality and Human Rights

(www.equalityhumanrights. com)

The Commission for Equality and Human Rights was established by the 2006 Equality Act, replacing the former Equal Opportunities Commission, the Commission for Racial Equality and the Disabilities Commission. Its website contains a range of publications that are relevant to its work, Codes of Practice and Guidance and the Commission's business plan.

Crime and Society Foundation

(www.crimeandsociety.org.uk)

The Crime and Society Foundation was set up within the Centre for Crime and Justice Studies at King's College London in 2003. A key role is to stimulate public debate on contemporary issues affecting the current and future operations of the criminal justice system. Its website contains a wide range of online material relating to publications, articles and speeches relating to the criminal justice system.

Crime Info

(www.crimeinfo.org.uk)

This extremely informative website is operated by the Centre for Crime and Justice Studies at King's College London and provides up-to-date information on a wide range of topics affecting the study of crime and the criminal justice system, including current publications. The site includes a discussion forum, an interactive exercise in which you can discover what it is like to be a judge and a topic of the month.

Criminal Cases Review Commission (CCRC)

(www.ccrc.gov.uk)

The website of the Criminal Cases Review Commission contains information related to the work of this body, an online case library that contains information on the cases handled by the CCRC, and for some of these a full copy of the Appeal Court's judgement is available at www.casetrack.com (although this is a subscription service). The CCRC website also contains a small publications list, some of which (including the annual report) are available on line.

Crown Prosecution Service (CPS)

(www.cps.gov.uk)

The CPS website includes online annual reports since 2000/1, business plans and provides access to material prepared by the 42 CPS areas. It also contains consultations initiated by the CPS which help inform their policy-making in areas that include the prosecution of domestic violence and rape, and gives access to the annual CPS lecture that was inaugurated in 2008. Additionally, the Code for Crown Prosecutors is available online together with CPS guidance on prosecution policy in connection with specific criminal offences including racist and religious crimes. The work of the CPS is monitored by the CPS Inspectorate, the CPSI (www.hmcpsi.gov.uk). Its website includes online annual reports since 2000/1, reports of thematic and joint reviews and provides access to reports prepared by the CPS areas and branches.

Europol

(www.europol.europa.eu)

Europol's website contains online reports on organized crime, specific aspects of serious crime, the annual report and press releases detailing current activities and operations.

Her Majesty's Courts Service

(www.hmcourts-service.gov.uk)

Her Majesty's Courts Service website provides online information into the work of the service, access to Crown Court annual reports since 2000/1 and County Court annual reports since 2002/3, HMCS frameworks and guidance to the legal professions and policy and strategy documents.

Home Affairs Committee

(www.parliament.uk/ parliamentary_committees/ home_affairs_committee.cfm)

The Home Affairs Committee of the House of Commons conducts periodic investigations into services administered by, and issues connected with, the Home Office. Many of these are concerned with aspects of the criminal justice system. Evidence submitted to the Committee during its investigations is published as and when it is presented and is then incorporated into the Committee's final report. These can be found by clicking onto 'Reports and Publications' which are available on line from the 1997/8 Parliamentary Session onwards.

Home Office

(www.homeoffice.gov.uk)

The Home Office website provides immediate access to a vast amount of up-to-date information that is available on line, including White Papers and strategic plans related to Home Office activities. The website is organized into a number of headings and the key ones include crime and victims, security, anti-social behaviour, drugs and the police.

The Research, Development and Statistics (RDS) is a Directorate within the Home Office that publishes a wide volume of information relevant to students of crime and criminal justice (available on line at: www.homeoffice.gov.uk/rds). This includes the British Crime Survey and crime statistics. It also provides a link to the Home Office Scientific Development

Branch (http://scienceandresearch. homeoffice.gov.uk/rds) which is concerned with applying technical solutions to combat crime.

The Home Office website also provides access to the Home Office Research Studies archive. These consist of reports undertaken by or on behalf of the Home Office on the areas over which the Home Secretary exercises responsibility and from 1969 to 2004 are available on line.

Home Office Circulars

(www.circulars.homeoffice. gov.uk)

Circulars give instructions on issues that include the implementation of legislation and policy administered by this department. Circulars from 2003 onwards are available on line.

Howard League for Penal Reform

(www.howardleague.org)

The Howard League is a penal reform charity, established in 1866. In addition to the *Howard Journal for Criminal Justice*, it publishes a wide range of material on issues connected with the criminal justice process that includes prisons, restorative justice, human rights, sentencing and victims. The website provides information on these publications, most of which are available for purchase.

Independent Police Complaints Commission (IPCC)

(www.ipcc.gov.uk)

This body is responsible for managing or supervising police investigations into complaints made by members of the public against police officers and can independently investigate the most serious cases of this nature. The website contains material that includes IPCC reports, guidelines and research, an archive of press releases, responses to IPCC reports and consultations, and an annual report which provides information on the operations of the complaints system.

Joint Committee on Human Rights

(http://www.parliament.uk/ parliamentary_committees/ joint_committee_on_human_ rights.cfm)

The Joint Committee on Human Rights consists of 12 members appointed from both the House of Commons and the House of Lords. It is responsible for human rights issues in the UK although its remit does not extend to the consideration of individual cases. Its website provides online access to a range of reports and publications from 2000/ 2001, many of which directly concern the operations of the criminal justice system.

Judicial Appointments Commission

(www.judicialappointments. gov.uk)

This non-departmental body composed of 15 Commissioners was established by the 2005 Constitutional Reform Act whose role is to select candidates for judicial office. The website contains information related to its selection procedures, current selection exercises, the annual report and statistical information since 2006/7.

Complaints made by candidates seeking judicial office (and also in connection with judicial discipline and complaints) are handled by the Judicial Appointments and Conduct Ombudsman (www. judicialombudsman.gov.uk) whose position was also created by the 2005 Constitutional Reform Act.

Justice

(www.justice.org.uk)

Justice is an influential legal and human rights organization that was established in 1957. It seeks to improve the legal system and quality of justice by advocating improvements to all aspects of the operations of the criminal justice process. A list of publications are available on its website. Many of these have to be purchased, although some material is available on line including the Justice Annual Lectures and key articles that appear in its journal, *Justice.*

Justice Committee

(www.parliament.uk/ parliamentary_committees/ justice.cfm

The Justice Committee is a select committee of the House of Commons that is responsible for the policy, administration and expenditure of the Ministry of Justice and for the work carried out by the Law Officers of the Crown, the Crown Prosecution Service and the Serious Fraud Office. The Committee also scrutinizes draft sentencing guidelines prepared by the Sentencing Guidelines Council. The website contains reports since 2002/3 dealing with aspects of the Committee's work that includes sentencing, terrorism and legal complaints. It also contains material concerned with the compilation of these reports – oral and written evidence and uncorrected oral evidence.

Law Society

(www.lawsociety.org.uk)

The Law Society of England and Wales website contains online copies of its annual report since 1999/2000 and publications on a range of issues affecting the profession. The website also contains access to the Law Society's online bookshop and a directory of the publications produced by the Law Society Strategic Research Unit that are available for purchase.

The website also provides a link to the Solicitors' Regulation Authority (www.sra.org.uk/consumers/consumers.page) which acts as an independent regulatory authority for all solicitors in England and Wales and to the Legal Complaints Service (www.legalcomplaints.org.uk) which investigates complaints made against solicitors.

Legal Action Group (LAG)

(www.lag.org.uk)

The LAG is a charity, established in 1972, that works with lawyers and advisers to promote equal access to justice for all members of society. The LAG produces a journal, *Legal Action*, which is available by subscription although some material that includes editorials and indexes is available online. The website also contains online reports concerning responses to consultations on criminal justice issues and information on its publications that are available for purchase.

Legal Services Commission (LSC)

(www.legalservices.gov.uk)

The LSC website has public information leaflets related to its operations, consultations on LSC policy development, newsletters, the annual report and strategic plan and specialized publications.

Liberty

(www.liberty-human-rights.org.uk)

This body was established in 1934, and was originally called the National Council for Civil Liberties. Its activities include lobbying Parliament, providing advice to the public and expert opinion and conducting research and publishing reports on a wide range of issues that have human rights or civil liberties implications in areas that include ASBOs, young people's rights, terrorism and torture. The website contains online reports, responses to consultations and briefings.

Ministry of Justice

(www.justice.gov.uk)

The Ministry of Justice website provides access to a range of online reports and consultation papers on the tasks for which it is responsible. An important publication is the annual *Statistics on Race and the Criminal Justice System,* prepared under Section 95 of the 1991 Criminal Justice Act that provides detailed information related to minority ethnic groups as suspects, offenders and victims. The website also contains online publications that include policy reports and circulars related to changes in legislation and research undertaken by the department related to its operation.

National Association for the Care and Resettlement of Offenders (NACRO)

(www.nacro.org.uk)

NACRO is a crime-related charity, established in 1966. Detailed information on the services with which NACRO is involved are available on line at its website which also provides access to the organization's publications catalogue which covers areas such as youth crime, mental health, race and criminal justice and crime reduction. Some of these are available on line and others can be purchased. NACRO also published the journal *Safer Society* until February 2008 when it was replaced by *The Community Safety Journal*. This is available by subscription, although aspects of the former journal are available online.

National Audit Office (NAO)

(www.nao.org.uk)

The National Audit Office is headed by the Comptroller and Auditor General and is responsible for auditing the accounts of all government departments, agencies and public bodies. The National Audit Office website contains reports related to investigations that it has conducted itself or in connection with which it has commissioned outside research. It also includes briefing that it provides to Parliamentary Select Committees. Online copies of the annual report since 1999 and the corporate plan since 2007 are also available.

National Offender Management Service (NOMS)

(www.justice.gov.uk/about/ noms.htm)

The NOMS website contains a number of online policy and consultation papers, and other useful publications that include prison performance ratings, action plans and the annual performance reports of the regions.

National Police Improvement Agency (NPIA)

(www.npia.police.uk)

The NPIA website contains its plan of action which details NPIA activities. It also provides information concerning its products and services portfolio which is organized into six categories. The NPIA business plan and report and accounts are also available online and the website contains links to

ACPO, the APA and the Home Office.

The Scottish Police Services Authority (SPSA), created 12 months before the NPIA, provides a similar service to the eight Scottish forces. (www.spsa.police. uk). Additionally, the SPSA has also a responsibility to oversee the Scottish Crime and Drugs Enforcement Agency (www.sdea. police.uk).

National Probation Service (NPS)

(www.probation.homeoffice. gov.uk)

The NPS website includes online news/updates, bulletins and briefing sections which provide up-to-date information on a wide range of issues affecting the service. It also includes a list of Local Probation Areas and Youth Offending Teams (YOTs) and access to their websites.

The NPS is inspected by Her Majesty's Inspectorate of Probation (HMIP). HMIP reports directly to the Home Secretary on the performance of the NPS and YOTs, in particular on the effectiveness of their work in relation to individual offenders, children and young people which aims to reduce re-offending and protect the public. The HMIP's website (http:// inspectorates.homeoffice.gov.uk/ hmiprobation) contains online reports of inspections of specific

Probation Areas and other activities performed by the HMIP.

Office for Criminal Justice Reform (OCJR)

(www.cjsonline.gov.uk/the_cjs/ departments_of_the_cjs/ocjr/ index)

The OCJR website provides online information on the operations of the criminal justice process and key publications related to the goal of a joined-up approach to criminal justice. Information related to operations of the National Criminal Justice Board can be obtained from its website (http://lcjb.cjsonline. gov.uk/ncjb/1.htm/). Information of the operations of the 42 local boards can also be accessed (http://lcjb. cjsonline.gov.uk).

Parliament

(www.parliament.uk)

Debates in the House of Commons and House of Lords are recorded in the publication *Hansard* which is available on line at www. publications.parliament.uk/pa/ pahansard.htm.

It is then possible to click on to daily debates (which are concerned with current legislation being considered by Parliament and also provide access to questions by MPs answered orally and in writing and statements made by Ministers), bound volume debates (which provide details of legislation considered in previous Sessions of Parliament) and Standing Committees considering Bills. Online bound volume debates commence in the 1988/9 Parliamentary Session in the House of Commons and 1994/5 Parliamentary Session in the House of Lords. Online debates in House of Commons Standing Committees commence in the 1997/8 Parliamentary Sessions.

Parole Board

(www.paroleboard.gov.uk)

The Parole Board's website contains online copies of its Annual report since 2002/3 and its three-year corporate plans since 2001–4. The site also contains information leaflets related to the board's work and policy statements dealing with areas that include risk assessment and race. There is also an online exercise *Judge for Yourself* relating to a decision to grant parole in a fictitious case.

Police Federation of England and Wales

(www.polfed.org)

The Police Federation's journal, *Police*, and editions published since 2005 are available online in the website's media centre. This also contains press releases and reports by the federation and federation news.

Police Forces

(www.police.uk/forces.htm)

The above website address produces a map providing access to individual force websites. The online information available includes matters such as performance statistics, matters of current importance and news updates to provide for communication between the police force and the public that it serves.

The activities performed by police forces in England and Wales are subject to scrutiny by Her Majesty's Inspectorate of Constabulary (HMIC). The HMIC website (www. inspectorates.homeoffice.gov.uk/hm ic/inspections) provides access to online reports concerned with force inspections, inspections of Basic Command Units, thematic inspections and best value reviews of specific activities conducted by individual forces. The annual report of the Chief Inspector of Constabulary (HMCIC) is available online from 1998/9.

Online information on all eight Scottish forces is available through the Scottish Police Forces website (www.scottish.police.uk). This provides information on individual force organization and policy and access to material including annual reports and performance indicators. There is also a link to ACPOS (www.acpos.police.uk).

The Police Service of Northern Ireland (PSNI) website (www.psni. police.uk) provides online access to

PSNI annual reports and statistical information and an archive of press releases since January 2001. The PSNI is supervised by the Northern Ireland Policing Board, whose website (www.nipolicingboard.org.uk) provides online access to a wide range of literature related to policing including the board's annual report since 2001/2, the corporate plan 2005–8 and the policing plan since 2003–7.

Policy Exchange

(http://www.policyexchange.org.uk/)

Policy Exchange is a research-led and evidence-based think tank that is especially interested in free market and localized solutions to public policy issues. Its research includes criminal and justice areas and its website contains online copies of a wide range of reports in areas that include policing, prisons, gang crime and youth offending.

Prison Reform Trust (PFT)

(www.prisonreformtrust.org.uk)

The PRT is a charity established in 1981. A considerable amount of material related to imprisonment is available online and the PRT website also contains a list of publications available for purchase which include books, pamphlets, briefing papers and consultation responses. The *Bromley Briefings Factfile* giving up-to-date statistical information on prisons is available online. The website further supplies links to other websites operated by organizations whose work is concerned with imprisonment.

Prison Service

(www.hmprisonservice.gov.uk)

The Resources Centre section of the Prison Service website contains online copies of annual reports (since 2001), the business plan (since 2000/1) and the corporate plan from (2001/4) onwards. It also contains publications and documents on issues such as prison performance standings and ratings and strategy documents. There is also an online prison virtual tour. The *Prison Service Journal* discusses issues of relevance to the prison service. This is a subscription journal, but articles in the most current issue are available on line. A compatible publication, *Prison Service News*, is available on line since November 2003.

Separate prison services exist for Scotland and Northern Ireland whose websites contain similar material to that of the site for England and Wales. The Scottish Prison Service (www.sps.gov.uk) is an executive agency of the Scottish Government and is responsible for Scotland's 15 custodial establishments. The Northern Ireland Prison Service (www.niprisonservice.gov.uk)

is an executive agency of the Northern Ireland executive and controls Northern Ireland's five custodial institutions.

Her Majesty's Inspectorate of Prisons provides independent scrutiny of the conditions for, and treatment of, prisoners and other detainees held in prisons, young offender institutions and immigration removal centres. Contracted-out prisons also fall within this official's remit. Its website (http://inspectorates.homeoffice.gov.uk/hmiprisons) contains online reports of inspections of specific institutions, thematic reviews and research publications. The annual report is also available from 1996/7 and the HMIP business plan since 2008/9.

Public Accounts Committee (PAC)

(http://www.parliament.uk/parliamentary_committees/committee_of_public_accounts.cfm)

The PAC was established in 1861 to examine 'the accounts showing the appropriation of the sums granted by Parliament to meet the public expenditure, and [since 1934] of such other accounts laid before Parliament as the committee may think fit'. Its website contains reports, oral and written evidence and government responses to PAC reports. Reports cover a wide range of subject areas, and include matters

connected with the criminal justice process. These are available on line commencing in the 1997/8 Parliamentary Session.

Restorative Justice Consortium (RJC)

(http://www.restorativejustice.org.uk/)

The RJC is a charity that was set up in 1997 to serve as the national voice for restorative justice in England and Wales. Its website contains a publication section that includes access to its newsletter, *Resolution*, annual reports from 2001 and a range of reports related to the principles and practice of restorative justice.

Scottish Government

(www.scotland.gov.uk)

The Scottish Government constitutes the devolved government for Scotland. The Justice Department of the Scottish Government is responsible for a wide range of activities concerned with the criminal justice process. These include the police service, the administration of the courts and legal aid. There are two executive agencies attached to the Justice Department: the Scottish Prison Service and the Scottish Courts Service. The website of the Scottish Prison Service (www.sps.gov.uk)

contains online information concerning headquarters policy statements and research publications. Copies of the annual report and accounts are available from 1999/2000 and the business plan for 2006–8. The website of the Scottish Courts Service (www.scotcourts.gov.uk) provides online access to the agency's business plan 2008–9, the corporate plan 2008–11, the annual report and accounts since 2002/3 and information leaflets related to its work.

Security Industry Authority (SIA)

(www.the-sia.org.uk)

The SIA website includes general publications, information on specific licensing sectors and financial and strategic information related to the agency. It also contains a number of case studies designed to highlight the benefits arising to companies from the work performed by the agency.

Security Service (MI5)

(www.mi5.gov.uk)

MI5's website contains much online information on the detailed activities of the organization, security advice and material related to the contemporary threats posed by espionage and terrorism to the UK.

Sentencing Guidelines Council (SGC)

(www.sentencing-guidelines.gov.uk)

The SGC website contains a wide range of online material which includes guidelines and draft guidelines and consultation papers and research reports related to aspects of crime and sentencing. The SGC's newsletter, *The Sentence*, and the body's annual reports are also available electronically.

Serious Organized Crime Agency (SOCA)

(www.soca.gov.uk)

SOCA's website contains literature related to its operations and work, the annual report from 2006/7 and the annual plan from 2006/7.

Social Exclusion Task Force

(www.cabinetoffice.gov.uk/social_exclusion_task_force)

This body was originally known as the Social Exclusion Unit and was set up in 1997, within the Cabinet Office. It was transferred to the Office of the Deputy Prime Minister in May 2002 and under its new name was placed within the Cabinet Office in 2006. Its key aims are to identify priorities for those suffering from social exclusion, to test solutions to tackle social exclusion and to facilitate collaboration across government departments. Much of its work is focused on specific projects.

Its website contains a range of documents related to the analysis and implementation of policy to alleviate social exclusion and it has a publications page that includes reports written for the former Social Exclusion Unit since 1997.

Statewatch

(www.statewatch.org)

Statewatch was established in 1991 and monitors state and civil liberties throughout the EU and seeks to identify developments that threaten to encroach or erode civil and political liberties. Its website contains online briefings on issues that include changes/projected alterations to state powers in connection with protest and developments affecting EU-wide policing. It also provides an extremely useful online link to UK legislation of relevance to the concerns of Statewatch. Statewatch publishes *Statewatch Bulletin* and *Statewatch Online* and the website also contains a publications list.

Victim Support

(www.victimsupport.org.uk)

Victim Support is an independent charity that seeks to help people cope with the effect of crime. Its website related to England and Wales contains online information related to the work of Victim Support. This includes leaflets and reports related to specific categories of crime, the annual report and accounts (available since 2000) and the national strategy 2005–8. The magazine *Victim and Witness View,* launched in November 2004, is also available online.

Youth Justice Board

(www.yjb.gov.uk)

The main purposes of the Youth Justice Board for England and Wales are to prevent offending and re-offending by children and young persons below the age of 18 and to ensure that custodial arrangements for them are safe, secure and address the cause of their offending behaviour. Its website provides up-to-date information on the organization's activities and also provides access to publications related to its work including Youth Justice Board position papers and access to key legislation affecting the youth justice system. Many of these reports and publications are available on line, others can be purchased. The website also includes online copies of the annual report and accounts since 2005/6 and the annual statistics. Free access to the bi-monthly *Youth Justice Magazine* is also available from this website.

The Youth Justice Board website also provides access to information relating to the operations of the 155 Youth Offending Teams in England and Wales including guidelines issued by the Youth Justice Board to YOTs on a wide range of policy matters. Online information includes the annual report since 2004 and copies of the programme of inspections into specific YOTs that commenced in 2003.

Index

Section One – Definitions

absolute discharge
   See sentences of the criminal
   courts 227–8
accountability 3–4
accredited programmes 5–6
actuarial assessment
   See assessment tool 11–12
administrative law 6–7
adversarial justice 7–8
Anti-social Behaviour Orders
   (ASBOs) 8–11
appellate court
   See criminal court system
   England and Wales 45
assessment tool 11–13
Association of Chief Police Officers
   (ACPO)
   See Police Staff Associations 184–5
Attorney General
   See political oversight of the
   criminal justice system 191–2
attrition 14–15
Audit Commission 15–16

bail 17–18
barristers
   See legal profession England and
   Wales 126–7
Basic Command Units (BCUs)
   19–20
Best Value 20–2
bifurcation 22–3
binding over
   See sentences of the criminal
   courts 229
boot camps 23–4
Bourbon system of policing 25–6
Bow Street Runners
   See thief takers 242
British Association for Women in
   Policing
   See Police Staff Associations 186–7
British Crime Survey
   See victimization surveys 247
'broken windows' 26–7

cautioning (formal) 28–30
charge reduction ('downgrading')
   See plea bargaining 170

Civil Justice Council
  See Law Commission 118
cognitive behavioural programmes
  30–1
cold case review
  See National DNA Database
  (NDNAD) 145
committal proceedings
  See criminal court system
  England and Wales 46
Common Law
  See law (sources of) 122–3
Community Order
  See non-custodial sentences 157,
  sentences of the criminal courts
  229–30
community safety
  See crime prevention 41
Comprehensive Area Assessments
  See joined-up government 108
Comprehensive Spending Review
  See Police Service England and
  Wales 177
concurrent sentence
  See sentences of the criminal
  courts 230
conditional caution
  See out of court disposals 163
conditional discharge
  See sentences of the criminal
  courts 228
consecutive sentence
  See sentences of the criminal
  courts 230
constabulary independence 32–3
consultation 33–4
contestability
  See new public management 155
control orders
  See internment 102
coroners 34–7

Crime and Disorder Reduction
  Partnerships (CDRPs) 37–9
crime prevention 39–42
crime statistics 42–5
criminal court system England and
  Wales 45–50
criminal court system Scotland 50–2
criminal record 52–3
Crown Prosecution Service (CPS) 53–5
cuffing
  See crime statistics 43–4
custodial sentence
  See sentences of the criminal
  courts 230, and also prisons 195

dark figure of crime
  See crime statistics 42–3
deferred sentence
  See sentences of the criminal
  courts 228–9
delegated legislation 56–7
derogation
  See European Convention on
  Human Rights 75
desistance 57–9
detection rates 59–61
deterrence
  See punishment (aims of) 200
Diplock Courts 61–2
discretion 62–3
displacement of crime
  See crime prevention 40
District Policing Partnership
  (Northern Ireland)
  See Police Service Northern
  Ireland 181–2
Dixon of Dock Green 64–5
doli incapax
  See youth justice system 255
domestic violence 65–7
double jeopardy 67–8

electronic monitoring ('tagging')
69–70
empowerment 70–2
equity
See law (sources of) 122–3
Eurojust 72–3
European Arrest Warrant 73–4
European Convention on Human
Rights 74–6
European Court of Human Rights
(ECHR) 76–7
European Court of Justice (ECJ) 78–9
Europol (the European Police
Office) 79–81
evaluation
See What works? 252
examining magistrates
See inquisitorial justice 96–7
expert witness 81–2

field research 83–4
fines
See sentences of the criminal
courts 229
fire brigade policing 84–6

General Council of the Bar (Bar
Council)
See legal profession England and
Wales 127
Green Paper
See law-making process 119–20

habeas corpus 88–9
hate crime 89–90
Her Majesty's Courts Service
See political oversight of the
criminal justice system 193–4
Home Detention Curfew (HDC)
See electronic monitoring
('tagging') 69–70

Home Office
See political oversight of the
criminal justice system 192
Home Office Circular 91
human rights 91–3

incapacitation
See punishment (aims of) 200
indictable offence
See criminal court system
England and Wales 46
informants (grasses/supergrasses) 94–5
inquisitorial justice 96–7
institutional racism 97–9
International Court of Justice (ICJ)
99–100
International Criminal Court (ICC)
100–1
International Law Commission
See Law Commission 119
internment 101–3
Interpol (International Criminal
Police Organization) 103–4

joined-up government 105–9
judges 109–11
Judges' Rules 111–12
Judicial Committee of the Privy Council
See criminal court system
England and Wales 49
judicial review 112–14
jury system 114–16
Justice and Home Affairs (JHA)
Council 116–17

Law Commission 118–19
law-making process 119–22
law (sources of) 122–4
Law Society
See legal profession England and
Wales 126

legal aid 124–5
legal profession England and Wales
125–9
Legal Services Board
See legal profession England and
Wales 128–9
lex talionis
See punishment (aims of) 201

magistrates 130–2
mandatory sentence 132–3
Megan's Law 133–5
Military Assistance to the Civilian
Authorities (MACA) 135–6
Ministry of Justice
See political oversight of the
criminal justice system 192–3
miscarriage of justice 136–8
moral panic 138–40
Multi-Agency Public Protection
Arrangements (MAPPAs) 140–2
mutual aid 142–3

narrowing the justice gap
See detection rates 60
National Black Police Association
See Police Staff Associations 186
National Crime Reporting Standard
See crime statistics 44
National DNA Database (NDNAD)
144–6
National Offender Management
Service (NOMS) 146–8
National Police Improvement
Agency (NPIA) 148–9
neighbourhood management 149–50
neighbourhood policing 150–1
net widening
See out of court disposals 162–3
new policing system (development
in nineteenth century) 152–4

new public management 154–6
non-custodial sentences 156–8

Offender Assessment System
(OASys)
See assessment tool 12
Office of Legal Complaints
See legal profession England and
Wales 128–9
old policing system 159–61
out of court disposals 161–3

PACE Codes of Practice 164–5
panopticon 165–6
paramilitary policing 166–8
Parole Board for England and Wales
168–9
Penalty Notices for Disorder (PNDs)
See out of court disposals 162
penology
See punishment (aims of) 199
plea bargaining 170–2
police authority 172–3
Police Community Support Officer
(PCSO) 173–4
Police Federation of England and
Wales
See Police Staff Associations
185–6
police property 175–6
Police Service England and Wales
176–8
Police Service Northern Ireland
178–82
Police Service Scotland 182–4
Police Staff Associations 184–7
Police Superintendents' Association
of England and Wales
See Police Staff Associations 186
policing by consent (development in
nineteenth century) 187–90

Policing Performance Assessment
Framework
See Best Value 21
policy transfer 190–1
political oversight of the criminal
justice system 191–4
pre-sentence report
See sentences of the criminal
courts 230–1
prisons 195–7
Probation Service 197–9
punishment (aims of) 199–203
purposeful activities 203–4

Queen's Counsel
See legal profession England and
Wales 127
Queen's evidence
See informants 94

reassurance policing 206–7
re-balancing the criminal justice
system 207–10
recidivism 210–11
reductivism
See punishment (aims of)
199–201
regulatory supervision 211–13
rehabilitation
See prisons 195
remand in custody
See bail 18
reprimands (juvenile justice)
See cautioning 29
resettlement
See recidivism 211
restorative justice 213–15
retributivism
See punishment (aims of) 201–2
right to silence 215–16
royal prerogative of mercy 216–17

rule of law 217–19
rules of evidence 219–20

Sarah's Law
See Megan's Law 134
Schengen Information System (SIS)
See Schengen initiatives 221–2
Schengen initiatives 221–3
Security Service (MI5) 223–5
self-policing society 225–6
self-report studies 226–7
sentencers
See bifurcation 22, also judges
109–11, magistrates 130–2
sentences of the criminal courts 227–31
Sentencing Advisory Panel (SAP)
See Sentencing Guidelines
Council 233
Sentencing Guidelines Council
(SGC) 231–3
sentencing tariff 233–5
separation of powers 235–6
Serious Organized Crime Agency
(SOCA) 236–7
similar fact evidence
See rules of evidence 219
solicitors
See legal profession England
and Wales 126–7
Solicitors' Regulation Authority
See legal profession England
and Wales 126–7
soundings
See judges 110
Special Constabulary ('the Specials')
237–9
summary justice
See out of court disposals 161
summary offences
See criminal court system
England and Wales 45–6

supergrass
  See informants 94
surveillance 239–40
suspended sentence
  See sentences of the criminal
  courts 228

thief takers 241–2
third sector
  See new public management 155
triable either way offences
  See criminal court system
  England and Wales 46
tripartite system of police
  governance 243–5

UK Border Agency
  See political oversight of the
  criminal justice system 193

verballing
  See Judges' Rules 112
victim-blaming
  See crime prevention 41, and
  victimology 250
victimization surveys 247–8
victimology 249–50
vigilante justice
  See self-policing society 225–60
Violent and Sex Offenders Register
  (ViSOR)
  See Megan's Law 134
voir dire
  See rules of evidence 219
Voluntary Bill of Indictment
  See criminal court system
  England and Wales 46

warnings
  See cautioning (formal) 29
What works? 251–2

White Paper
  See law-making process 119–20
women's police department 253–4
World Court
  See International Court of Justice
  99–100

youth justice system 225–8
Youth Offender Panel (YOP)
  See youth justice system 257–8
Youth Offending Team (YOT)
  See youth justice system 256

zero tolerance 259–60

Section Two – Key Acts affecting criminal justice

Magna Carta (1215) 263
The Statute of Winchester (1285)
  263–4
The Justices of the Peace Act (1361)
  264
The Bill of Rights (1689) 264–5
The Penitentiary Acts (1779 and
  1794) 265–6
The Vagrancy Act (1824) 226
The Metropolitan Police Act (1829)
  266–7
The County and Borough Police Act
  (1856) 267
The Prison Act (1878) 267–8
The Prison Act (1898) 268
The Probation of Offenders Act
  (1907) 268
Murder (Abolition of the Death
  Penalty) Act (1965) 268
The Police and Criminal Evidence
  Act (1984) 269
The Prosecution of Offences Act
  (1985) 269–70

The Police and Magistrates' Courts
Act (1994) 270
The Crime and Disorder Act (1998)
271
The Human Rights Act (1998) 272
The Police Reform Act (2002) 272–3
The Criminal Justice Act (2003) 273–4
The Constitutional Reform Act
(2005) 274
The Private Security Industry Act
(2005) 274

Section Three – Key documents affecting criminal justice

The Gladstone Report (1895): prison
reform 277
Royal Commission on the Police
(1962): police reform 277–8
The Mountbatten Report (1966):
prison security 278–9
The Scarman Report (1981): urban
disorders 279
The Royal Commission on Criminal
Procedure Report (1981): reform
of the criminal process 279–80
The Morgan Report (1991): crime
prevention 280–1
The Woolf Report (1991): prison
conditions 281–2
The Learmont Report (1996): prison
security 282–3

Misspent Youth (1996): reform of
the youth justice system 283–4
The Macpherson Report (1999): the
criminal justice system and
racism 284–5
The Patten Report (1999): policing
in Northern Ireland 285–6
The Auld Report (2001):
reorganization of the court system
in England and Wales 286–7
The Halliday Report (2001):
sentencing reform 287–8
The Cantle Report (2001):
community cohesion 288–9
The Carter Report (2003): the
formation of the National
Offender Management Service
(NOMS) 289–90
The Bichard Inquiry (2004):
information-sharing between
police forces 290–1
The O'Connor Report (2005): police
force amalgamations 291–3
The Corston Report (2007): women
and the criminal justice system
293–4
The Carter Review (2007): prison
policy 294–5
The Casey Review (2008): reform
of the criminal justice system
295–6
The Flanagan Reports (2007 and
2008): police reform 296–7